D0201134

MOTHER-WORK

WITHDRAWN
ST. MARYS COLLEGE LIBRARY

WOMEN IN AMERICAN HISTORY

Series Editors
Mari Jo Buhle
Jacquelyn Dowd Hall
Nancy A. Hewitt
Anne Firor Scott

A list of books in the series appears at the end of this volume.

362.7
L121

MOTHER-WORK

Women, Child Welfare, and the State, 1890–1930

Molly Ladd-Taylor

UNIVERSITY OF ILLINOIS PRESS

Urbana and Chicago

LIBRARY ST. MARY'S COLLEGE

© 1994 by the Board of Trustees of the University of Illinois
Manufactured in the United States of America
C 5 4 3 2 1

This book is printed on acid-free paper.

Library of Congress Cataloging-in-Publication Data

Ladd-Taylor, Molly, 1955–
    Mother-work : women, child welfare, and the state, 1890–1930 /
Molly Ladd-Taylor.
        p. cm. — (Women in American history)
    Includes index.
    ISBN 0-252-02044-8 (cloth : acid-free paper)
    1. Child welfare—United States—History.   2. Child rearing—
United States—History.   3. Motherhood—United States History.
I. Title. II. Series.
HV741.L33 1994
362.7'1'0973–dc20   93-9926
                                                                      CIP

For My Mother

Hylda Higginson Taylor

1921–90

Contents

Acknowledgments

Since I began working on this book, there has been an explosion of scholarship on women and the welfare state. I have benefited immensely from the collegiality and collective wisdom of scholars working in this area. I would especially like to thank the participants and organizers of three conferences: the Conference on Gender and the Origins of the Welfare State, held at Harvard University's Center for European Studies in 1987–88; the Women in the Welfare State Conference at the University of Wisconsin-Madison in 1989; and the Mini-Conference on Gender and Social Policy, held in conjunction with the annual meeting of the Social Science History Association in 1990.

The research and writing of this book were funded in part by a Woodrow Wilson Foundation Research Grant in Women's Studies, the Lena Lake Forrest Fellowship of the Business and Professional Women's Foundation, the Bush Center for Child Development and Social Policy, a Johnston Graduate Fellowship from Oberlin College, and a Joyce and Knight Foundations faculty development grant from Carleton College.

Many librarians and archivists provided invaluable assistance. Aloha South of the National Archives was exceptionally helpful. I would also like to thank the staffs of the Schlesinger Library at Radcliffe College, the University of Minnesota's Social Welfare History Archives, the Sophia Smith Collection at Smith College, the Library of Congress, the University of Chicago's Regenstein Library, Yale University's Sterling Memorial Library, and Carleton College Interlibrary Services.

I accumulated many other debts over the years. I am grateful to colleagues, mentors, and friends who generously commented on all or part of the manuscript: Eileen Boris, Ann Braude, Mari Jo Buhle, Nancy F. Cott, Linda Gordon, Nancy A. Hewitt, Sonya Michel, David Montgomery, Susan Reverby, and Lynn Y. Weiner. Eileen Boris and Nancy Cott were particularly helpful in shaping the direction of the book. Susan Putz was an able research assistant. Claire Ericksen and the teachers at Northfield Day Care kept my daughter happy and healthy so I could concentrate on the book. My colleagues in the Carleton College History Department, especially Clifford E. Clark, Jr., Jamie Monson, and Harry Williams, also gave me their encouragement and support.

My oldest and greatest debts are to Nancy F. Cott and Ann Braude. Nancy Cott supervised the dissertation on which this book is based. Her astute comments on numerous drafts helped me see more clearly what I was trying to say and how to sharpen the analysis; her warm encouragement and rigorous questioning are a model for feminist scholars. Ann Braude's friendship and superb editing skills kept me going in graduate school and, by the curious twist of fate that brought us to the same Minnesota college, supported me at the project's end. For her intellectual and personal generosity, I am continually grateful.

My family helped me throughout the research and writing. I am especially grateful to Carter and Frank Williams, who provided a cat-free home-away-from-home near the National Archives, and to Michael and Karin Clifford, who welcomed me into their family. Paul Clifford gave me love and encouragement, taking time from his own work so that I could do mine. Disa Clifford provided a continual and welcome reminder that there are many things more important than book-writing.

It is my greatest regret that my mother, Hylda Higginson Taylor, did not live to see this book in print, for she nurtured the project as well as its author from the beginning. She gave me material and emotional assistance during graduate school and beyond, and she taught me about the joys and sorrows of "mother-work." Like many of the women in this book, my mother suffered the tragic loss of an infant daughter and worked hard so that I, her surviving daughter, might have a better life than she. Her strength and courage in difficult times were an inspiration.

Introduction

In the years I worked on this book, I was often asked the title. Invariably, when I answered "mother-work," it was assumed I meant "working mothers," women with children employed outside the home. Despite more than twenty years of second-wave feminism, "mother-work" — meaning women's unpaid work of reproduction and caregiving — still seems to many like a contradiction in terms.

The response to my term "mother-work" reflects the contradictory character of motherhood in the late twentieth-century United States. Mothering is both public and private, both work and leisure. Though it mostly takes place at home, childrearing is the most public of acts, as any mother knows. From the first evidence of pregnancy, the mother is deluged with advice and observations from relatives, friends, and even strangers on her child's weight, sleeping habits, and behavior. Bookstores are full of how-to books on childrearing, and the media bombards us with images of both good mothers and bad. Still, mothering remains private — done mostly by women at home, alone. Because childrearing takes place at home and is done out of love, it is not considered work, and it is not paid; rather it is assumed to be a personal matter, benefiting only the individual family, and not a political and societal concern. Thus, even as a Reagan-Bush-appointed judiciary politicizes reproduction by restricting access to abortion and expanding "fetal rights," the United States makes no provisions for federally funded child care, family allowances, or maternal and child health care.

The contradictory attitudes and public policies affecting mothers today have their roots in the first years of the twentieth century, when maternal and child welfare first became national political concerns. The ideology and administrative forms of today's child welfare system were developed during the Progressive era, and women played a central role in their development.

Convinced that they were naturally sensitive to the needs of children because of their capacity for motherhood, organized women established private-sector child welfare services and lobbied the government for reform. Because the United States lacked a labor party or strong socialist movement, activist women were responsible for some of the biggest welfare accomplishments of the Progressive era: the passage of mothers' pensions (later Aid to Families with Dependent Children) and protective labor legislation for women workers, the 1912 establishment of the U.S. Children's Bureau, and the 1921 passage of the Sheppard-Towner Maternity and Infancy Protection Act, the first national welfare measure, which provided federal matching grants for infant health clinics.[1]

This book examines the politicization of women's traditional work of child care and the establishment of child welfare services in the early twentieth-century United States. I begin with the premise that women's unpaid reproductive labor in both its private and public forms has been central to the development of the American political and economic system. At home, mothers raised children to be citizens, workers, and soldiers; in the community, women volunteers were the principal campaigners for the expansion of public health and welfare programs affecting children.[2] By examining the two components of "mother-work"—childrearing in the home, and the maternalist reform activity characterized as "social motherhood"—I hope to shed light on the intersection of private life and public policy. For example, while personal experience with infant mortality led many women to organize for child welfare reform, the services they established helped reduce infant mortality and thus altered women's experience of mothering.

Despite the growing scholarly interest in both motherhood and women's welfare activism, the connection between women's private and public mother-work has remained largely unexplored. Welfare historians focus on women's public activism and "maternalist" ideology, while historians of childbirth and childrearing explore women's daily lives, but generally ignore politics.[3] Yet women's private experiences of mothering were deeply connected to political developments, especially to the expanding public health, education, and welfare services. Indeed, there was no purely "private" experience of childrearing—both because mothers raised children to be citizens and workers for the nation, and because mothers' working conditions were determined as much by labor and farm policies affecting their family income as by legislation directly concerned with welfare and reproduction. The extraordinary popular support for programs such as mothers' pensions and publicly funded maternal and infant health care in the first decades of the century cannot be understood simply as a manifestation of maternalism or of women's sentimental ideas about home and motherhood; it was rooted in their experience of childrearing. As feminist lawyer and peace activist, Crystal Eastman, remarked in 1925, "These matters of ordinary human welfare are their own trade interests, their professional concerns. Women resent the waste of child life with a special passion, as an architect resents the wanton destruction of beautiful buildings."[4]

Maternalism and Women's Welfare Activism

As the concept of maternalism gains currency among scholars of gender and the welfare state, it is important to clarify its meaning. In this work, I use the term maternalism to denote a specific ideology whose adherents hold (1) that there is a uniquely feminine value system based on care and nurturance; (2) that mothers perform a service to the state by raising citizen-workers; (3) that women are united across class, race, and nation by their common capacity for motherhood and therefore share a responsibility for all the world's children; and (4) that ideally men should earn a family wage to support their "dependent" wives and children at home. This restricted definition of the word maternalism, which has been used to describe everyone who campaigned for child welfare or who used the language of motherhood to justify her activities, avoids the pitfall of conflating very different ideologies and types of organizing that relied on the rhetoric of motherhood.[5]

A wide range of political perspectives and positions on woman suffrage can be included within this definition of maternalism. However, if we want to "distinguish among women's choices in reform," as historian Nancy Cott rightly urges us to do, then maternalists cannot properly be called feminists. Maternalists were wedded to an ideology rooted in the nineteenth-century doctrine of separate spheres and to a presumption of women's economic and social dependence on men. By contrast, Cott points out, feminists "differentiated themselves from earlier participants in the 'woman movement.'... [and] regarded their constellation of demands for female individuality, political participation, economic independence, and sexual freedom as a new challenge to the social order."[6] Nevertheless, maternalism and feminism coexisted and at times overlapped during the Progressive era; it was only in the 1920s, with the bitter debate over the Equal Rights Amendment, that they clearly diverged.

As an ideology and a social movement, maternalism was made possible by changes in the household economy of the Anglo-American middle class. Beginning in the eighteenth century and continuing well into the twentieth, the removal of industrial production from the home, the availability of labor-saving devices, and the decline in family size reduced the length of time middle-class urban women spent on household chores and "freed" them for full-time caregiving. As well-off women spent less time on household "maintenance," such as sewing and cooking, they had more time for household "management" and child care, and for club work and welfare activities that took them outside the home. These changes in women's work, along with families' growing dependence on men's wage labor, augmented the apparent split between home — the private sphere of women — and "work" — the public world of men. Women's aptitude for caregiving was idealized, while their social and economic contribution to the family economy was devalued, and they became more economically dependent on men.[7]

The changes in domestic work were accompanied by new concepts of childhood and maternal responsibility that lay the foundation for maternalist politics. Before the mid-eighteenth century, the idea of childhood as a distinct stage of life was unknown. However, by the time of the American Revolution, economic specialization and the new religious and political interest in individual rights had altered the dominant thinking about children and the family. No longer was the family seen primarily as a unit of production; instead, it was considered a site of love and affection. Children were valued for their natural goodness and not their economic productivity, and childhood was conceived as a period of growth rather than submission. Authors of childrearing tracts, describing the purpose of education as developing a capacity for self-government, lessened the father's disciplinary authority over children and elevated the mother's purportedly gentler and more natural role in childrearing. They urged Anglo-American wives to be Republican Mothers whose patriotic duty was to educate their sons to be moral and virtuous citizens.[8]

The concept of motherhood popular at the turn of the twentieth century was in many ways a continuation of the family ideals formed in the early national period. "Scientific motherhood," as the later ideology was called, resembled and perpetuated Republican Motherhood and the Victorian cult of domesticity in three ways: it considered motherhood women's chief duty and function; it assumed that children should be raised in their own homes; and it emphasized women's need for instruction on their domestic responsibilities. However, the importance attached to science and medical expertise represented a shift away from the religious and moral themes of the antebellum years.[9] Writing in women's magazines and childrearing books, proponents of scientific motherhood maintained that maternal instinct needed to be supplemented with scientific education and training; they considered love (provided by women) and science (provided by men) equally necessary ingredients of child care in the modern age.[10]

Although the ideology of maternalism was grounded in the changes in middle-class domestic work and tied to the doctrine of scientific motherhood, its appeal cannot be understood apart from the white protestant alarm over "race suicide" in the late nineteenth and early twentieth centuries. The rapid influx of immigrants from southern and eastern Europe, the ambiguous status of the first generation of emancipated African Americans, and U.S. expansion into Puerto Rico, Cuba, and the Phillipines left middle- and upper-class Americans increasingly aware of the diverse racial and ethnic makeup of the United States. Many Anglo-Americans responded to their new consciousness of cultural differences, and to the disrupting effects of industrialization and urban growth, with fear verging on hysteria about crime, disorder, and the breakdown of the family (meaning the Anglo-American family). As the birth rate among native-born whites declined and the divorce rate rose, conservative maternalists and some progressive reformers, most notably Theodore Roosevelt, expressed concern about the seemingly high birth rates and unfamiliar childrearing practices of immigrants and women of color and criticized the growing independence of modern "American" mothers. They looked to education as the solution: to remind Anglo-American women of their moral and civic responsibility to bear (and stay at home with) children and to teach immigrants "American" family patterns.[11]

Maternalists' genuine concern for the welfare of women and children of other racial and ethnic groups—combined with their culturally specific ideas about proper family life and children's needs—made assimilating immigrants into "American" culture a vital part of their child welfare work. Many immigrants came from rural communities where the family was the unit of production and the father still exerted control over the property, earnings, and labor power of family members. Thus, Anglo-American reformers believed that they could protect children from what they considered patriarchal abuse and injustice by modernizing immigrant families and "helping" them adjust to "American" culture. They hoped to limit patriarchal power by replacing it with the seemingly more benign—and maternal—authority of the state. Asserting their place in the public sphere at a time when there were few opportunities for women to do so directly, maternalists instructed racial ethnic and working-class women on "proper" nutrition, hygiene, and childrearing methods, and lobbied for child labor and compulsory school laws that would extend the period of dependency in childhood. They insisted that the recognition of motherhood as a profession and (Anglo-American) women's control over childrearing as mothers and as social workers, nurses, and educators ("social mothers") were essential both to women's sense of dignity and to the well-being of the nation.

Today, the maternalist assumption that women are united by a capacity for motherhood seems at best mistaken, but in some ways the material realities of motherhood in the first years of the twentieth century gave women of different social and economic groups more in common than their counterparts today. For one thing, despite significant differences in standards of living and access to health care, women from all social and economic groups faced frightening rates of infant and maternal mortality. For another, job discrimination, low wages, and inequitable child custody laws meant that well-off and poor mothers alike were economically and socially dependent on their families. All women in the Progressive era were denied legal, political, and economic equality; they could not vote, sit on juries, or receive equal pay for equal work. It is thus not surprising that even unmarried professionals used the language of motherhood to carve out a place for themselves in the public sphere. My point is not that women of different economic and cultural groups had similar caregiving experiences or ideologies of motherhood, but that the maternalist assumption of similarity grew out of the social and economic vulnerability of Anglo-American middle-class women—a vulnerability somewhat diminished in the 1920s as a result of improvements in health care, the right to vote, and increasing employment opportunities for educated women in the welfare system and expanding service sector.

By the end of the 1920s, the maternalist movement had changed the political landscape and altered women's relationship to the state. Ironically, this magnified the differences among women, for while working-class and poor women became the primary consumers of child welfare services, more affluent and educated women became the employees and administrators of the growing welfare system. Child health and welfare programs were increasingly run by men and women whose authority derived from their professional expertise, rather than by women—volunteer or professional—whose authority was based on motherhood. Although maternalists achieved their goal of professionalizing child welfare services and getting the government to take over their funding and administration, in the long run professionalization had the unintended result of reducing women's control over the services. This is partly because the absorption of child welfare programs into the government bureaucracy made maternalism less political in the sense that it was less capable of politically motivating or organizing women at the grassroots.

The depoliticization of maternalism in the mid-1920s adversely affected the position of middle- as well as working-class mothers. As doctors, social workers, and psychologists triumphed over mothers as the recognized experts on childrearing, praise for scientific motherhood was supplanted by condemnation of "oversolicitous" mothers. While most childrearing experts writing before World War I maintained that effective childrearing depended on both science and mother-love, authors of the 1920s insisted that it required only science. Following the behaviorist John Watson, they described mother-love as a "dangerous instrument" from which the child had to be protected.[12]

Mass culture also manifested an anti-mother mood. The postwar decade saw the expansion of a consumer economy that privileged youth and defined women primarily as wives and companions, not as mothers. Popular films and women's magazines promoted the image of the flapper, whose interest in fun, heterosexuality, and personal fulfillment was a significant departure from the socially concerned mother who was the womanly ideal of the Progressive period.[13] At the same time, a backlash against progressive politics and the women's movement diminished the maternalist movement's political force. By the end of the decade, most advocates of government responsibility for maternal and child welfare couched their argument in terms of assistance, not entitlement, and asked only for aid to the poor. For middle-class women of the 1920s, childrearing was to be an individual, not a social concern.

Maternalists and Feminists

The following pages distinguish between three groups of early twentieth-century women activists: sentimental maternalists, or club mothers, in the National Congress of Mothers and Parent-Teacher Associations; progressive maternalists, or progressive women reformers, allied with the U.S. Children's Bureau; and feminists, most of whom were affiliated with the National Woman's Party (NWP). Although there were sharp and often bitter differences between the three groups, the distinctions between them must not be drawn too sharply. Individuals in each group often had close working relationships, and there was considerable overlap in membership. For example, Florence Kelley, director of the National Consumers' League, was both a progressive maternalist devoted to child welfare reform and a member of the NWP's National Executive Committee — until the debate over the Equal Rights Amendment (ERA) in the 1920s drove the final wedge between maternalism and feminism.

I chose the three groups in this study because they had greater influence with politicians and civic leaders than other women, and because their ideas about family life form the basis of child welfare policy and feminist politics today. By examining the motherhood ideology of three types of mostly Anglo-American women activists, I hope to illuminate both the variations within maternalism and the differences between maternalism and other types of activism based on motherhood. For example, even though feminists used motherhood rhetoric during the 1910s, they were not maternalists because they asserted women's individual right to economic independence and thereby challenged the maternalist concept of the family. Recognizing the distinction between the language of maternalism and other types of motherhood rhetoric adds to our understanding both of early twentieth-century maternalism—and of the potential for using motherhood as the basis for organizing women today.

The discussion of maternalism begins with the sentimental maternalists in the National Congress of Mothers, the organization principally responsible for the passage of mothers' pensions legislation in the 1910s. The National Congress of Mothers, which evolved into the National Congress of Parents and Teachers (PTA) in 1924, was traditionalist in thinking; for example, it never endorsed woman suffrage. Congress leaders were convinced that women's highest calling was marriage and childrearing, and they were enthusiastic supporters of psychologist G. Stanley Hall and the child study movement. Believing that mothers should stay home with their children, club mothers limited their social welfare vision to protecting "dependent" mothers and children who did not have male breadwinners. They did not discuss extending government aid to working-class men or wage-earning women.[14]

Scholars of women and welfare have generally overlooked the PTA, but progressive maternalists—the second group in my study—have been the subject of a number of studies that emphasize the influence of their female reform network on social welfare policy.[15] Although the term "progressive maternalist" could be applied to a broad group of women in the social justice wing of the progressive movement, I focus specifically on those settlement workers, and particularly Hull-House residents, who participated in the creation and administration of the U.S. Children's Bureau. The members of the Hull-House/Children's Bureau network lobbied for and administered such key welfare reforms as protective labor legislation, maternal and child health care, and mothers' pensions. Unlike club mothers, who tended to be elite or middle-class mothers without college degrees, progressive women reformers were typically unmarried, highly educated career women who lived—and often loved—in a female world. Despite their personal biographies, however, most progressive maternalists assumed that the majority of women wanted to marry and stay home with their children. Active and outspoken suffragists, they asserted women's right to choose between marriage and career (they were convinced that women could not choose *both* marriage and career). The Children's Bureau staff rejected the sentimental language of mother-love used by the National Congress of Mothers, stressed the importance of social science and professionalism, and showed an unusual sensitivity to the material conditions of mothers' work. They saw maternal and child welfare reform as a step toward broader government protection for male as well as female members of the working class.

In contrast to maternalists, who made the establishment of child welfare services a priority, feminists were relatively unconcerned with social welfare reform. Yet, because they played an important part in politicizing motherhood during the Progressive era—and because the debate over the Equal Rights Amendment in the early 1920s was a critical juncture in the history of maternalism—I have included them as the third group in my study. Before the ERA debate, feminists frequently used the language of motherhood and sexual difference to challenge male dominance and the ideology of the family wage. Some, like Charlotte Perkins Gilman and Crystal Eastman, proposed alternatives to the nuclear family—such as socializing housework or endowing motherhood (paying women a government salary for childrearing)—in order to free mothers from economic and psychological dependence on men. By the mid-1920s, however, most feminists in the National Woman's Party rejected rhetoric and social policy based on motherhood and gender difference in favor of the Equal Rights Amendment and an almost exclusive focus on creating equal opportunities for women outside the home.[16] Comparing maternalist and feminist politics of motherhood reveals both the limits of maternalist social policy and the failure of most feminists to demand the state-funded welfare services necessary for women's fuller entrance into public life.

Despite the political differences among them, women from all three groups in this study shared an understanding of motherhood that was shaped by the specific experience of middle- and upper-class Anglo-Americans. For example, although few men actually earned enough money to be the sole support of their wives and children—and many married women, particularly African Americans, worked outside the home—both maternalists and feminists equated motherhood with economic dependence on men and confinement to the private nuclear family household. In their view, motherhood meant a rigid separation of spheres that gave women responsibility for childrearing and men the obligation of breadwinning. At the same time, it meant a roof over their heads, a common bond with other women, and the rewards of watching children grow. Motherhood was, as Nancy Cott has observed about the nineteenth-century concept of woman's sphere, "both the point of oppression and the point of departure" for activist women in the Progressive era.[17]

Any historian trying to link private life and public activism faces the problem of limited sources. Thus this study of "mother-work" relies heavily on the publications and records of one organization, the U.S. Children's Bureau. Established in 1912 as a division of the Department of Commerce and Labor, the Children's Bureau was the first federal agency to be headed and staffed almost entirely by women, and it acted as the women's branch of the government in the 1910s and 1920s. (The Women's Bureau, which was not established until 1920, dealt with women only in their capacity as wage earners.) The Children's Bureau was initially conceived as a research and education agency; it published and distributed childrearing literature, spearheaded a nationwide birth registration campaign, and conducted investigations on infant mortality and child labor. In the 1920s, it administered the Sheppard-Towner Act. The agency's published reports on infant mortality, child labor, and mothers' pensions, along with staff members' extraordinary correspondence with grassroots women, provide the most complete documentation available on the lives of typical mothers. The Children's Bureau records are rich in detail about mothers' daily lives and working conditions; they also provide a wealth of information about the ideas and administrative methods of progressive maternalists.

As rich as the Children's Bureau records are, approaching mother-work through the lens of the Bureau is not without problems. The information contained in Bureau studies of maternity care and child labor was filtered not only through the agency's investigators in the field, but also through Bureau officials who were anxious to defend the Children's Bureau and its reform perspective from the agency's many enemies in Washington. Moreover, neither the agency's research investigations nor its correspondence with mothers captures the experiences of a complete cross-section of American women. The most revealing documents, the letters from mothers, no doubt came disproportionately from white farm mothers who shared many of the Bureau's cultural values. The diversity of the Children's Bureau's correspondents is impressive, but immigrants, women of color, and those who could not write English are underrepresented in the agency's correspondence. Much more research is needed on class and cultural differences in both public and private mother-work; this book is a beginning and an appeal for further study.

The organization of *Mother-Work* is more topical than chronological. The first section, "Mother-Work at Home," sets maternalist welfare activism in context by exploring the concerns of mothers in real families and communities. The second section, "Mother-Work in the Community," investigates maternalism and the feminist politics of motherhood between 1890 and 1930. Chapter 2 examines sentimental maternalism from the 1897 founding of the National Congress of Mothers to the organization's turn away from reform politics at the end of the 1920s. Chapter 3 focuses on the progressive maternalism of the Hull House/Children's Bureau network. It describes maternalists' 1912 entrance into the federal government (that is, the Children's Bureau) and assesses their impact on child welfare policy. Chapter 4 examines the feminist politics of motherhood in the 1910s and 1920s. It concludes with a discussion of the debate over the Equal Rights Amendment, the first feminist challenge to motherhood rhetoric. The final section, "Mothers and the State," consists of case studies of two maternalist reforms that laid the basis for the 1935 Social Security Act. Chapter 5 describes the enactment and administration of mothers' pensions in the

1910s and 1920s, and chapter 6 investigates the passage and implementation of the 1921 Sheppard-Towner Act. The Sheppard-Towner Act represents both the climax and defeat of the maternalist movement; its repeal in 1929 marked the end of politicized motherhood, and so marks the conclusion of this book.

NOTES

1. There has recently been an explosion of scholarship on women's role in American welfare state formation. See, for example, Linda Gordon, ed., *Women, the State and Welfare* (Madison: University of Wisconsin Press, 1990); idem, "Social Insurance and Public Assistance: The Influence of Gender in Welfare Thought," *American Historical Review* 97 (Feb. 1992): 19–54; Theda Skocpol, *Protecting Soldiers and Mothers: The Politics of Social Provision in the United States, 1870s-1920s* (Cambridge: Harvard University Press, 1992); Seth Koven and Sonya Michel, "Womanly Duties: Maternalist Politics and the Origins of Welfare States in France, Germany, Great Britain, and the United States, 1880–1920," *American Historical Review* 95 (Oct. 1990): 1076–1108; idem, *Mothers of a New World: Maternalist Politics and the Origins of Welfare States* (New York: Routledge, 1993); Kathryn Kish Sklar, *"Doing the Nation's Work": Florence Kelley and Women's Political Culture, 1860–1930* (New Haven: Yale University Press, 1994).

2. On women's caregiving work in and outside the home, see Ann Ferguson, *Blood at the Root: Motherhood, Sexuality and Male Dominance* (London: Pandora Press, 1989); Kari Waerness, "On the Rationality of Caring," in *Women and the State,* ed. Anne Showstack Sassoon (London: Hutchinson, 1987); Lisa Leghorn and Katherine Parker, eds., *Woman's Worth: Sexual Economics and the World of Women* (Boston: Routledge, 1981); Rae Andre, *Homemakers: The Forgotten Workers* (Chicago: University of Chicago Press, 1981); Selma James and Mariarosa Dalla Costa, *The Power of Women and the Subversion of the Community,* 3d ed. (Bristol, England: Falling Wall Press, 1972); Wendy Edmond and Susie Fleming, eds., *All Work and No Pay* (Bristol, England: Falling Wall Press, 1975).

3. Exceptions in U.S. history include Nancy Schrom Dye and Daniel Blake Smith, "Mother Love and Infant Death," *Journal of American History* 73 (Sept. 1986): 329–53; Richard W. Wertz and Dorothy C. Wertz, *Lying-In: A History of Childbirth in America,* 2d ed. (New Haven: Yale University Press, 1989); Linda Gordon, *Heroes of Their Own Lives: The Politics and History of Family Violence* (New York: Viking, 1988). Other works on the history and politics of motherhood include Jane Lewis, *The Politics of Motherhood: Child and Maternal Welfare in England, 1900–1939* (London: Croom Helm, 1980); Ann Taylor Allen, *Feminism and Motherhood in Germany, 1800–1914* (New Brunswick, N.J.: Rutgers University Press, 1991); Deborah Dwork, *War is Good for Babies and Other Young Children: A History of the Infant and Child Welfare Movement in England, 1898–1918* (London: Tavistock, 1987); Katherine Arnup, Andrée Lévesque and Ruth Roach Pierson, eds., *Delivering Motherhood: Maternal Ideologies and Practices in the 19th and 20th Centuries* (London: Routledge, 1990); Ann Dally, *Inventing*

Motherhood: The Consequences of an Ideal (New York: Schocken, 1982); and Elisabeth Badinter, *Mother Love, Myth and Reality: Motherhood in Modern History* (New York: Macmillan, 1981).

4. Crystal Eastman, "The British Labour Women's Conference," *Equal Rights* 12 (July 4, 1925): 166.

5. Koven and Michel, "Womanly Duties," and Skocpol, *Protecting Soldiers and Mothers,* both use the term broadly to apply to all women welfare activists who used the rhetoric of motherhood. The idea that there is a specifically female ethic of care is articulated in two influential works: Sara Ruddick, "Maternal Thinking," *Feminist Studies* 6 (Summer 1980): 342–67, and Carol Gilligan, *In a Different Voice: Psychological Theory and Women's Development* (Cambridge: Harvard University Press, 1982).

6. Nancy F. Cott, "What's in a Name? The Limits of 'Social Feminism'; or, Expanding the Vocabulary of Women's History," *Journal of American History* 76 (Dec. 1989): 821. See also her *The Grounding of Modern Feminism* (New Haven: Yale University Press, 1987), 3–10. Many maternalists would be considered feminists according to Karen Offen's definition of "relational feminism" in "Defining Feminism: A Comparative Historical Approach," *Signs* 14 (Fall 1988): 119–57, and Naomi Black's description of "social feminism" in *Social Feminism* (Ithaca: Cornell University Press, 1989). Note that my restricted use of both "maternalism" and "feminism" makes it possible to distinguish between maternalists who accepted married women's economic (if not necessarily political) dependence on men and feminists like Ellen Key, who exalted motherhood and gender difference but proclaimed women's individuality, economic independence, and sexual freedom. Some African American scholars use the term "womanism" to refer to welfare politics specific to black women. See Elsa Barkley Brown, "Womanist Consciousness: Maggie Lena Walker and the Independent Order of Saint Luke," *Signs* 14 (Spring 1989): 610–33. The book that coined the durable term "social feminism," which until recently was the term most frequently used to describe women welfare activists, is William L. O'Neill, *Everyone Was Brave: A History of Feminism in America* (Chicago: Quadrangle, 1971.)

7. See Ruth Schwartz Cowan, *More Work for Mother: The Ironies of Household Technology from the Open Hearth to the Microwave* (New York: Basic, 1983); Susan Strasser, *Never Done: A History of American Housework* (New York: Pantheon, 1982); Glenna Matthews, *"'Just a Housewife': The Rise and Fall of Domesticity in America* (New York: Oxford University Press, 1987); Joann Vanek, "The Time Spent in Housework," in *The Economics of Women and Work,* ed. Alice Amsden (New York: St. Martin's Press, 1980). On early nineteenth-century changes in the household economy, see Nancy F. Cott, *The Bonds of Womanhood: "Woman's Sphere" in New England, 1780–1835* (New Haven: Yale University Press, 1977); Jeanne Boydston, *Home and Work: Housework, Wages, and the Ideology of Labor in the Early Republic* (New York: Oxford University Press, 1991).

8. See Sylvia D. Hoffert, *Private Matters: American Attitudes toward Childbearing and Infant Nurture in the Urban North, 1800–1860* (Urbana: University of Illinois Press, 1989); Bernard Wishy, *The Child and the Republic: The Dawn*

of *Modern American Child Nurture* (Philadelphia: University of Pennsylvania Press, 1968); Philip J. Greven, Jr., *The Protestant Temperament: Patterns of Child-rearing, Religious Experience, and the Self in Early America* (New York: Knopf, 1977); Carl Degler, *At Odds: Women and the Family in America from the Revolution to the Present* (New York: Oxford University Press, 1980); Steven Mintz and Susan Kellogg, *Domestic Revolutions: A Social History of American Family Life* (New York: Free Press, 1988), 52–60; Mary P. Ryan, *The Empire of the Mother: American Writing about Domesticity, 1830–1860* (New York: Haworth Press, 1982); Ruth Bloch, "American Feminine Ideals in Transition: The Rise of the Moral Mother, 1785–1815," *Feminist Studies* 4 (June 1978): 101–26. The term *Republican Mother* is from Linda Kerber, *Women of the Republic: Intellect and Ideology in Revolutionary America* (Chapel Hill: University of North Carolina Press, 1980).

9. By contrast, the effort to combine science with housework dates back at least until the 1840s, with Catharine Beecher's *A Treatise on Domestic Economy* (New York: Schocken, 1977, orig. 1841). See Kathryn Kish Sklar, *Catharine Beecher: A Study in American Domesticity* (New York: W.W. Norton, 1973); Boydston, *Home and Work.*

10. Quoted in Rima D. Apple, *Mothers and Medicine: A Social History of Infant Feeding, 1890–1950* (Madison, Wis.: University of Wisconsin Press, 1987), 100. Apple's book contains an excellent discussion of the ideology of scientific motherhood.

11. See Linda Gordon, *Woman's Body, Woman's Right,* 2d ed. (New York: Penguin, 1991), esp. chap. 7; Gwendolyn Mink, "The Lady and the Tramp: Gender, Race, and the Origins of the American Welfare State," in *Women, the State and Welfare,* ed. Gordon, 92–122; Robert H. Wiebe, *The Search for Order, 1877–1920* (New York: Hill and Wang, 1967); Susan Tiffin, *In Whose Best Interest? Child Welfare Reform in the Progressive Era* (Westport: Greenwood Press, 1982), 14–37; John Higham, *Strangers in the Land* (New York: Atheneum, 1965). Anna Davin, "Imperialism and Motherhood," *History Workshop* 5 (Spring 1978), 9–65, examines this issue in England.

12. Douglas A. Thom, *Everyday Problems of the Everyday Child* (New York: D. Appleton, 1927), 36; John B. Watson, *Psychological Care of Infant and Child* (New York: W.W. Norton, 1928), 87.

13. See Stuart Ewen, *Captains of Consciousness: Advertising and the Social Roots of the Consumer Culture* (New York: McGraw-Hill, 1976); Roland Marchand, *Advertising the American Dream: Making Way for Modernity, 1920–1940* (Los Angeles: University of California Press, 1985); Matthews, "Just a Housewife," 172–96.

14. The National Congress of Mothers was formed in 1897. The name was changed to the National Congress of Mothers and Parent-Teacher Associations in 1908 and to the National Congress of Parents and Teachers in 1924. Throughout this study, I refer to the organization as the Mothers' Congress or use the modern acronym PTA to avoid confusion over the name change. Historical studies that touch on the Mothers' Congress include Steven Schlossman, "Before Home Start:

Notes toward a History of Parent Education in America, 1897–1929," *Harvard Education Review* 46 (Aug. 1976): 436–67; Theda Skocpol, *Protecting Soldiers and Mothers*; Sheila M. Rothman, *Woman's Proper Place: A History of Changing Ideals and Practices, 1870 to the Present* (New York: Basic, 1978); and Barbara Ehrenreich and Deirdre English, *For Her Own Good: 150 Years of the Experts' Advice to Women* (Garden City: Anchor, 1979).

15. See, for example, Robyn L. Muncy, *Creating a Female Dominion in American Reform, 1890–1935* (New York: Oxford University Press, 1991); Ellen Fitzpatrick, *Endless Crusade: Women Social Scientists and Progressive Reform* (New York: Oxford University Press, 1990); Kathryn Kish Sklar, "Hull House in the 1890s: A Community of Reformers," *Signs* 10 (Summer 1985): 658–77. Susan Ware, *Beyond Suffrage: Women in the New Deal* (Cambridge: Harvard University Press, 1981), discusses the influence of the women's network in the 1930s.

16. Cott, *Grounding*; Susan D. Becker, *The Origins of the Equal Rights Amendment: American Feminism Between the Wars* (Westport: Greenwood Press, 1981).

17. Nancy F. Cott, "Feminist Theory and Feminist Movements: The Past Before Us," in *What is Feminism?* ed. Juliet Mitchell and Ann Oakley (New York: Pantheon, 1986), 51. For an excellent discussion of the irrelevance of white women's assumptions about motherhood to black women, see Patricia Hill Collins, "The Meaning of Motherhood in Black Culture and Black Mother/Daughter Relationships," *Sage* 4 (Fall 1987): 3–9.

PART ONE

Mother-Work
at Home

For the willingness to go down to the gates of death, to face its possibility for long weary months, to *know* that suffering and to fear that death stands as a sure and inevitable host at the end of a long journey — to know this, and to be willing to face it for the sake of others, is a heroism, a bravery, a self-abnegation so infinitely above and beyond the small heroism of camp or battlefield that comparison is almost sacrifice.

— Helen Gardener, "The Moral Responsibility
of Women in Heredity"

We just worked and had babies.

— Michiko Tanaka, *Through Harsh Winters*

1

The Work of Mothering

When Robert and Helen Lynd investigated childrearing in Muncie, Indiana, in the 1920s, they were struck by the "eagerness" of mothers in both the working and business classes "to lay hold of every available resource for help in training their children." The Lynds found that women of all social and economic groups avidly read baby books, women's magazines, and the child care bulletins published by the federal Children's Bureau. Elite women took classes in parent education and discussed scientific works on child development in their reading circles and mothers' clubs. Outside Muncie, working-class and farm women attended government-sponsored health clinics and classes. They also encountered the dominant childrearing advice in newspapers and farm journals, and from visiting nurses, social workers, and their children, who learned it at school. By 1929, according to one estimate, the mothers of one-half of all babies born in the United States had been touched by the government's childrearing advice. Many of them changed at least some of their behavior to bring it in line with the current medical wisdom.[1]

Mothers have always sought advice and assistance with childrearing from female friends and family members, but their growing dependence on help from government and medical experts outside their own networks was new to the twentieth century. In most cultures, and in Anglo-American communities well into the nineteenth century, mothers labored in a predominantly female world of reproduction, caregiving, and household chores. Child care was not the sole responsibility of an individual mother; rather, it was a social obligation shared by female friends and family. Women who shared household or farm chores frequently exchanged ideas about childrearing, and girls grew up familiar with childbirth and nursing, often helping to raise younger children. In some traditions, women's collective respon-

sibility for children was formalized. For example, Mexican American grand-
mothers or other older female relatives were called "comadres" who sponsored christenings, shared childrearing and disciplinary responsibilities, and
took care of children in the all-too-frequent instances of maternal death.
All women were expected to assist with childbirth and care for the sick,
although a few exceptionally skilled female healers and midwives stood out
in every community. Practicing what one historian aptly labeled "social
medicine," these experienced healers provided advice on nursing and childrearing as well as care during childbirth and illness.[2]

Although women's work of child care was always social in that it took
place within a web of female relationships, maternalists strove to make it
political, the subject of grassroots activism and public policy. Between the
1890s and the 1920s, maternalist activists—most of them Anglo-American
and middle-class—demanded that doctors and the state take action to protect
the health and well-being of children and their mothers. The popular appeal
of the maternalist movement, and the extraordinary impact it had on both
private medical care and public policy, can only be understood in the context
of mothers' daily experience of childbearing and childrearing. Thus this
study of maternalism begins with an examination of women's work of
mothering.

Any discussion of women's work of childbirth and childrearing must
begin with the recognition that it varied tremendously according to class,
culture, circumstance, and personality. While some women were well informed about sex and reproduction, others had no experience in child care
and lacked vital information about reproduction and their bodies. While
some women had a strong network of friends, relatives and neighbors to
help them care for their babies, others nursed sick children and coped with
difficult pregnancies virtually unaided. Many mothers gave birth with female friends and neighbors at their side, but others delivered their children
alone. Some women had husbands who helped with child care and household tasks, although most were married to men who stayed away from
what they considered women's work. (In contrast, women often helped out
with "men's work" in the fields or family business.) Some women were
married to men who viewed health care (especially prenatal care) as an
unnecessary indulgence; still others were reluctant to bother their husbands
with what they saw as "women's" concerns.[3]

The most significant thing turn-of-the-century mothers had in common
was fear of death, their own and their children's. Women from every social
and economic group had personal knowledge of infant and maternal death,
even though mortality rates were significantly higher among the poor and
people of color.[4] In 1915, approximately 10 percent of all infants—but almost
20 percent of infants of color—died in the U.S. birth registration area (where

statistics were collected) before they were one year old.[5] Approximately six white, or ten nonwhite, women died for every thousand live births between 1900 and 1930. According to historian Judith Walzer Leavitt, this meant that approximately one woman in thirty might be expected to die over the course of her fertile years. Moreover, many who survived suffered long-lasting and debilitating injuries.[6]

Until the early twentieth century, when improvements in public health and maternalists' well-publicized baby-saving campaign raised people's expectations for health, most women probably understood maternal suffering and infant death as God's will. Upper- and middle-class Anglo-Americans expressed what one historian called a "passive acceptance" of infant death throughout the nineteenth century. As late as the 1910s, Lithuanian immigrants in Connecticut still thought it impossible to prevent the deaths of those "ordained to die" in infancy, and African American midwives reportedly believed that "women are born to suffer and it's wrong to interfere" and "if the baby is born to die, nothing can be done."[7] According to physician S. Josephine Baker, the pioneering reformer who headed the New York Bureau of Child Hygiene, immigrant mothers grieved deeply when their babies died, but "they were just horribly fatalistic about it while it was going on. Babies always died in summer and there was no point in trying to do anything about it. . . . I might as well have been trying to tell them how to keep it from raining."[8]

Such fatalistic attitudes notwithstanding, most mothers did everything they could to keep their children alive and well. They called on physicians or traditional healers, followed suggestions from female friends and relatives, and made liberal use of patent medicines and home remedies. Most families treated minor complaints with home remedies. In the case of more serious illness, however, some families turned to medical doctors, while others relied on traditional healers. Many immigrant mothers used folk medicine to prevent disease. For example, Italian immigrants tied talismans of garlic around children's necks and used charms to ward off the evil eye. Rural women, both black and white, made frequent use of dollar medicines and home treatments made from drugs on hand, such as salts, camphor, oil, calomel, and quinine. African Americans customarily relied on herbal teas. Even relatively well-off women, such as Magnolia Le Guin, a doctor's daughter, combined patent medicines and home remedies with medical treatment and prayer.[9]

Women's dread of infant and maternal death set the stage for the medicalization of childbirth and infant care, and for the maternalist welfare movement. Urban Anglo-Americans were the first to look beyond their female support networks for help. Elite mothers, convinced that physician-attended births were safer and more respectable, began hiring male physicians to attend normal deliveries in the middle of the eighteenth century; by the middle of the next century, most babies born to middle- and upper-class urban women were delivered by doctors. During the same period, many mothers also began to rely on published health manuals, many of them ostensibly authored by doctors, to supplement advice from female relatives and friends. However, even though they believed that medical treatment and good mothering could enhance a child's chances of survival, most continued to think of infant death as inevitable and to view it as a private family sorrow. Not until the turn of the twentieth century did women turn their private agony into public action, joining with others in the maternalist movement to urge medical professionals and the government to assume their share of responsibility for the welfare of the nation's children.[10]

Pregnancy and Childbirth

Long after childbirth had been medicalized for middle-class whites, working-class and racial ethnic mothers continued to rely on traditional sources of support. They viewed pregnancy and childbirth through a folk or religious lens that bore little resemblance to the medical model. Looking to midwives and religious healers instead of physicians for assistance during pregnancy and delivery, immigrants and women of color generally observed the practices prescribed by their religions and cultures.

Folk healers had many techniques to protect the expectant mother and her unborn child. Like twentieth-century medical doctors, who maintained that consuming certain things (such as fresh vegetables and milk) and avoiding others (such as alcohol) would produce a healthy baby, traditional healers directed pregnant women and new mothers to eat — or avoid — certain foods. In some Native American communities, for example, it was thought that eating the feet of an animal or touching a crawfish would cause the baby to be born feet first, that eating berries would leave a birthmark on the baby, and that eating nuts would make it difficult for the baby to break through the amniotic sac.[11] People in many cultures believed that what the mother saw or felt, such as looking at a deformed or injured person or animal or thinking evil thoughts, would injure or "mark" an unborn baby. Thus, a Milwaukee woman of unknown ethnicity worried that she had marked her unborn baby by putting her hand on her face after having a craving for strawberries that she was unable to satisfy, and a Missouri mother attributed her infant's death to her witnessing the birth of a calf while pregnant. Maria Chona, a Papago Indian woman, told an anthropologist that she was kind to the people in her village who looked sick or ugly, and never laughed at them, so that her unborn baby would have a strong body. Indeed, the belief in marking a baby was so common that medical experts devoted considerable energy to refuting it.[12]

Many of the rituals of pregnancy were intended to facilitate childbirth and the child's later health. For example, the Tewa of New Mexico forbade pregnant women from lingering at a door, or from starting to go out and then not going, lest the unborn child start out and then draw back or take a long time to come out. A Japanese immigrant wrapped her belly in cotton cloth in order to "bear small, raise big." In contrast, Jewish expectant mothers were warned against doing anything special at all. Engaging in public preparations for a new baby by sewing baby clothes or following a special health regimen were feared to bring bad luck.[13]

Although most customs of pregnancy adduced expectant mothers to take care of themselves, working-class and farm women frequently found that their household and farm responsibilities made it impossible for them to do so. A great many pregnant women worked right up until delivery. In rural Mississippi, for example, three-fourths of the white and almost all of the black women in one sample did housework and laundry while they were pregnant; one-third of the whites and four-fifths of the blacks worked in the fields as well. A North Carolina mother of five picked forty-five pounds of cotton and cooked a big dinner for her family the morning her baby was born. Even in prosperous areas, such as the dairy farms of northern Wisconsin, as many as one-half of the mothers worked in the fields while they were pregnant. They also carried water, tended the garden, cared for chickens and livestock, milked cows, churned butter, separated cream, and cleaned dairy equipment. Nor could women working in the beet fields of Colorado afford to quit work during pregnancy. "One mother remarked that 'Annie was almost born in the beet field,' and another 'topped until 6 A.M. and Lucy was born at 7 A.M.' "[14]

The working conditions of farm mothers were not necessarily improved by their husbands' prosperity. Women on large farms were responsible for feeding and cleaning up after work crews in addition to their own families. And when children were born during harvest season, farm wives had little time to rest. A Kansas woman attributed her slow recovery from a difficult pregnancy to the fact that she had to board six extra men to help with the harvest. Another lamented, "Just now I am expecting threshers — about 30 men for two days, and, while I will have help, I have to go ahead and get things ready for others. . . . I am so tired! If I could only rest a while, but I don't see any chance. I have had my children so fast and have had so much to do I am worn out. There are seven in the family now and I am only 26. What will it be like in ten years more, if I live?"[15]

The dangers of overwork were compounded by repeated pregnancies. A thirty-seven-year-old Pennsylvania mother, who had been pregnant twelve

times but had only six living children (two had died in infancy), and a
twenty-three-year-old New Hampshire woman who had only one living
child out of four pregnancies, were not atypical. An analysis of letters written
to Margaret Sanger found that the multiparas (those who had more than
one child) had an average of five children each. One-half of those who
reported the frequency of their pregnancies had become pregnant at intervals
of eighteen months or less. And their childbearing years were long: 80
percent had married before age twenty. Many women were terrified by
pregnancy, both because they could not afford more children and because
it brought illness and the possibility of death. "I always became depressed
when I got pregnant because I couldn't work, and without work I couldn't
feed my children," explained California farm worker Michiko Tanaka, who
eventually bore eleven children. "Once I remember pouring cold water over
my stomach and even jumping off a peach tree, but I was healthy and
couldn't abort. But I never thought of taking medicine to abort. I just thought
of it as an act of *kamisama* [the gods]." A thirty-year-old mother of four,
whose mother had sixteen children before dying at the age of thirty-eight,
confided to Margaret Sanger: "My soul cries out to die rather than have
more babies. . . . I'd be happy if I wasn't constantly under the shadow of
more babies."[16]

Because birth control and abortion were illegal, poor women often resorted
to desperate measures to end pregnancy. Emma Goldman, a midwife in the
1890s, remembered being overwhelmed by poor women's "fierce, blind
struggle" against frequent pregnancies. "It was incredible what fantastic
methods despair could invent: jumping off tables, rolling on the floor,
massaging the stomach, drinking nauseating concoctions, and using blunt
instruments," she wrote. "It was harrowing, but it was understandable.
Having a large brood of children, often many more than the weekly wage
of the father could provide for, [meant that] each additional child was a
curse, 'a curse of God,' as orthodox Jewish women and Irish Catholics
repeatedly told me." Some women had as many as twelve abortions. Although many women had safe abortions, others nearly died from botched
ones. "I have been practicing abortion though I know it will kill me in
time," a twenty-three-year-old mother of two confided to Margaret Sanger.
"I would rather die than have any more children when we cannot take
care of them."[17]

Sickness and the expense of large families and repeated pregnancies placed
a heavy strain on marital relations. Although many women were fortunate
to have caring and sensitive husbands, some men resented their pregnant
wives' ill health and objected to their desire for prenatal care as "foolishness"
or an unnecessary luxury. One woman who had to give up housekeeping
because she was sick wrote to Margaret Sanger that her husband and his

family were "mad with fury that he has such hard luck with me, [and] didn't feel sorry for me but for him as he had to pay doctor bills." Another worried because her husband "seems to think it is all my fault. All he seems to think about is the expense it will be to him, not the suffering I have to go through to bring it in to the world and the care of it afterwards, for he certainly doesn't bother his head about their little wants, its always mother that has to do their things for them. And when they are right little I really believe he fairly hates them."[18]

Women were able to face the difficulties of caring for their families during pregnancy and confinement by depending on support from female family members, friends, and healers. Throughout the nineteenth century, and into the twentieth, middle-class women gave birth at home with women friends as well as physicians by their side. Most immigrants and mothers of color also employed female attendants. In 1910, long after childbirth had been medicalized for middle-class whites, midwives attended at least half of all births in the United States. A study of Waterbury, Connecticut, conducted between 1913 and 1915, found that four out of ten foreign-born women (and almost seven out of ten Italians) were attended by midwives, even though physicians attended the deliveries of nine-tenths of Waterbury residents born in the United States. Similarly, midwives delivered 61 percent of Polish babies in a Wisconsin county, but only 16 percent of Anglo-Americans. In rural Mississippi, 88 percent of African American mothers used midwives, while 79 percent of white mothers were delivered by doctors.[19]

Many traditional mothers preferred midwives because they considered childbirth a female concern and because they wanted a woman's support. Midwives typically arrived when labor began and either stayed for several days after the birth or visited every day for one or two weeks until mother and child were comfortable. In addition to delivering babies and, in some cases, performing abortions, midwives looked after older children, cared for sick family members, prepared meals, did the wash, and cleaned the house. They also provided moral support and advice. "Granny helps in your misery," observed one Texas mother. "Midwife . . . gives tea etc., and helps with her hands," said another. Furthermore, midwives were less expensive than doctors, and they delivered babies even when doctors refused to do so because of racial or ethnic prejudice, difficult access, or the patient's inability to pay. Committed to doing the "Lord's work," many midwives were willing to work in exchange for crops or services, or even no payment at all. Indeed, payments to Hispanic parteras "were called gifts, because they were free-will offerings," reflecting the personal nature of the midwife-mother relationship.[20]

Most midwives were old women who had borne many children and were highly respected members of their communities. Religious women whose skills were passed down between generations, they saw their skills as a gift from God; the African American description of the midwife's job as "catching babies" reflects the perception that midwives merely assisted God's work. While physicians used drugs and medical instruments to hasten labor and facilitate delivery, lay midwives relied on prayer, massage, and herbal medicine to make birth safer and less painful. "Honey, I don' do nothin'; I jus' lights my pipe an' waits," explained an African American midwife when asked what she did after arriving on a case.[21]

The healing techniques used by traditional birth attendants were rooted in religious and symbolic ritual. Southern African American midwives hastened labor by placing the ashes of hen feathers under the mother's bed or by giving her tea made from a dirt-dauber's nest. They stopped hemorrhaging by serving ginger tea, applying cobwebs and cloths soaked in vinegar or tansy on the abdomen or birth canal, and advised the mother not to change her clothes for several days after birth. Birthing mothers in the black community wore the hat of the baby's father in order to have an easier delivery, and midwives "cut the pain" by placing an ax under the bed or a pocket knife under the mattress of a birthing mother. Russian Jews set a pan of water under the mother's bed to prevent bedsores and keep away poisons; after the baby was born, the mother blew into a bottle to make sure the placenta was safe delivered and all would be well.[22]

Whether their babies were delivered by traditional methods or medical ones, most birthing mothers were assisted by an experienced attendant. However, rural women who lived many miles from a doctor or midwife often had to rely exclusively on family members and female friends. A 1917 study of maternity care in a homesteading county in Montana found that neighbor women attended over half the deliveries, while husbands delivered one baby out of eight. "One neighbor does it for another out here," one mother explained. Women living close by were "always ready to lend a helping hand." Although most went "as a favor" because no one else was available, a few acquired a reputation for skill and charged for their services. In Wyoming, an especially compassionate mother attended the deliveries of a number of her neighbors, even adopting the baby of one who died. On at least one occasion, she moved an expectant mother and her three children to a cabin on her farm. She did the family's cooking and wash (on top of all her own work), and she was the sole attendant at the baby's birth. Yet not even this remarkable mother could help every woman who needed her. "So many of my neighbors die at giving birth to their children," she grieved.[23]

Even rural women who made arrangements for a physician-attended delivery might find themselves without care at the last minute. "We had planned to have a physician, but the snow was so bad it was impossible to send for him," a Montana mother explained. A Minnesota farm wife called a doctor during each of three deliveries, but he arrived in time for the birth only once. Still, she said of her last delivery, "being a more experienced Mother and having my mother and a neighbor Lady with me, we got along fine." Not all women were so experienced or so fortunate, however. A nineteen-year-old in Montana was totally alone when she had her first child. She delivered the baby, cut and tied the cord, cared for the newborn, and did all her own cooking and housework until her husband arrived with help two days later. Although not permanently injured, the young mother was weak and could not work for six months. "Nearly every neighborhood had known of a death or a narrow escape from death on account of childbirth," observed the author of a study on maternity care in Montana. "Again and again mothers would say, 'I've never been well since.' "[24]

For most working-class and racial ethnic women, it was not difficult access but discrimination and the high cost of medical care that made a physician-attended birth out of the question. "If I had a doctor, then when winter came there would be nothing for clothes," a Mississippi African American declared; "Poor families can't have such things as doctors." California farm worker Michiko Tanaka, who came to the United States in 1923, explained: "In the country, doctors were not available, and when they were, either they would not treat us [Japanese] or their services were too expensive. So as a rule, the midwives substituted for doctors in the delivery of the baby or the woman did it herself."[25] The following case of a Polish immigrant living in a Pennsylvania steeltown documents the matter-of-fact approach to childbirth common among women who had little opportunity to take care of themselves:

> At 5 o'clock Monday evening went to sister's to return washboard, having just finished day's washing. Baby born while there, sister too young to assist in any way; woman not accustomed to midwife anyway, so she cut cord herself; washed baby at sister's house; walked home, cooked supper for boarders, and was in bed by 8 o'clock. Got up and ironed next day and day following; it tired her, so she then stayed in bed two days. She milked cows and sold milk day after baby's birth, but being tired hired some one to do it later in week.[26]

Although this woman survived, overwork and inadequate maternity care could be deadly for mothers and babies alike. More women aged fifteen to forty-four died from childbirth than any other cause except tuberculosis, and many deaths attributed to tuberculosis and other diseases were hastened by pregnancy and childbearing. Excessive work and poverty were also correlated with infant death. Throughout the 1910s, studies found that the lowest income groups had the highest infant mortality. As one researcher, remarking on the fact that 46 percent of infant deaths occurred in the first month of life, observed, "Many of these children fail to survive because of conditions antedating birth."[27]

Mortality rates were especially high among the poor, but death and injury due to inadequate or incompetent medical care affected women of all classes. Georgia housewife Magnolia Le Guin was permanently injured after the birth of her first child, who died within a week. Although she eventually had eight more children, Le Guin blamed her chronic discomfort on the ignorant maternity care given her by her (brother-in-law) physician. "When I first became a mother he wrecked my health—and in some respects wrecked [it] for life," Le Guin wrote years later in her diary. "I was in a serious state for a year." African American clubwoman Mary Church Terrell "sank down into the very depths of despair" after losing her third baby two days after birth. Terrell was "tormented by the thought that . . . its little life might have been spared" if a proper incubator had been available. "I could not help feeling that some of the methods employed in caring for my baby had caused its untimely end."[28]

Even physician Dorothy Reed Mendenhall, a graduate of Johns Hopkins University Medical School and later a member of the federal Children's Bureau staff, lost her first child and suffered permanent injury as a result of bad obstetrics. Mendenhall was badly torn and became ill from puerperal sepsis because her doctor did a vaginal examination without washing his hands; her daughter died of a cerebral hemorrhage because he incorrectly performed a version, a procedure in which the fetus is turned within the uterus to facilitate vaginal delivery. Other college-educated women had similar experiences. A Minnesota woman had a nervous breakdown after being badly torn during childbirth and poorly treated by a "reputable" physician. "I have suffered endless torture and unnecessary worry and pain because of this doctors carelessness or ignorance, I don't know which," she lamented; "Life for me will never be as full."[29]

Double Duty: Housework and Child Care

Most cultures designated a certain period of time after childbirth for rest. Japanese custom provided for a twenty-one day rest after delivery; Mexican Americans observing the dieta stayed inside for fifteen days and in bed for eight. Anglo-American experts advised new mothers to "refrain from full activity" for six weeks. In reality, however, many women had to resume heavy housework and wage-earning responsibilities within a few weeks or even days after giving birth. For example, a new mother from Manchester, New Hampshire, began doing the housework and helping in her husband's store when her baby was one week old. Another woman from the same city returned to housework three days after delivery and to her job in a cotton mill after one month. A Polish American woman in rural Wisconsin went back to her normal responsibilities (which included milking cows, churning butter, chopping wood, and hauling manure) two weeks after the birth of a new baby, who was her fourth child under five years old. Another farm wife, apparently trying to take it easy, was found in bed "with her dough board in front of her trying to make biscuits" the day after she had given birth.[30]

Cooking was one of the most demanding household chores in the early twentieth century, and one of the most important, for gastrointestinal diseases were a major cause of infant death, especially in summer. Many mothers tried to prevent mortality through proper infant feeding.[31] Native-born white women living in cities typically followed the dietary recommendations of their doctors, while working-class and farm mothers were more likely to seek help from experienced mothers in their family and neighborhood. As late as 1917, white Montana homesteaders reportedly "received with surprise" the suggestion that they consult a physician about infant diet. Most immigrants and farm wives breastfed their babies, although they typically combined breast milk with food from their own tables — "just the same as I eat myself." Many, following the common belief that giving an infant a taste of everything the mother ate would prevent colic, fed babies "chewed rations" until their teeth arrived (that is, they chewed the infant's food before giving it to him or her). A study of Johnstown, Pennsylvania, found one-month-old infants given bread, potatoes, eggs, and crackers. Older babies were fed apples, sauerkraut, cabbage, bacon, bread soaked in lard, cakes, pies, coffee, tea, and beer.[32]

Many working-class and farm wives who wanted to follow the modern medical advice on infant diet found it virtually impossible to do so. Some found it hard to breastfeed their babies because poor nutrition and overwork depleted their milk. However, bottlefeeding was also risky, for bottlefed babies were three times as likely to die during their first month as breastfed ones. Safe bottlefeeding was an expensive and time-consuming operation that required money to buy pure milk and the necessary equipment (bottles, nipples, and an ice box), and time to prepare and heat formula and sterilize the bottles. Furthermore, many women could not find or afford the fresh fruit, vegetables, milk, or meat recommended for older children. "I am trying to carry out your orders in regard to feeding my baby," a Kentucky woman wrote her state department of health, "but it is a little hard, as we have no money to go on, but I am trying to raise green things in my little garden that the children need. We have good milk at least." A California mother of six, whose husband was unable to work, worried that her children "do not get what they ought to have to eat. They never see a glass of milk."[33]

As if inadequate rest and nutrition were not enough, many working-class mothers faced the additional burden of second-rate housing. Poor urban and rural women frequently lived — and worked — in overcrowded housing without running water, electricity, heat, or ventilation. It was not uncommon, especially in the south, to find homes with few windows for light or air and no floor but the ground. Many southern homes lacked screens to keep flies and mosquitoes (and malaria) out of the house; in one rural Texas county, 75 percent of black homes and 28 percent of white ones had neither toilets nor screens. In urban working-class neighborhoods, where dirt from steel mills and railroad tracks blew in open windows and mud from unpaved streets was often tracked inside, it was virtually impossible to keep a sanitary and well-ventilated house. Fewer than half of the mothers surveyed in a Pennsylvania steeltown kept their windows open at night; it was simply too difficult to keep the house warm and clean. Moreover, many working-class homes lacked closets and cupboards, so dishes and food had to be kept on tables, shelves, or on the stove, vulnerable to insects, animals, and dirt.[34]

Awful housing conditions not only added to the mother's workload and stress; they were also unhealthy, for respiratory and contagious diseases moved faster through inadequate and overcrowded housing. In one industrial city, 21 percent of babies living in homes with low rent, compared to less than 9 percent of infants of homeowners, died before their first birthday. A study of Johnstown, Pennsylvania, found that babies who lived in homes with more than two people per room were 2 1/2 times as likely to die as those who lived in homes where there was more than one room per person (that is, where no one slept in the kitchen and the child might have a separate bedroom). Infant mortality doubled when infants shared a bed with siblings or parents. Cramped quarters also increased the likelihood of children getting burned or injured by a hot stove or washtub, or of falling from a tenement window. Nevertheless, women in "crowded" homes had more companionship and perhaps even more household help than those who lived in single-family homes. Female family members and neighbors helped one another during pregnancy, childbirth, and sickness, and shared the care of infants and young children when mothers worked outside the home.[35]

Poor and working-class mothers depended on the assistance of female relatives and friends, for few had appliances or labor-saving devices that might ease the burden of housework. Only 2 percent of women surveyed in Mississippi between 1916 and 1918 had washing machines or refrigerators. Many impoverished women and children had to carry water and haul coal or wood long distances or up several flights of stairs; some had to prepare dinner in wood or coal stoves or over an open hearth. Only 8 white women, out of 295 whites and 380 blacks in the Mississippi study, had water in the house. Water was also rare in the homes of the Texas cotton families in a survey conducted in 1920 and 1921. Indeed, one-half of the black families in one county, where conditions were particularly bad, had to carry water 30 feet or more; 21 percent carried it 300 feet or more. Some Texas families (both black and white) still cooked over an open hearth, requiring parents and older children to keep a watchful eye on toddlers lest they wander too close to the fire. Doing laundry was also arduous work, for it required hauling water, scrubbing with a wash board, boiling clothes, and making soap. As always, young children added to the workload. Diapers had to be sewn as well as washed, and infrequent changings probably led to nasty bouts of diaper rash as well as more serious disease.[36]

Since few working-class men earned enough to support their families, many wives had to supplement the family income by working inside or outside the home. Taking in boarders was one of the most common ways mothers of young children earned money; as many as one-third of households in white and black working-class districts took in boarders at any given time. In Akron, Ohio, two-thirds of Italian women with infants under one year old took in boarders; boarding was also the chief wage-earning occupation for Mexican American wives in Colorado mining towns. Women who kept boarders spent long hours on cleaning and food preparation, often having meals and dinner buckets ready at irregular hours to accommodate men working in factories at different shifts. Trying to keep children quiet so that boarders could sleep during the day surely added to mothers' workload and stress.[37]

Besides taking in boarders, working-class mothers also earned wages at home by working as washerwomen, seamstresses, or industrial homeworkers. Finishing garments, making artificial flowers, shelling nuts, or rolling cigars at home permitted women to watch their children while contributing to the family income. African American women found that working in their own homes had the additional advantage of freeing them from the daily supervision and harassment of whites. Mothers forced to toil well into the night faced enormous strain, for it was nearly impossible to keep children quiet and attend to their needs while earning the necessary income. Moreover, small tenement dwellings crowded with garments and other materials created a fire hazard, and scalding hot wash tubs caused not a few burns.[38]

Although most turn-of-the-century mothers stayed home with their children, some impoverished mothers went to work outside the home. Most probably did outside wagework sporadically, depending on their husbands' income, the availability of child care, and the ability of older children to contribute to the family earnings. A 1928 study of wage-earning mothers in Philadelphia found that 21 percent of women with children under sixteen were employed six months out of the year. African American wives and single mothers were especially likely to work outside the home, no doubt because of their greater financial need. In the Philadelphia study, 44 percent of black mothers, in contrast to 19 percent of white ones, were gainfully employed. Studies found that the proportion of mothers doing wagework dropped as their husband's wages increased. In Manchester, for example, almost two-thirds of mothers whose husbands earned less than $550 were employed the year after the baby's birth, compared to fewer than 10 percent of mothers whose husbands earned more than $1,250. A survey of 725 Philadelphia mothers in industry found only 10 who said they did wagework because they wanted to. "Apparently, the mother works when she must," observed the author of another study, "and when necessity is less stringent she relaxes her efforts outside and gives more attention to her home."[39]

For the wage-earning mother, a sympathetic observer declared, "There is no hour of her day but has its duty, no day of her week but has its labor." According to Katharine Anthony, author of a 1914 study of *Mothers Who Must Earn,* most employed mothers held two jobs because they were responsible for housework as well as their paying jobs. Wage-earning mothers had to toil long hours to keep up with their household chores. Southern factory workers, for example, would rise at 5:00 A.M. in order to be at the mill by 6:00; they returned home twelve hours later to cook, sew, and do the laundry well into the night. In the beet fields of Colorado, "many [women] said that they rose at daylight, and that Saturday, when the family washing was done, became Sunday morning before they went to bed." A Michigan beet worker described her day: "In order to get my work done before going to the field I often have to get up at 3 o'clock. I bathe the children and prepare the food before going out. Then at night I must bake and clean house, so that there are many nights when I do not get more than 3 hours' sleep. The work is too hard for any woman. By the time you have worked 12 or 13 hours a day bending over you don't feel much like doing your cooking and housework."[40]

Many urban and rural wives took care of children and did household chores with little or no help. During the beet-growing season, for example, only 14 out of 454 Colorado mothers engaged in fieldwork had help with meal preparation from another adult in the household. Only 42 had even a child to help them. Similarly, more than one-third of wage-earning mothers in a Chicago study did all the housework themselves. An additional one-third had help from their children; only one-fifth had help from their husbands, a figure that may reflect the large proportion of single mothers engaged in wagework. As laundry was the most arduous of household chores, it is significant that over one-half of the Chicago women did all their own washing. Only 4 percent asked their children to help with the laundry, perhaps out of concern for protecting their health.[41]

Arranging for adequate child care was a particular challenge for wage-earning mothers. Because there were few day nurseries — and the majority were unsanitary and inconveniently located — most of the 843 wage-earning mothers in a Chicago study left their children with neighbors, relatives, or older siblings. One-quarter made no provision for child care outside of school.[42] Many employed mothers arranged their work schedules around their children. Some worked at night so they could be with their children during the day; others worked during the day, but returned home at noon to check on children and catch up on household chores. Countless mothers took their children with them to work. Agricultural workers left babies in boxes, baskets, or canvas tents while they worked in the fields, and let older children, from three to five years old, play about the area. The mother or an older child made sure the little ones did not fall into an irrigation ditch or get too badly bitten by flies or mosquitoes. Some women also took babies and preschool children to factories, although they had to watch them carefully because children who could crawl or run were vulnerable to accidents. "I take the children [aged 6 and 3 years] to the factory with me" one cannery worker explained; "I have to keep my eye on them and I lose a lot of time that way. They like to run around and play but it is too dangerous, and I try to make them stay near me."[43]

Although trying to watch a child while running a machine or working in the fields was stressful and could pose a danger to both worker and child, in most instances it was probably safer and warmer than the alternatives, such as leaving children home alone. Yet, some mothers — wanting to protect children from dangerous machinery, disease-carrying insects, or the hot sun — left children alone in the house and tried to look in on them during the day. Government investigators found at least fifteen children under five years old, and three children under three years old, left alone while their mothers worked in the Michigan beet fields. A nine-month-old baby was left at home alone while his mother worked from 5 A.M. until 7:30 P.M., with one hour off at mid-day. In Texas, a four-year-old girl was found caring for two babies while her mother was at work picking cotton.[44]

Most wage-earning women tried to care for their children as best they could, but the triple burden of wage earning, housework and child care took a toll on both mothers and children. In one industrial city in New Hampshire, 28 percent of babies whose mothers returned to wagework within four months died before their first birthday — more than twice the rate of babies whose mothers were not gainfully employed. Some women workers lost as many as five children during infancy! Furthermore, fatal accidents were not uncommon, especially (but not only) where parents were distracted by household and wage-earning responsibilities or forced to leave children unattended. In rural Mississippi, for example, a significant number of black children died as a result of burns because their families still cooked and heated their homes over an open hearth. Sadly, but not surprisingly, some mothers blamed themselves for their babies' deaths and the harsh conditions of their children's lives. "I was *mucha kucha* [careless] with my children but *kamisama* looked after them," lamented Michiko Tanaka, a California farm worker who tried both taking her children to work and leaving them at home. "Not a single one got hurt. . . . I was lucky. When I think of my children, I feel sorry for them. The way I raised them was unpardonable, regrettable. Despite the poverty they all faced, they all treat me so well with no resentment."[45]

The lives of middle- and upper-class mothers were not nearly as onerous or as dangerous as those of the poor. However, they too suffered from the frequent illnesses, accidents, and deaths of their children. Moreover, many middle-income women had household and social responsibilities that took time and attention away from child care. All but a few spent long hours cooking, sewing, and cleaning, even if they were fortunate enough to be able to pay someone to do "heavy work" such as washing, ironing, and scrubbing floors. A study of comfortable families in the 1910s found that housewives spent an average of fifty-six hours per week on housework. Harried mothers complained that exhaustion and fatigue left them little time to enjoy their children. "Would that I didn't have to live in such a strain — my strength so overtaxed!" sighed Georgia housewife Magnolia Le Guin; "If I had enough leisure and less strain I could and would be a better mother in many ways. I have not the time to be a companion for my children and am to[o] tired to talk with them much of the time." A Seattle mother of three felt the same way. "I am busy all day and all evening but my work is never done. I am tired enough to drop when night comes and in the morning look with dread upon the day ahead of me," she cried. "I want to play with my babies, I want to have time to love them and laugh with them. I love them until it hurts and know that . . . I can never forgive myself for not making more of these precious years."[46]

Mothers' Work and Maternalist Reform

The difficult working and living conditions of working-class and farm mothers, the demanding lives of middle-class mothers, and the fear of illness and death all mothers shared, gave rise to, and sustained, the maternalist child welfare campaign. Beginning in the 1890s, growing numbers of middle-class women, newly convinced that scientific information about child development could prevent most infant mortality, tried to turn their knowledge into action and save children's lives. As Children's Bureau chief Julia Lathrop put it, "Science refuses to accept the old fatalistic cry 'The Lord gave, the Lord hath taken away, blessed be the name of the Lord.' "[47] Optimistic about the possibilities of scientific motherhood — and disturbed by what they considered the dangerous and ignorant practices of traditional mothers — maternalists educated themselves about scientific childrearing and taught working-class women new methods of care. They wanted to make the benefits of modern science and medicine available to all children.

Native-born white women were the first and most enthusiastic proponents of the scientific childrearing advice and maternalist reforms. They had the smallest family size (and lowest birth rate) of any ethnic group, and consequently were more likely to be isolated in the home without the support of female family and friends. They were also more exposed to the science — and apparent complexities — of child psychology. "No man or woman of even average ability could read some of the admirable books and articles on child study without becoming painfully conscious of the shortcomings in themselves," a leading maternalist declared in 1900. "Life was simpler for my mother," an Indiana mother reflected twenty-five years later. "In those days one did not realize that there was so much to be known about the care of children. I realize that I ought to be half a dozen experts, but I am afraid of making mistakes and usually do not know where to go for advice."[48]

The first three decades of the twentieth century thus marked a transition between traditional social medicine and the modern medical management of childbirth and childrearing. Between 1910 and 1930, the proportion of midwife-attended births dropped from 50 to 15 percent, and the number of women taking sick children to doctors and following the medical advice on infant diet increased.[49] By the end of the 1920s, women from virtually every social and economic group had begun to look outside their female support networks to new sources of expertise on child care. No longer able to depend on relatives, friends, and neighbors for ongoing help with housework and child care, inexperienced mothers turned increasingly to physicians and to the childrearing advice found in government pamphlets and women's magazines for information and encouragement that had once been handed down informally. Still, few completely abandoned their traditional ways; most mothers combined the "scientific" advice from doctors and baby books with prayer, home remedies, and suggestions from relatives and friends.

The most dramatic development in early twentieth-century mothering was the substantial drop in infant mortality. Between 1915 and 1930, the proportion of infant deaths fell from 99 to 60 for every 1,000 live births for white infants, and from 181 to 100 for babies of color.[50] Behind these numbers lay the invisible work of mothers, who nursed children through serious illnesses, supervised their diets, and organized for health and welfare reform. The extraordinary improvement in children's life chances significantly eased the physical and emotional burdens of mothers' work, and it surely altered women's feelings about motherhood.

The middle-class women reformers who disseminated the scientific child-rearing advice and lobbied the government for child welfare reform played a critical role in the transformation of mothers' work. Increasingly well informed about the extent of the infant mortality problem — and affected by infant and maternal death themselves — maternalists empathized with the grief of poor mothers and judged their own feelings about motherhood to be universal. Ellen Glasgow's 1913 novel *Virginia* captures their sentiment well. After nursing her son through the deadly diphtheria, a white society matron was brought to a stunning recognition of the universal experience of motherhood: "The pang of motherhood — this was what she was suffering — the poignant suspense, the quivering waiting, the abject terror of loss, the unutterable anguish of the nerves, as if one's heart were being slowly torn out of one's body." Although caring for her sick child left Virginia feeling distant from her husband, it created a "feeling of oneness" with her mother and a mulatto servant, "whom she had always regarded as of different clay from herself." In this privileged vision of universal motherhood, all mothers were bound together by their love for children and responsibility for their care.[51] Maternalists believed that, as experienced mothers and educated women who kept abreast of the latest scientific theories of child care, they were uniquely positioned to lead the movement for child welfare reform. It is to their efforts — to mother-work in the community — that we now turn.

NOTES

Portions of this chapter previously appeared in my article, "'Grannies' and 'Spinsters': Midwife Education Under the Sheppard-Towner Act," *Journal of Social History* 22 (Winter 1988): 255–75.

1. Robert S. Lynd and Helen M. Lynd, *Middletown: A Study in American Culture* (New York: Harcourt Brace Jovanovich, 1956, orig. 1929), 149; U.S. Children's Bureau, *The Promotion of the Welfare and Hygiene of Maternity and Infancy for the Fiscal Year Ending June 30, 1929,* Publication No. 203 (Washington, D.C.: Government Printing Office, 1929), 21. The Children's Bureau arrived at this statistic by comparing the estimated number of live births with the number of registered births in states where new parents were sent childrearing literature.

2. Laurel Thatcher Ulrich discusses "social medicine" in *A Midwife's Tale: The Life of Martha Ballard, Based on Her Diary, 1785–1812* (New York: Vintage, 1991), 61–62. On women's collective responsibility for childbirth and child care, see also Judy Barrett Litoff, *American Midwives, 1860 to the Present* (Westport:

Greenwood Press, 1978), 27; Sarah Deutsch, *No Separate Refuge: Culture, Class, and Gender on an Anglo-Hispanic Frontier in the American Southwest, 1880–1940* (New York: Oxford University Press, 1987), 48–49; and Sheila Kitzinger, *Women as Mothers* (New York: Vintage, 1980).

3. For evidence of the diversity of mothers' experience, see the letters reprinted in Molly Ladd-Taylor, *Raising a Baby the Government Way: Mothers' Letters to the Children's Bureau, 1915–1932* (New Brunswick, N.J.: Rutgers University Press, 1986).

4. This point is made in two pioneering studies: Nancy Schrom Dye and Daniel Blake Smith, "Mother Love and Infant Death, 1750–1920," *Journal of American History* 73 (Sept. 1986): 329–53; and Judith Walzer Leavitt, *Brought to Bed: Childbearing in American Society, 1750–1950* (New York: Oxford University Press, 1986).

5. The infant mortality rate (the number of deaths within the first year per 1,000 live births) was 98.6 for white infants and 181.2 for nonwhites. U.S. Bureau of the Census, *Historical Statistics of the United States, Colonial Times to 1970, Part I* (Washington, D.C.: Government Printing Office, 1975), 57. See also Richard Alan Meckel, *Save the Babies: American Public Health Reform and the Prevention of Infant Mortality, 1850–1929* (Baltimore: Johns Hopkins University Press, 1990), 238–39.

6. U.S. Children's Bureau, *Maternal Deaths: A Brief Report of a Study Made in 15 States,* Publication No. 221 (Washington, D.C.: Government Printing Office, 1933), 6; Leavitt, *Brought to Bed,* 25.

7. Sylvia D. Hoffert, *Private Matters: American Attitudes toward Childbearing and Infant Nurture in the Urban North, 1800–1860* (Urbana: University of Illinois Press, 1989), 195; U.S. Children's Bureau, *Infant Mortality: Results of a Field Study in Waterbury, Ct., Based on Births in One Year,* Publication No. 29 (Washington, D.C.: Government Printing Office, 1918), 32; idem, *Maternity and Child Care in Selected Rural Areas of Mississippi,* Publication No. 88 (Washington, D.C.: Government Printing Office, 1921), 22.

8. S. Josephine Baker, *Fighting for Life* (New York: Macmillan, 1939), 58.

9. Michael M. Davis, Jr., *Immigrant Health and the Community* (New York: Harper & Brothers, 1921), 129–42; Children's Bureau, *Infant Mortality in Waterbury,* 76–77; idem, *Maternity and Child Care in Mississippi,* 46–47; idem, *Rural Children in Selected Counties of North Carolina,* Publication No. 33 (Washington, D.C.: Government Printing Office, 1918), 40–41; Charles A. LeGuin, *A Home-Concealed Woman: The Diaries of Magnolia Wynn Le Guin, 1901–1913* (Athens: University of Georgia Press).

10. See Catherine Scholten, "'On the Importance of the Obstetrick Art': Changing Customs of Childbirth in America, 1760–1825," *William and Mary Quarterly* 34 (1977): 426–45; Hoffert, *Private Matters;* Dye and Smith, "Mother Love and Infant Death."

11. See Ruth Underhill, *The Autobiography of a Papago Woman* (New York: Kraus Reprint Co., 1969, orig. 1936), 41; Truman Michelson, *The Autobiography of a Fox Indian Woman: Fortieth Annual Report of the Bureau of American*

Ethnology to the Secretary of the Smithsonian Institution, 1918–1919 (Washington, D.C.: Government Printing Office, 1925), 315–21; Carolyn Niethammer, *Daughters of the Earth: The Lives and Legends of American Indian Women* (New York: Collier, 1977).

12. Ladd-Taylor, *Raising a Baby,* 56–57, 125; Underhill, *The Autobiography of a Papago Woman,* 41. For an example of medical refutation, see U.S. Children's Bureau, *Prenatal Care,* Publication No. 4 (Washington, D.C.: Government Printing Office, 1913), 20.

13. Elsie Clews Parsons, "Tewa Mothers and Children," *Man* 24 (Oct. 1924): 148; Akemi Kikumura, *Through Harsh Winters: The Life of a Japanese Immigrant Woman* (Novato, Calif.: Chandler & Sharp, 1981), 43; Neil M. Cowan and Ruth Schwartz Cowan, *Our Parents' Lives: The Americanization of Eastern European Jews* (New York: Basic, 1989), 119.

14. Children's Bureau, *Maternal and Child Care in Mississippi,* 9, 35–39; idem, *Rural Children in North Carolina,* 34; idem, *Maternity and Infant Care in Two Rural Counties in Wisconsin,* Publication No. 46 (Washington, D.C.: Government Printing Office, 1919), 29–40; idem, *Child Labor and the Work of Mothers in the Beet Fields of Colorado and Michigan,* Publication No. 115 (Washington, D.C.: Government Printing Office, 1923), 54.

15. U.S. Children's Bureau, *Maternity and Infant Care in Rural Kansas,* Publication No. 26 (Washington, D.C.: Government Printing Office, 1917), 32–39; Ladd-Taylor, *Raising a Baby,* 132.

16. U.S. Children's Bureau, *Infant Mortality: Results of a Field Study in Johnstown, Pa., Based on Births in One Calendar Year,* Publication No. 9 (Washington, D.C.: Government Printing Office, 1915), 81–82; idem, *Infant Mortality: Results of a Field Study in Manchester, N.H., Based on Births in One Year,* Publication No. 20 (Washington, D.C.: Government Printing Office, 1917), 98–9; Mary Sumner Boyd, "Appendix," in Margaret Sanger, *Motherhood in Bondage* (New York: Brentano's, 1928), 442–43; Kikumura, *Through the Harsh Winters,* 39; Sanger, *Motherhood in Bondage,* 408–9. See Sydney Stahl Weinberg, *The World of Our Mothers: the Lives of Jewish Immigrant Women* (Chapel Hill: University of North Carolina Press, 1988), 218–33.

17. Emma Goldman, *Living My Life* vol. 1 (New York: Dover Publications, 1970, orig. 1931), 185–86; Kate Simon, *Bronx Primitive: Portraits in a Childhood* (New York: Viking Press, 1982), 70; Sanger, *Motherhood in Bondage,* 394–410. A Children's Bureau study of maternal mortality attributed one-fifth of all childbirth-related deaths of married women and one-third of the deaths of unmarried mothers to abortion. U.S. Children's Bureau, *Maternal Deaths: A Brief Report of a Study Made in 15 States,* Publication No. 221 (Washington, D.C.: Government Printing Office, 1933), 34–35.

18. Sanger, *Motherhood in Bondage,* 67–68, 399–400. See also Ladd-Taylor, *Raising a Baby,* 53, 132, 148–58.

19. Leavitt, *Brought to Bed,* 87–115; Litoff, *American Midwives,* 27; Children's Bureau, *Infant Mortality in Waterbury,* 45, 48; idem, *Maternity and Infant Care in Wisconsin,* 32; idem, *Maternity and Child Care in Mississippi,* 27.

20. "Report on the Midwife Survey in Texas, January 2, 1925," reprinted in *The American Midwife Debate: A Sourcebook on its Modern Origins*, ed. Judy Barrett Litoff (Westport: Greenwood Press, 1986), 77–79; WPA investigator on Hispanic midwives quoted in Deutsch, *No Separate Refuge*, 47.

21. "Midwife Education," in "Semi-Annual Report of Work Done Under the Federal Maternity and Infancy Act in the State of Virginia," July 1, 1924 to Jan. 1, 1925, File 11–50–8, Children's Bureau Records, Correspondence & Reports Relating to Surveys and Programs, 1917–54, Record Group 102, National Archives, Washington, D.C (hereafter cited as C&R, CB). See Molly Ladd-Taylor, "'Grannies' and 'Spinsters': Midwife Education Under the Sheppard-Towner Act," *Journal of Social History* 22 (Winter 1988): 255–75.

22. "Report of Midwife Classes Held in Halifax County, Virginia," in "Semi-Annual Report of Maternity and Infancy Work [Virginia]," July 1, 1924 to Jan. 1, 1925, File 11–50–8, C&R, CB; Ionia Whipper, "Superstitious Practices of Georgia Midwives," Folder 36a, Dorothy Kirchwey Brown Papers, Arthur and Elizabeth Schlesinger Library on the History of Women in America, Radcliffe College, Cambridge, Mass.; Davis, *Immigrant Health and the Community*, 192.

23. One-fifth of the Montana mothers left the area to have their babies. U.S. Children's Bureau, *Maternity Care and the Welfare of Young Children in a Homesteading County in Montana*, Publication No. 34 (Washington, D.C.: Government Printing Office, 1919), 27–31; Mrs. A. P., Wyoming, to Julia Lathrop, Nov. 1, 1916, and Mrs. A. P. to Julia Lathrop, Oct. 19, 1916, File 4–3–0–3, Children's Bureau Records, Central Files, 1914–50, Record Group 102, National Archives, Washington, D.C.

24. Children's Bureau, *Maternity Care . . . in Montana*, 28–31; Ladd-Taylor, *Raising a Baby*, 55.

25. Children's Bureau, *Maternity and Child Care in Mississippi*, 33; Kikumura, *Through Harsh Winters*, 31.

26. U.S. Children's Bureau, *Infant Mortality: Results of a Field Study in Johnstown, Pa., Based on Births in One Calendar Year*, Publication No. 9 (Washington, D.C.: Government Printing Office, 1915), 32.

27. U.S. Children's Bureau, *Maternal Mortality from All Conditions Connected with Childbirth in the United States*, Publication No. 19 (Washington, D.C.: Government Printing Office, 1917), 7–8; Leavitt, *Brought to Bed*, 24–25; Julia Lathrop, "Income and Infant Mortality," *American Journal of Public Health* 9 (Apr. 1919): 270–74.

28. Le Guin, *A Home-Concealed Woman*, 78; Mary Church Terrell, *A Colored Woman in a White World* (Washington, D.C.: Ransdell Inc., 1940), 107.

29. Dorothy Reed Mendenhall, Unpublished Autobiography, Typescript, Box 3, Folder H., p. 2, Folder I, pp. 12–17, Sophia Smith Collection, Smith College, Northampton, Mass.; Ladd-Taylor, *Raising a Baby*, 177–78.

30. Sucheng Chan, *Asian Americans: An Interpretive History* (Boston: Twayne, 1991), 110; Fran Leeper Buss, *La Partera: Story of a Midwife* (Ann Arbor: University of Michigan Press, 1980), 38; Children's Bureau, *Prenatal Care*, 31; idem, *Infant Mortality in Manchester*, 89, 99; idem, *Maternity and Infant Care in Wisconsin*, 48.

31. According to the best-selling pamphlet *Infant Care,* nine-tenths of all infant illnesses were due to "improper feeding." U.S. Children's Bureau, *Infant Care,* Publication No. 8 (Washington, D.C.: Government Printing Office, 1914), 64. In an approximate sampling of letters in the Children's Bureau's Central Files (file group 4–4) between 1914 and 1928, I found over half (733) to be primarily about food (including nursing, weaning, formulas, and diet for older children), while 629 were on other topics.

32. Children's Bureau, *Maternity Care in Montana,* 72; Ladd-Taylor, *Raising a Baby,* 75; Children's Bureau, *Rural Children in North Carolina,* 38–39; idem, *Infant Mortality in Johnstown,* 81–84. See Rima D. Apple, *Mothers and Medicine: A Social History of Infant Feeding, 1890–1950* (Madison: University of Wisconsin Press, 1987), for an excellent discussion of the medicalization of infant feeding.

33. U.S. Children's Bureau, *Causal Factors in Infant Mortality: A Statistical Study Based on Investigations in Eight Cities,* Publication No. 142 (Washington, D.C.: Government Printing Office, 1925), 89; Mrs. M. P. C. to Annie Veech, June 1, 1925, enclosed in Veech to Dorothy Kirchwey Brown, Apr. 15, 1929, Box 2, Folder 40, Dorothy Kirchwey Brown Papers, Schlesinger Library; Ladd-Taylor, *Raising a Baby,* 187.

34. U.S. Children's Bureau, *The Welfare of Children in Cotton-Growing Areas of Texas,* Publication No. 134 (Washington, D.C.: Government Printing Office, 1924), 38–39; idem, *Infant Mortality in Johnstown,* 24–26; idem, *Child Labor and the Work of Mothers in Oyster and Shrimp Canning Communities on the Gulf Coast,* Publication No. 98 (Washington, D.C.: Government Printing Office, 1922), 76–77, 81.

35. Julia Lathrop, "Income and Infant Mortality," 272; Children's Bureau, *Infant Mortality in Manchester,* 109–12; idem, *Infant Mortality in Johnstown,* 24–25. On shared kin responsibilities, see Judith Ellen Smith, *Family Connections: A History of Italian and Jewish Immigrant Lives in Providence, Rhode Island, 1900–1940* (Albany: State University of New York Press, 1985), 99–107.

36. Children's Bureau, *Maternity and Child Care in Mississippi,* 36; idem, *Welfare of Children in Cotton-Growing Areas of Texas,* 38–39. On the technology of housework, see Ruth Schwartz Cowan, *More Work for Mother: The Ironies of Household Technology from the Open Hearth to the Microwave* (New York: Basic, 1983).

37. Jacqueline Jones, *Labor of Love, Labor of Sorrow: Black Women, Work, and the Family from Slavery to the Present* (New York: Basic, 1985), 189; Children's Bureau, *Infant Mortality in Akron,* 19; Deutsch, *No Separate Refuge,* 92; Children's Bureau, *Infant Mortality in Johnstown,* 29, 47, 82; Lathrop, "Income and Infant Mortality," 273.

38. See Eileen Boris and Cynthia R. Daniels, eds., *Homework: Historical and Contemporary Perspectives on Paid Labor at Home* (Urbana: University of Illinois Press, 1989); and Eileen Boris, *In Defense of Motherhood: The Politics of Industrial Homework in the United States,* (New York: Cambridge University Press, 1994).

39. U.S. Children's Bureau, *Children of Working Mothers in Philadelphia,* Publication No. 204 (Washington, D.C.: Government Printing Office, 1931), 5–6;

Lathrop, "Income and Infant Mortality"; Gwendolyn Hughes, *Mothers in Industry* (New York: New Republic, 1925), 5; Katharine Anthony, *Mothers Who Must Earn* (New York: Russell Sage Foundation, 1914), 128–29. See also Lynn Y. Weiner, *From Working Girl to Working Mother: The Female Labor Force in the United States, 1820–1980* (Chapel Hill: University of North Carolina Press, 1985).

40. Anthony, *Mothers Who Must Earn,* 90; Jacquelyn Dowd Hall et al, *Like a Family: The Making of a Southern Cotton Mill World* (Chapel Hill: University of North Carolina Press, 1987), 169–70; Children's Bureau, *Child Labor and the Work of Mothers in the Beet Fields,* 55, 108.

41. Children's Bureau, *Child Labor and the Work of Mothers in the Beet Fields,* 55; idem, *Children of Wage-earning Mothers,* 38–40.

42. Chicago had forty-five day nurseries, each with an enrollment limit of twenty. Only two accepted African American children. Children's Bureau, *Children of Wage-Earning Mothers,* 17–23.

43. Children's Bureau, *Child Labor and the Work of Mothers in the Beet Fields,* 111; idem, *Child Labor and the Work of Mothers in Oyster and Shrimp Canning Communities,* 67.

44. Children's Bureau, *Child Labor and the Work of Mothers in the Beet Fields,* 111; idem, *Welfare of Children in Cotton-Growing Areas of Texas,* 7.

45. Children's Bureau, *Infant Mortality in Manchester,* 52–53, 88–89; idem, *Maternity and Child Care in Mississippi,* 45; Kikumura, *Through the Harsh Winters,* 40, 32.

46. Cowan, *More Work for Mother,* 154–60; Laura Cowley Brossard, "A Study of the Time Spent in the Care of Babies," *Journal of Home Economics* 18 (Mar. 1926): 123–27; Le Guin, *Home-Concealed Woman,* 175–76; Ladd-Taylor, *Raising a Baby,* 129–30.

47. Julia Lathrop, Address before the International Congress of Working Women, Nov. 1919, Box 60, Folder 10, Edith and Grace Abbott Papers, Regenstein Library, University of Chicago.

48. Presidential Address by Mrs. Theodore W. Birney, *Proceedings of the Third Annual Convention of the National Congress of Mothers,* in *National Congress of Mothers: The First Conventions,* ed. David J. Rothman and Sheila M. Rothman (New York: Garland Publishing, 1987), 196; Lynd and Lynd, *Middletown,* 151.

49. Litoff, *American Midwives,* 114.

50. Bureau of the Census, *Historical Statistics of the United States,* 57.

51. Ellen Glasgow, *Virginia* (Garden City: Doubleday, Page & Co., 1913), 351.

PART TWO

Mother-Work in the Community

If woman would keep on with her old business of caring for her house and rearing her children, she will have to have some conscience in regard to public affairs lying quite outside of her immediate household. The individual conscience and devotion are no longer effective.

— Jane Addams, "Why Women Should Vote"

A new standard is rising — the woman's standard. It is based not on personal selfishness but on the high claims of motherhood, motherhood as social service instead of man-service. This new motherhood shines before us like a sunrise.

— Charlotte Perkins Gilman,
"The New Mothers of a New World"

2

"When the Birds Have Flown the Nest, the Mother-Work May Still Go On": Sentimental Maternalism and the National Congress of Mothers

By 1914, so many middle-class mothers had taken up social service work that novelist Dorothy Canfield Fisher concluded that all the publicity given to child care had caused "most matrons to turn naturally to some phase of similar activity in the community." According to Fisher, middle-aged women were making "themselves more useful to the world than ever before by applying to various forms of social uplift the experience, the poise, the knowledge of life which they have acquired in the years of their mothering."[1] Moved by the seemingly universal "pang of motherhood" — and certain that they had a special role to play in the community by virtue of being mothers — middle- and upper-class women joined mothers' clubs and parent-teacher associations in the thousands. Working on the local level and in the National Mothers' Congress, they educated themselves about the science of child development, distributed childrearing information to the poor, and got involved in political matters relating to child welfare. Their maternalism was a bridge between mothers and experts, grassroots activists and political reformers, and between traditional and modern concepts of child care.

Motherhood was a central organizing principle of Progressive-era politics. Although it was also a unifying theme for a wide array of voluntary associations in the nineteenth century, between 1890 and 1920 it became an overtly political concern, inextricably tied to state-building and public policy.[2] Virtually every female activist used motherhood rhetoric, and virtually every male politician appealed to motherhood. This and the next two chapters examine the ideology of motherhood held by three groups of activists: sentimental maternalists of the National Congress of Mothers, progressive maternalists at the Children's Bureau, and feminists. All three groups built on the organizing power of motherhood during the Progressive era, using motherhood rhetoric both to improve conditions for children and to advance women's status. All three also backed away from motherhood rhetoric in the 1920s, when tensions over women's role in public life and the state's responsibility for social welfare provoked a backlash against feminism and reform, and a bitter split among women activists. Despite, or perhaps because of, maternalist welfare successes during the 1910s, motherhood rhetoric stopped being a viable organizing tool for reform-minded women activists after 1925. Progressive appeals to motherhood were for the most part politically ineffective, and the language of motherhood increasingly became the preserve of conservative politicians and organizers.[3]

This chapter focuses on the National Congress of Mothers, which gave a unified voice to the thousands of white women who participated in mothers' clubs and parent-teacher associations between 1890 and 1930. Although it has generally been ignored by historians, the National Congress of Mothers played a critical role in the popularization of parent education and child psychology and in the expansion of American public education, health, and welfare services—especially mothers' pensions—in the early twentieth century.[4] By 1915 the National Congress of Mothers and Parent-Teacher Associations (the name was changed in 1908) had a paid membership of 60,000, a monthly journal called the *Child-Welfare Magazine,* and ties with mothers' organizations throughout the world. Five years later membership had reached 190,000, and by 1930 the National Congress of Parents and Teachers boasted almost 1.5 million members.[5] Each mothers' club or PTA paid dues to the National Congress and received the *Child-Welfare Magazine,* but the activities of local chapters varied widely. Some clubs, especially in the early days, were primarily discussion groups on child study; others were vehicles for socializing and entertainment. Some PTAs focused on the schools, while others were involved in a wide range of community activities. As the national organization grew, it became increasingly oriented to the schools.

The diversity in membership, autonomy of local groups, and fact that few clubs appear to have left records make the activities of the PTA difficult to document, but a tentative portrait of the organization can be drawn from published materials and local reports included in the *Child-Welfare Magazine* during the 1900s and 1910s. Like nineteenth-century clubs and charities, the Mothers' Congress distributed alms and was steeped in the ideology of friendly visiting; unlike them, it also called on federal and state governments to protect child health and welfare. Local clubs raised money for school supplies, such as playground equipment, and programs, such as kindergartens and hot lunches for children, until school districts began to provide funds themselves. Club mothers helped establish juvenile courts and baby clinics; they lobbied for state mothers' pensions laws, federal health care legislation, financial aid to the schools, and censorship of "immoral" books and films.

In the 1920s, state and local PTAs helped the federal Children's Bureau administer the Sheppard-Towner Act. Yet despite working closely with government leaders to develop child welfare policies, PTA leaders insisted that woman's place was in the home and refused to endorse controversial issues such as woman suffrage.[6]

Most members of the National Congress of Mothers agreed on the dual aim of maternalism: to teach mothers how to care properly for their own children and to awaken their maternal responsibility to improve social conditions affecting all children. "The young mothers have all they can do within the home," wrote PTA president Hannah Schoff, "but when the birds have flown from the nest, the mother-work may still go on, reaching out to better conditions for other children." Underscoring both the private and public responsibilities of motherhood, Schoff insisted that "parents can never do their full duty for their own children . . . until they make it their business to see that all children have proper treatment and proper protection."[7] The two sides of maternalism are reflected in the aims of the National Congress: "To carry the mother-love and mother-thought into all that concerns or touches childhood in home, school, church or state; to raise the standards of home life; to develop wiser, better-trained parenthood; to bring into closer relation the home and the school"[8]

Sentimental maternalists were not only interested in child welfare; they also wanted to advance women's status. Yet while feminists and progressive women reformers embraced modernity and women's expanding social roles, the leaders of the National Congress of Mothers held fast to the late nineteenth-century ideology of scientific motherhood. To the extent that they wanted to professionalize motherhood by bringing science and education to childrearing, it was at least initially because they wanted women to be more content to stay at home in their traditional roles. "It is because most women have not had the knowledge and training which would enable them to evolve the beautiful possibilities of home life that they have in many instances found that sphere narrow and monotonous," explained the organization's founder Alice Birney.[9]

The contradictions inherent in maternalism — that is, in idealizing women's place in the home while asserting their influence in politics and government — are illuminated in the history of the National Congress of Mothers. Internal politics and changing times brought a significant shift in the organization's public image. Initially a model of respectability, opposed to woman suffrage and to women's professional involvement in social welfare administration (President Hannah Schoff even opposed the creation of the Children's Bureau in 1912), the National Congress of Mothers worked closely with progressive maternalists in the late 1910s. In the early 1920s, the PTA was listed as part of the international socialist conspiracy on the infamous Spider Web Chart, an effective piece of right-wing propaganda alleging a communist plot to take over the United States.[10] The resulting dissension within the PTA led the organization to withdraw from political controversy and to focus instead on parent education. By the end of the decade, the right-wing backlash to advances in social welfare policy and to women's visibility in public life had brought about the depoliticization of motherhood — and of the national PTA.

The National Congress of Mothers

At the end of the nineteenth century, many women exhibited a great deal of interest in an organization of mothers. When Alice Birney called the first meeting of the National Congress of Mothers in 1897, she expected seventy-five women to attend. Instead, over two thousand women and a handful of men poured into the meeting hall. They listened to lectures by G. Stanley Hall and moral crusader Anthony Comstock and heard papers on maternal responsibility for home life, heredity, and character-building. At the end of the meeting, they passed a series of resolutions on moral reform, child welfare, and parent education, which reflected the wide scope of their concerns. A White House reception, the wide press coverage, and the enthusiasm of the women who attended the first gathering attest to the broad interest in both the private and public aspects of mother-work.[11]

From its inception, the Mothers' Congress seemed as interested in preserving what it thought to be the traditional home as in distributing scientific information on childrearing to its members. Congress leaders idealized motherhood, took for granted the biological differences between men and women, and did not question men's authority in the family. According to Birney, mothers had been "divinely appointed to be the caretaker of the child," and they needed a "system of mutual aid" to help them meet this awesome responsibility. Membership in the National Congress of Mothers was not limited to biological mothers, however; it was also open to men and unmarried women, who "through their works have shown themselves possessed of the maternal instinct." Indeed, at one point the advisory council of the Mothers' Congress was comprised entirely of men. The "love of childhood is a common tie, which should unite us in holiest purpose," Birney explained.[12]

The ideology of the Mothers' Congress was shaped to a great extent by the child study movement and its founder, psychologist G. Stanley Hall. Hall was an educational reformer who criticized traditional rote learning as unnatural and insisted that children's health would improve if educational programs were shaped according to their "natural" needs. "The guardians of the young should strive first of all to stay out of nature's way," he

proclaimed. Applying Darwin's theory of evolution to psychological development in his well-known theory of recapitulation, Hall maintained that
every individual passed through successive developmental stages that retraced
the evolution of the human race. Children's physical and mental well-being
thus depended on their being treated differently at each developmental stage.
Hall believed that preschool children should be allowed to express their
instinctive (animal) desire for freedom and play, while older children in the
"savage" stage needed external controls and habit training. Not until a
young white man entered university did the psychologist think reason and
intellectual learning should take precedence over physical health.[13]

Hall's evolutionary theory informed his understanding of woman's social
role. Convinced that men and women had separate social functions because
of their biological differences, he argued that (Anglo-American) women
were by their very nature more intuitive and emotional than men and thus
better suited to be moral teachers. The "body and soul" of womanhood was
"more generic . . . nearer the child and shares more of its divinity than does
the far more highly specialized and narrowed organism of the man," he
told the National Congress of Mothers in 1905. Women's education should
therefore focus not on intellectual development, but on training for motherhood. "I do not know . . . whether the Holy Mother . . . knew how to read,
but the whole world has united in reverence of her because she illustrated
the complete glory of motherhood."[14]

Hall's idealized view of maternity, his racial concept of child development,
and his scientific authority made him popular with the conservative leaders
of the Mothers' Congress, who made him a featured speaker at their first
convention. Elite club mothers saw in Hall's child study movement a way
to dignify Anglo-American motherhood; as one female follower explained
approvingly, child study would not "revolutionize all our educational methods . . . [but] confirm some good old-fashioned ways of training." Moreover,
the imprecise methodology of the "science" of child study gave women a
prominent, if subordinate, place in the movement. Hall declared that child
study "should be preeminently the woman's science," and he encouraged
mothers to make their own contributions to knowledge by studying their
children. He got women to turn their homes into laboratories for child
study and to keep "life books" recording the size, weight, and character
development of their children. Even after 1900, when the theory of recapitulation fell into disfavor among psychologists, sentimental maternalists
held on to child study ideas.[15]

Perhaps to defend the new — and unprecedented — mothers' organization
from the criticism of conservatives, Alice Birney declared that all the women
on the Board of the Mothers' Congress were "emphatically women of the
home." In reality, however, their lives often contrasted with the domestic

image they were trying to convey. Although Birney insisted that she spent most of her time at home with her children "where all mothers belong unless they are so situated as to be compelled to earn a livelihood," she herself did not stay at home. Born in 1858 in Georgia and educated for one year at Mount Holyoke, Alice McLellan hoped for a career in medicine. She married in 1879, but was soon widowed and left with a small daughter to support, so she earned money selling advertisements in New York City. In 1892, she married prominent Washington attorney Theodore Weld Birney, by whom she had two daughters. Birney came from a strong free-soil background and apparently encouraged his wife to establish a mothers' organization. When he died shortly after the National Congress of Mothers was founded, Alice Birney devoted herself to the organization. Her mother helped care for her children.[16]

Hannah Kent Schoff, who took over the presidency after poor health forced Birney to resign in 1902, also built an impressive career during her administration, which lasted until 1920. Despite her stated allegiance to traditional feminine values, Schoff operated successfully in the predominantly male political world. Wife of a prominent Philadelphia businessman and mother of seven, she fashioned the Mothers' Congress into an organization influential in local and national affairs. As president of the Philadelphia Juvenile Court and Probation Association, she drafted and secured the passage of bills setting up juvenile courts and a probation system for youth offenders in several states. Schoff persuaded President Theodore Roosevelt to endorse the juvenile court system and was the first woman invited to speak before the Canadian Parliament on the subject. She served as a consultant to the U.S. Bureau of Education, worked with the State Department to organize an International Conference on Child Welfare in 1908, and in 1910 was appointed U.S. delegate to the International Congress for Home Education in Brussels.[17]

Indeed, none of the early leaders of the Congress could be called typical mothers. Phoebe Hearst, the wife of the California senator and mother of publisher William Randolph Hearst, was the financial backer of the organization. The officers included the wives of the vice-president, postmaster general and three Cabinet members, the sister of the Secretary of Agriculture, and two daughters of the Secretary of Navy. Theodore Roosevelt sat on the Advisory Council, and Frances Cleveland, wife of President Grover Cleveland, took an intense interest in the organization. Others well known in reform circles also participated in the Mothers' Congress. African American writer and activist Frances Ellen Watkins Harper and suffragist freethinker Helen Gardener spoke at the first meeting. Among the delegates to the first Congress were Mrs. Luther Gulick, wife of the playground reformer, and

Mrs. Max West, who sixteen years later would write the Children's Bureau publications on child care.[18]

Given their backgrounds, it is not surprising that the leaders of the Mothers' Congress believed that women had influence and did not need to vote. Although some club mothers were suffragists, and Congress leaders requested and received letters of support from Susan B. Anthony and Elizabeth Cady Stanton, they tried to suppress discussion of woman suffrage "lest inharmony arise."[19] In general, the National Congress of Mothers, like conservative women's groups today, was primarily concerned with asserting women's proper place in the home. Schoff, for example, believed that woman's influence was and should be based on motherhood. She thought that the "new woman" was more interested in self-fulfillment than the well-being of her children, and vigorously opposed what she considered the "warped" values of wives who preferred "self-ownership," financial independence, and careers outside the home to childrearing. Theodore Roosevelt, an ardent supporter of the National Congress of Mothers, commended club mothers for their superiority to the "new woman" who sought a life outside of childbearing. A good mother was "sacred," he told them, but the woman who "shirks her duty, as wife and mother, earns the right to our contempt."[20]

As Roosevelt's attack on the new woman suggests, the maternalism of the Mothers' Congress derived much of its appeal from the gender and race apprehensions of the Anglo-American elite. At a time when immigration, the uncertain status of African Americans, and white women's increasing visibility in the public sphere generated cultural anxieties about "race suicide" and the decline of the family, Anglo-American club mothers clung to the traditions and social structure that appeared to provide them with dignity, authority, and security. They believed their status enhanced by rhetoric about maternal responsibility for racial progress and took advantage of the fear of race suicide by using eugenic arguments to insist that women should be treated with respect. As suffragist freethinker Helen Gardener told delegates at the 1897 convention, "The race which is born of mothers who are harassed, bullied, subordinated, or made the victims of blind passion or power . . . can not fail to continue to give the horrible spectacles we have always had of war, of crime, of vice, of trickery . . . and, alas! of insanity, idiocy, and disease added to a fearful and unnecessary mortality."[21]

Maternalist politics were necessarily racial politics. As followers of G. Stanley Hall, PTA members naturally accentuated the role of heredity in the natural development of the child and in the "progress" of the race. They celebrated healthy and virtuous (white) women as mothers of the nation's citizen-soldiers and censured those whose heredity, homes, and family lives did not fit the ideal. "To bring a child into the world without a prospect of being able to provide food and clothes for its body, or instruction and training for its mind, is not only a crime against the unfortunate offspring," a speaker told the Mothers' Congress in 1897, "but a crime against society itself." More than a decade later, Hannah Schoff proclaimed that "every wrong condition that confronts our nation" could be traced to the home. "Infant mortality, juvenile delinquency, increase in divorce, race suicide, municipal and political corruption . . . have their root in the kind of care and training received in the home and its relation to that received out of it."[22]

Club mothers, no doubt convinced that heredity had made them fit to be parents, avowed that privileged women had a special responsibility for the nurture and care of the world's less fortunate children. Believing in the natural goodness of all children, yet appalled by cultural differences in childrearing and the grim conditions of urban poverty, the leaders of the Mothers' Congress urged their followers to become moral teachers of the poor. They called on "enlightened" club mothers to educate poor women about scientific methods of housekeeping and childrearing and about the "laws" of heredity. "Some people say that the first need of the submerged world is better tenements," a speaker told delegates to the first Congress. "But it seems to me that we must first elevate the woman herself, and then she will be capable of using a better tenement. The woman, the mother, must be helped by other women." Another speaker evinced the double edge of maternalism's regard for all children's welfare when she called on elite women to "love the children that belong to other people" while justifying their intercession into the family lives of the poor. "Your children belong to me, to the neighbors, to everybody else, to every one with whom they come in touch," she declared. "You can not keep them to yourself; you can not keep them within the narrow home circle — they belong to the world, and they should be so taught. They are only lent to you to care for, to help, until they can stand on their own feet and live their own lives independently of you." It was the duty of elite women to help disadvantaged children become good citizens by teaching their mothers scientific methods of housekeeping and childrearing and an appreciation of Anglo-American ways.[23]

The Work of the PTA

In its early years, the National Congress of Mothers focused more on educating individual mothers about child study and proper home life than on providing social services or welfare-state building. Under Birney's leadership, the Congress supported local child welfare charities and promoted parent-teacher cooperation, but made child study a priority. Club members discussed Hall's theories about child development in mothers' classes and clubs, and distributed his questionnaires on imagination, religious sentiment, and fear to their children. Disseminating Hall's work to a wide audience, they played a leading role in popularizing child study.[24]

Following Hall, PTA leaders claimed that scientific knowledge about child development proved the need for school and welfare reform. By 1910, most mothers' clubs combined child study and maternal education with a variety of charitable and social services. The activities of the Gardner, Massachusetts, Parent-Teacher League were typical. In 1911, the League reported to the *Child-Welfare Magazine* that it published weekly newspaper articles and book lists on child development, ran a library on child welfare, and raised funds for educational projects, a playground, and a hot lunch program at a local school. In addition, it set up a pure milk station, collected money for a local tuberculosis society and fresh air camp, distributed Thanksgiving dinners and Christmas baskets to the poor — and provided child care during meetings so that more women would be able to attend.[25]

The move from friendly visiting to service-providing to politics is evident in the PTA's work on child health, the preservation of which president Hannah Schoff called the "first duty of parents and society." Five of the twenty-three papers presented at the founding meeting in 1897 concerned health, a fact reflecting women's responsibility for taking care of ill children as well as the ideology of child study and eugenics. Initially, the health work of the Mothers' Congress was mostly educational and was organized on a private and voluntary basis; for example, club members distributed literature on the prevention of tuberculosis and organized classes and clinics on nutrition and hygiene. For the most part, such activities separated maternal education from other social reform efforts and attributed child death and disease to women's ignorance, rather than to poverty or the environment. "Infant mortality exists because of lack of knowledge on the part of mothers as to care of babies," Schoff wrote; "only as mothers are instructed in infant hygiene can babies' lives be saved."[26]

In the 1910s, club mothers across the country made the provision of child health services a priority. A number of PTAs ran infant health clinics, where physicians and nurses, many of them women, examined, weighed, and measured children, and instructed their mothers on nutrition and hygiene. In Providence, Rhode Island, the PTA conducted baby clinics in every school district. Volunteers treated sick infants and offered information and "cheer and encouragement" in Yiddish, Italian, French, Portuguese, Polish, and English. In 1914, the Springfield (Missouri) Mothers' Congress announced in the *Child-Welfare Magazine* that it held fourteen free clinics, established a baby ward in a local hospital, and employed a visiting nurse. The same year, 845 women and 425 babies attended a child welfare station run by club mothers in Poughkeepsie, New York; 120 children between the ages of eight and twelve enrolled in their Little Mothers' Leagues. Another 503 mothers enrolled in a PTA-run Los Angeles children's center the first two months it was open in 1916. Significantly, the clinic did not serve the city's most disadvantaged families; the majority of clients were "American" and the wives of office employees or skilled workers (although the largest percentage had only an eighth-grade education). Several groups reported that, despite initial troubles getting women to attend, their health clinics had become so popular they had to turn people away. The services established by the PTA (and other voluntary women's organizations in the same years) served as a model for the prenatal and well-baby clinics later funded by the federal government under the Sheppard-Towner Act.[27]

Although many mothers' clubs provided much-needed health care to local women, some PTA baby contests and clinics focused more on physical beauty and eugenics than the elimination of disease. The Erie, Pennsylvania Mothers' Congress reported enthusiastically that better baby contests "standardized" the physical and mental equipment of childhood and gave mothers the chance to learn from physicians "wherein their children may be falling away from the point of perfection."[28] By publicizing a "normal" standard of health and development, such clinics legitimized a racially biased concept of health and beauty. This no doubt increased the anxiety of women who did not fit the ideal while elevating the status of Anglo-American mothers, whose social worth was enhanced by the supposedly superior physical characteristics of their children.

For many PTA members, it was but a short step from the voluntary provision of health services to involvement in politics. Finding the demand for health care great, but their own funds inadequate to meet the need, hundreds of local mothers' clubs lobbied the government for publicly funded child health services and worked with the federal Children's Bureau on its baby-saving campaign. The National Congress of Mothers and Parent-Teacher Associations helped the Bureau distribute its child care bulletins, publicize the need for birth registration, and organize government-sponsored health conferences; it was the only private organization acknowledged in the introduction to the Children's Bureau pamphlet, Prenatal Care. The PTA's association with the Children's Bureau continued into the 1920s, when parent-teacher associations in forty-two states helped the Children's Bureau administer the child health programs of the Sheppard-Towner Act. Many clubs also worked with the Bureau of Education on the "summer round up" of preschool children, giving examinations to preschool children so that they would enter the first grade free of remediable physical "defects."[29] They thus went beyond their initial emphasis on education and friendly visiting to establish permanent publicly funded health services.

PTA efforts to improve education, like its work for health care, revealed the fluid boundaries between public and private. Local parent-teacher associations funded and administered numerous school programs before local governments began to do so. In 1914, for example, the Parent-Teacher League in Gardner, Massachusetts, gave the local school money for a music teacher, a piano, a playground apparatus, a manual training program, student hot lunches, an emergency medicine cabinet, individual towels, liquid soap, and electric lights. The Springfield, Missouri, Mothers' Club furnished books, clothes, and balls to school children, and organized a crusade against cigarette smoking by schoolboys. PTA members throughout the country funded improvements on school buildings and grounds, taught cooking and sewing to schoolgirls, supervised the janitors who cleaned school buildings, and sought with varying degrees of success to influence the curriculum and format of the report card. They provided scholarships and clothing to poor children, and raised money for higher teacher salaries and for better country roads so that rural children would find it easier to attend school.[30]

As Birney was inspired by a meeting with kindergarten supporters to organize the Mothers' Congress, it was only natural that the PTA should make kindergartens a high priority. Delegates at the founding meeting passed a resolution calling for kindergartens in the public schools; in the 1910s the National Congress of Mothers and Parent-Teacher Associations worked with the National Education Association, the National Kindergarten Association, and the U.S. Bureau of Education to secure public funding for kindergartens. In 1913, after the California chapter secured legislation requiring school districts to establish kindergartens upon the petition of the parents of twenty-five children, the number of kindergartens in the state doubled within two years. After the Erie, Pennsylvania, Board of Education decided to abolish public kindergartens because they were too expensive and merely relieved "lazy" mothers of the care of their children, the PTA collected four thousand signatures on a petition and prevented their demise. By 1915, approximately 12 percent of the nation's children were educated in public kindergartens.[31]

Like other maternalists, elite PTA activists believed that they had both a special responsibility and a unique ability to nurture disadvantaged children. Convinced of the therapeutic power of mother-love, they worked to incorporate maternal values and "a little love" into the law and called on the state to protect and discipline children when their families could or would not. Countless mothers' clubs thus campaigned aggressively for mothers' pensions laws. Committed to the idea that "the personal care of a loving and wise mother is the greatest need of every child," sentimental maternalists expected that state-funded allowances to "deserving" mothers would permit poor women to stay home and nurture their children, instead of neglecting them by doing outside work or putting them in institutions.[32]

PTA leaders also tried to bring a motherly influence to bear on the criminal justice system. Indeed, president Schoff made juvenile correction her personal priority, revealing the deep connection she and other conservative maternalists perceived between childrearing and the prevention of crime and disorder. Schoff drafted several states' bills for juvenile courts, detention homes for children awaiting trial, and probation systems, and she served on the committee that appointed Philadelphia's first probation officers. Juvenile delinquents, truants, and runaways were "not hopeless criminals," she declared, "[but] . . . victims of conditions for which they are not responsible." Most juvenile crime could be prevented if every child had "sympathetic, individual and intelligent guidance." Schoff believed that the juvenile court could provide individualized and parent-like care for troubled children. Under the probation system, "wayward" children were permitted to live at home, but they were supervised by a social worker who taught the entire family "better" ways of housekeeping and childrearing.[33]

Schoff's fear of crime and disorder also determined her views on child labor. In contrast to progressive women reformers—and many rank-and-file club mothers—who wanted to restrict all wagework of children under fourteen, Schoff worried that "extreme and rigid" child labor laws would result in "compulsory idleness" and crime. She insisted that work developed "manliness and the sense of responsibility" in boys, directing their boundless energy "into safe channels." If they were prevented from working, she contended, many would turn to criminal lives. Although she supported welfare state protection for "dependent" mothers and children, Schoff adamantly opposed it for able-bodied men and boys.[34]

Elite club mothers thus asserted themselves as guardians of all the nation's children. They tried to protect their morals by banning the sale and consumption of liquor and censoring books and films they considered immoral. In 1917, for example, the Denver PTA presented a petition with ten thousand signatures to the Film Exchange Board and won a permanent committee to judge the suitability of films.[35] During World War I, the National Congress of Mothers and Parent-Teacher Associations supported the country's policymakers and enthusiastically joined the war effort. Schoff, like many club mothers, saw the war as a vindication of her views on education and health; she attributed the war to Germany's authoritarian educational system and pointed to the large number of men doing poorly on military physicals as evidence of the need for better education about hygiene. Although the leaders of the Mothers' Congress opposed government attempts to introduce military training in schools—children needed the "chance to be children"—they eagerly disseminated pro-American propaganda to immigrants and encouraged local chapters to form committees on food and energy conservation. In 1918, according to the *Child-Welfare Magazine,* all twenty-two

PTAs in Memphis, Tennessee, sold Thrift stamps, worked with the Red Cross, planted victory gardens, and discussed patriotism in meetings. Most also made sure that the American flag hung over local schools.[36]

Congress members also tried to protect the morality of the "boys" in military service. Club mothers provided a "home influence" for young soldiers by inviting them home for Sunday dinner and by setting up clubs equipped with pianos, victrolas, pool tables, books, and magazines close to military training stations. "The conditions of camp life are necessarily abnormal," explained the *Child-Welfare Magazine;* "there is a special need of personal influence and hospitality of good mothers, who can be camp protectors."[37] While the boys protected world democracy, sentimental ma-ternalists — in a dauntless effort to maintain control of the moral order — protected the boys.

Maternalism and the Politics of Race

The social and political perspective of mothers' club members was deter-mined not only by their gender, but by their race and class as well. White women's understanding of woman's place, their concept of race "progress," and their readiness to use the state to promote a certain kind of home life reflected the experience and social position of the Anglo-American elite. Still, the official view of the Congress on race was liberal for its time. Leaders of the National Congress of Mothers believed that women all over the world were joined in motherhood and subjection to male lust and could unite "on the common ground of their children's welfare." "The National Congress of Mothers, irrespective of creed, color, or condition, stands for all parenthood, childhood, home-hood," declared founder Alice Birney. "Its platform is the universe; its organization, the human race."[38]

Such liberal rhetoric notwithstanding, many white club mothers were ambivalent about the participation of racial ethnic women in their move-ment. The National Congress of Mothers encouraged immigrant and African American women to form (their own) mothers' clubs but rarely treated them as equal partners in the mothers' movement. The maternalist ideology of Anglo-American club mothers thus had a double edge. On the one hand, the idea that motherhood made women particularly concerned about chil-dren's welfare promised to cut across distinctions of race and ethnicity; on the other, the view that women were responsible for the bearing and raising of citizens established a hierarchy among mothers that distinguished between those raising desirable citizens and those raising bad ones. White club women's culturally specific understanding of "home-hood" and "human race" took the family lives of white middle-class protestants as the norm; they frequently had little meaning for women of other social groups. For example, the PTA assumption that married woman's place was in the home implicitly reproached many African American wives, who were five times as likely as married whites to work outside the home.[39]

From its founding through the 1910s, the National Congress of Mothers and Parent-Teacher Associations saw itself as an organization speaking for women of all races and cultures. The *Child Welfare Magazine* contained reports from mothers' clubs in foreign countries, including Palestine, Persia, China, Mexico, and England. It discussed conditions for women and children in these places and urged Americans to help women there establish mothers' clubs and kindergartens. Perhaps reflecting the abolitionist heritage of a few of its leaders, the Mothers' Congress also invited some prominent African Americans to speak at its annual meetings. At the founding convention, writer and activist Frances Ellen Watkins Harper took advantage of the inclusive rhetoric of maternalism and delivered an eloquent address urging white mothers to treat black women with dignity and to help fund their mothers' clubs. "Has not the negro also a claim upon a nation?" Harper implored. "If you want us to act as women, treat us as women." "That the children of any race are the hope of that race is doubly true of all backward races," declared Anna Murray of the Colored Women's League, using language understandable to Anglo-American club mothers. Speaking at the 1905 convention of the National Congress of Mothers, she urged white women to nurture and guard as "the jewel of our civilization" children of every race.[40]

PTA interest in mothers' clubs in foreign countries and African American communities was doubtless motivated by genuine concern for child welfare, but it also manifested a colonial spirit. The same year that white club mothers listened to Anna Murray's plea for fair treatment of black children, they enthusiastically applauded Columbia University professor Samuel Lindsay's speech urging them to become "truly missionary" and extend their "noble endeavors" to the "less favored" people of Puerto Rico. "They will receive us, as their people received the armed troops of the United States in 1898, with joy and hospitality," Lindsay declared; "and we can thus help fulfill for them their highest hopes that dawned the day the American flag was first raised as a symbol of their new sovereignty."[41]

During World War I, Anglo-American club mothers avidly joined the wartime Americanization campaign. In 1918, the National Congress of Mothers and Parent-Teacher Associations established its own Department of Americanization, which promoted English language classes for mothers and kindergartens for immigrant children. Americanization literature characterized ethnic women as "timid," "shy," and "diffident," innocent victims of social upheaval and male lust, childlike in their need of guidance and assistance. Convinced that foreign-born women were more abused by their husbands than they were, PTA members assumed that immigrant women's inability to speak English and their isolation in the home devalued them in the eyes of their more Americanized husbands and children. They believed that immigrant men forced their wives into domestic servitude, factory work, or street life; and they tried to save immigrant women by promoting American values. Once foreign-born women learned American ways, maternalists thought, they would no longer allow their husbands to treat them as slaves.[42]

The maternalistic attitude PTA officials had toward immigrants and women of color pervaded their literature and clearly influenced their charity and welfare work. However, the activities of the Mothers' Congress should not be seen simply as an attempt by elite matrons to impose their values on the poor, for it is likely that many club mothers learned something from the contact they had with working-class women. Like clients of other social service agencies, immigrant and working-class women who attended PTA classes were probably "active negotiators in a complex bargaining."[43] Maternalist ideas about universal motherhood may have made space for them to make their own demands. Although future research is needed to determine the influence of the participants in PTA-run mothers' classes on the National Congress of Mothers, it is possible that contact with working-class women contributed to the organization's growing interest in social welfare reform.

In any case, white club mothers' condescending attitude toward immigrant women coexisted with a romanticized view of "simple" hard-working mothers. Elite women who felt idle and useless often idealized poor women who had jobs, earned wages, and thus contributed to the upkeep of their families. "Happy the woman whose husband is so poor that her actual labor is honestly needed in the house," mused popular novelist Dorothy Canfield Fisher. "She is still in those halcyon days of economic simplicity. But woe to the prosperous woman, who . . . wastes and perverts her valuable productive energy."[44] Articles in the *Child-Welfare Magazine* urged club mothers to treat poor women with dignity. Like childrearing experts who told mothers they could learn from their children, Congress leaders reminded their members that they could learn from the poor. According to the *Child-Welfare Magazine,* the "silk-clad woman" was "generally clever enough to appreciate and to admire" the spirit and determination of poor mothers who faced years of self-denial and poverty for the sake of their children. "The feeling of inferiority, of uselessness . . . may humiliate the idle woman," one author wrote, "but it is bound to do her good. It will certainly deprive her conversation of sweeping criticism on lives and conditions unknown to her. It will also utterly do away with many of her prejudices against the foreigner and it will make the 'let them eat cake' attitude impossible."[45]

While the *Child-Welfare Magazine* frequently ran articles on club mothers' relations with immigrants, it contained little discussion of PTA work among African Americans. There is no evidence of an explicit policy on race in the records of the National Congress of Mothers and Parent-Teacher Associations, but it is likely that, like the General Federation of Women's Clubs and the National American Woman Suffrage Association, the Congress discriminated against African Americans. Although a handful of black women participated in the predominantly white mothers' clubs and PTAs, integrated groups were apparently rare, no doubt due to racially segregated schools and housing patterns as well as prejudice among white women. Separate "colored" mothers' clubs and parent-teacher associations appeared during the 1920s. The National Congress of Colored Parents and Teachers formed in 1926 (the same year the first Native American parent-teacher association was established in North Dakota). By 1930, it had 14,000 members.[46]

A 1926 survey of PTA officers about "extension work" among African Americans reveals white women's ambivalence about people of color in the national organization. Only two-thirds (168 of 248) of Colored Parent-Teacher Associations surveyed were even affiliated with the state or national Congress of Parents and Teachers. Most state PTAs did not allow black women to participate as equals; a leader of the Ohio Mothers' Congress observed with apparent astonishment that "some colored [women] seem to resent the fact that they are not invited to be a member of committees or take part on program of local meetings." White women were reluctant to have black leaders in groups that were predominantly white. Although a black woman successfully served as president of the nearly all-white Washington PTA, the California experience was undoubtedly more common: "While colored people are a small minority all is well, but if they become active, white women drop out." Although some groups avoided the race question because they had separate organizations, conventions and banquets seemed to pose a particular problem when black mothers' clubs were affiliated with white groups. In Tennessee, black women were allowed to attend PTA conventions as visitors, but had to sit in the rear, apart from other delegates. The Ohio Congress provided separate banquet tables for black and white women.[47]

Despite the active role African American women played in mothers' clubs and PTAs, there is only scattered reference to their activities in the *Child-Welfare Magazine.* The few reports from African American clubs describe activities almost identical to those undertaken by white clubs, perhaps because those activities were given special emphasis in a magazine whose readership was mostly white. For example, in 1916, the *Child-Welfare Magazine* reported that the six members of the Poplarville, Mississippi, Colored Mothers' Club paid tuition and bought books for orphaned students, furnished wood and crayons for their school, and were beginning to raise funds for a domestic science teacher.[48]

Although some black women worked with the National Congress of Mothers and Parent-Teacher Associations, most were active in clubs and organizations within the African American community. The most influential organization in the period of this study was the National Association of Colored Women (NACW), founded one year before the National Congress of Mothers, in 1896. Within twenty years, the NACW represented fifty thousand women in over a thousand clubs across the country.[49] Despite the many differences between the NACW and the PTA, a brief comparison of the two organizations reveals both the different nature of black women's welfare activism, and the ways in which the politics of Anglo-American club mothers were determined by their race. White and black club women were similar in a number of ways: they used the rhetoric of motherhood, found close friendships and meaningful work through club activism, and emphasized both the private and public aspects of mothers' work—child-rearing and child welfare. Both groups of women ran classes for mothers on childrearing and domestic science, and donated clothing, fuel, food, and medicine to the poor. Both established social welfare institutions, such as schools, orphanages, and old age homes, and ran these services until their funding and administration were were taken over by local governments.[50]

Yet, the leadership of the National Congress of Mothers and the National Association of Colored Women—and therefore the political styles of the two organizations—could hardly be more different. First, while no well-known white woman had the Mothers' Congress or the General Federation of Women's Clubs as her primary organizational affiliation, the NACW provided a home base for such prominent activists as Mary Church Terrell, Ida B. Wells, and Mary McCleod Bethune. (In that way, as well as in its support of women's right to vote, the NACW was more a counterpart of the predominantly white social settlements or suffrage organizations.) Second, the National Congress of Mothers had only two presidents between 1897 and 1920, while the NACW had six presidents in the same period, perhaps suggesting different ideas about leadership, democracy, and power. A third difference was the greater likelihood of African American club women to be highly educated married women with careers. In contrast to sentimental maternalists, most of whom were married women but did not have a paying job, and progressive maternalists, who tended to be single women with careers, a profile of 108 NACW members between 1896 and 1920 found that three-quarters were married and nearly three-quarters worked outside the home. (Only one-quarter had children, however).[51]

Overcoming obstacles that white club mothers did not have to face, NACW leaders listed impressive accomplishments outside the home, especially in the area of education. Mary Church Terrell, the organization's first president, was a graduate of Oberlin College and the first black woman appointed to the Board of Education in the District of Columbia. Margaret Murray Washington, second wife of Booker T. Washington and Dean of Women at Tuskegee Institute, was the editor of the NACW journal, *National Notes,* and served as its president from 1914 to 1918. Mary Talbert, NACW president from 1916 to 1920, was another Oberlin graduate. She served as assistant principal of a church in Little Rock, Arkansas, and went on to become the national director of the Anti-Lynching Crusaders in the 1920s. Mary McLeod Bethune, arguably the most influential African American woman in the first half of the twentieth century, served as NACW president from 1924 to 1928 before going on to found the National Council of Negro Women in 1935. One of seventeen children of slaves freed by the Civil War, Bethune rose to national prominence as founder and head of the school that became the Bethune-Cookman College and as president of the Florida Federation of Colored Women. She reached the peak of her influence during the New Deal, when as director of the division of Negro Affairs in the National Youth Administration, she ensured that at least some of the benefits of the expanding U.S. welfare system reached the African American community.[52]

Black and white members of mothers' clubs also differed in their understanding of home and motherhood.[53] Both groups accepted women's responsibility for childrearing and used maternal imagery to further their cause. For example, Ida B. Wells described motherhood as "one of the most glorious advantages of the development of . . . womanhood," and Chicago club activist Fannie Barrier Williams urged women to "become the civic mothers of the race."[54] However, the realities of mothering in a racist society made it impossible for African Americans to idealize motherhood in the same way as elite whites. For them, the legacy of slavery—when motherhood meant producing slave labor and possibly losing one's children through sale—and infant and maternal mortality rates at least double those of whites defined the maternal experience. Mary Church Terrell, who herself lost three children within days of their births, eloquently explained the differences to the National Congress of Mothers:

> Contrast, if you will, the feelings of hope and joy which thrill the heart of the white mothers with those which stir the soul of her colored sister. Put yourselves for one minute in her place, (you could not endure the strain longer) and imagine, if you can, how you would feel if situated similarly—As a mother of the weaker race clasps to her bosom the babe which she loves as fondly as you do yours, her heart cannot thrill with joyful anticipations of the future. For before

her child she sees the thorny path of prejudice and proscription which his little feet must tread. . . . So rough does the way of her infant appear to many a poor black mother that instead of thrilling with the joy which you feel, as you clasp your little ones to your breast, she trembles with apprehension and despair.[55]

For Anglo-American women, the home was a locus of socialization to train young children to be good citizens. For African Americans, it was a training ground for struggle as well. It was the place for "building up strength and righteousness in its sons and daughters, and equipping them for the inevitable battles of life which grow out of the struggle for existence."[56] African American mothers were responsible not only for teaching children to be honest and industrious workers and citizens but also for helping them fight discrimination and live with dignity in a racist world.

Black and white women activists also differed in their attitude toward the poor. Like white club mothers, African American activists were concerned with "proper" home life and social uplift, and assumed the task of imparting these values to the poor. Membership in African American clubs was limited to members of "worthy" families, and organizational activities often reflected a condescending attitude toward the poor. At the second NACW convention in 1897, for example, Mary Church Terrell urged club women to establish kindergartens so that the "waifs and strays of the alleys [could] come in contact with intelligence and virtue." Nevertheless, elite black women were much more likely than Anglo-Americans to perceive their fate as being tied to that of the poor. As Fannie Barrier Williams explained, "The club movement among colored women reaches into the sub-social condition of the entire race. Among white women, clubs mean the forward movement of the best women in the interest of the best womanhood. Among colored women, the club is the effort of the few competent on behalf of the many incompetent; that is to say that the club is only one of many means for the social uplift of a race."[57]

The NACW motto, "Lifting as We Climb," expressed black club women's desire to close the gap between different social classes even as it reinforced the social values of the elite. NACW leaders shared the view, widely held by whites, that many poor black families were unstable; unlike whites, they attributed family instability not to individual moral failure but to the historical sexual exploitation of black women under slavery. Thus, while Anglo-American club mothers tended to blame individual men or women for what they considered dysfunctional families, NACW leaders considered the "improper" home life of an African American "more his misfortune than his fault."[58]

While white club mothers tried to preserve the concept of woman's sphere (at least in theory), racism made the ideology of separate spheres a luxury few blacks could afford. Unlike the Mothers' Congress, which generally disavowed politics even while it developed close relationships with government leaders and influenced the direction of public welfare policy, the NACW openly asserted the need for political power. For them, there was a special urgency to the maternalist dictum that mothers' responsibilities should extend beyond the private home to improve social conditions affecting children. Like white club mothers, the NACW was concerned with moral and domestic matters, such as temperance, social purity, and child study. Beyond them, black women also agitated around obviously political subjects not directly related to child welfare, such as lynching, the convict lease system, police brutality, and jim crow laws. A comparison of the 1904 resolutions of the National Congress of Mothers and the NACW is instructive. The Mothers' Congress advocated moral training in the public schools, opportunities for deaf children equal to those of "normal" youth, stricter laws against divorce, child labor legislation, and a probation system. The same year, the NACW endorsed temperance, educational mothers' meetings, and the elimination of immoral literature; it also condemned lynching, called for a boycott of segregated street cars, and urged members to study and prepare for woman suffrage.[59]

The welfare institutions established by black club women, like those established by whites, reveal the fluid boundaries between public and private agencies. Kindergartens, a priority because education was crucial to African American advancement and because so many mothers worked outside the home, were established through the effort of the entire community. Churches supplied fuel and rent money; individuals and organizations donated milk, bread, and clothing. In Washington, D.C., the Colored Woman's League ran seven free kindergartens and several day nurseries serving more than one hundred children until they were incorporated into the public school system. The Gate City Free Kindergarten Association of Atlanta ran five kindergartens and two day nurseries in poor neighborhoods. Even after the Kindergarten Association became eligible for public funding by joining the Atlanta Community Chest in 1923, it continued to be financed largely by private fund-raising drives.[60]

African American women activists, with little hope of influencing white policymakers, naturally focused more on community self-help and building private welfare institutions than on public welfare reform. Still, some organizations — most notably the Atlanta Neighborhood Union — combined self-help and political pressure. Organized in 1908 by Lugenia Burns Hope, wife of the president of Atlanta University, the Union made health care a priority, offering classes in prenatal and infant care, hygiene, and the treatment of tuberculosis. It also ran a dental clinic and enlisted volunteer nurses

and doctors to visit patients in their homes. Yet despite its success at institution building within the black community, the Union was unable to
make significant and lasting improvements in white-controlled services. A
vigorous campaign to improve the public schools succeeded in establishing
an additional school for black children and in raising the salaries of black
teachers, but ultimately had little impact on Atlanta's racist school system.[61]

The inability of African American women to influence policymakers is
especially striking when compared to white women's success. Between 1890
and 1920, European American women gained unprecedented influence in
government and won important legislative victories, such as mothers' pensions, protective labor laws, and the vote. African American women and
children, however, faced tightening segregation laws and increasing racial
violence. Most were not covered by mothers' pensions and protective legislation, and, even after the passage of the woman suffrage amendment,
many were denied the right to vote. Blacks were also excluded from the
alliance white maternalists forged with government agencies; not until the
1930s did Mary McLeod Bethune have the ear of federal officials. Yet most
white club mothers did not see racial discrimination or violence as child
welfare concerns. The racial exclusivity of the National Congress of Mothers
and its members' narrow understanding of child welfare — along with legal
segregation, jim crow laws, and the stinginess of white taxpayers and politicians — ensured that public child welfare services remained inferior or
unavailable in black communities even as they were improving in white
ones.

Politics and the PTA in the 1920s

While the NACW asserted the importance of women's political activism
from its inception, the increasing political involvement of the National
Congress of Mothers and Parent-Teacher Associations during the Progressive
era seemed to many a significant break from the past. In the 1890s, white
club mothers concentrated on discussing child study and distributing alms
to the needy; twenty years later, even rank-and-file members helped run
social service organizations and lobbied their legislators themselves. However,
in the anticommunist climate of the early 1920s, PTA leaders divided over
the direction they felt the organization should take. Moderates like Katharine
Chapin Higgins (president from 1920 to 1923) made restructuring the organization and increasing membership a priority, while national secretary
Florence Watkins and Legislative Department head Elizabeth Tilton focused
on progressive welfare reform. Under Watkins' leadership, the National
Congress of Mothers and Parent-Teacher Associations joined the National
Council for the Prevention of War and the Women's Joint Congressional

Committee, a lobbying coalition of the major women's reform organizations. As a result, the PTA was listed on the widely circulated Spider Web Chart as one of fifteen "Socialist-Pacifist" women's organizations that were "an Absolutely Fundamental and Integral Part of International Socialism."[62]

The Red Scare of the early 1920s brought the long-standing political differences within the PTA to the surface. Members were sharply divided over the questions of women's involvement in politics and the state's responsibility for social welfare. The president of the Washington, D.C., PTA accused Florence Watkins of being a communist. Archconservative Brigadier-General Amos Fries, head of the Chemical Warfare Service of the War Department, and a PTA member and father of four, attacked the National Council for the Prevention of War as communist, leading PTA president Higgins to order Watkins to withdraw from the peace organization. (She had been a member of its executive board.) In 1923, several delegates to the PTA convention attempted to remove the peace and child labor planks from the platform. They had the support of ex-president Hannah Schoff, who urged delegates to stand by their government against advocates of disarmament and the child labor amendment, but the liberal platform prevailed.[63]

Most PTA members seem to have welcomed the Progressive-era politicization of motherhood, but the organization's growing involvement in civic and legislative work did not go unquestioned. A 1919 letter to the *Child-Welfare Magazine* objected that the PTA's political activities violated the principle of helping its *"own members* to be more capable in developing the bodies, minds and hearts of *their own* children." "The average homemaker is not and never should become a public woman," the author complained. "Discussion and analysis of the essentials of true home life and child character, seem to have given place to restoration through Juvenile Courts and general legal and social service work."[64]

Such political conservatism affected the style and program of the National Congress of Mothers and Parent-Teacher Associations, as the uncontroversial task of membership building gained prominence over child welfare. The slogan, "A PTA in every school," was adopted in 1922. In 1923, national membership reached 532,000, up from 200,000 just three years earlier. Although the National Congress continued to support progressive legislation, such as disarmament, the child labor amendment, and a World Court, these were the efforts of an active minority led by Watkins, and not the major focus of the organization. For example, although the PTA endorsed the child labor amendment and the outlawry of war in its 1927 resolutions, these issues took a back seat to less controversial aims such as "worthy home membership, sound health, mastery of tools, technics and spirit of learning, useful citizenship, and wise use of leisure."[65]

The decision to drop "mothers" from the name of the National Congress

of Mothers and Parent-Teacher Associations in 1924 acknowledged the growing influence of experts and teachers in the organization — and indicated
the end of sentimental maternalism. While the early leaders all claimed to
be "women of the home," the PTA's fifth president, Ina Caddell Marrs, listed
among her credentials a ten-year teaching career, as well as nine years of
activism in the state and National Congress of Parents and Teachers and
marriage to the superintendent of the Texas State Department of Education.
Furthermore, as the PTA began to focus on parent education and the schools,
its officers benefited from new career opportunities in those fields. In 1930
the organization received a grant from the Laura Spelman Rockefeller Memorial Foundation for a specialist in parent education and for publication
of a *Parent Education Yearbook.* PTA leaders taught parent education in
colleges, summer schools, elementary schools, and libraries.[66]

The changing focus of the National Congress of Parents and Teachers
was reflected in the *Child-Welfare Magazine.* The journal stopped publishing
reports on the activities of local mothers' clubs, the section on "State News,"
and articles on foreign-born mothers. Instead, it discussed health and safety
in the schools, ways to protect children from "immoral" influences, and
how to raise a "normal" child. The magazine published study questions,
reading lists, advice from child psychologists and educators, and excerpts of
popular childrearing books, such as Douglas Thom's *Child Management,*
Dorothy Canfield Fisher's *Mothers and Children,* and *Wholesome Childhood,* by Ernest Groves. Child psychology and parent education replaced
benevolence and social reform as its focus. In contrast to the Gilded Age
and Progressive era, when the ideal mother was portrayed as a "social"
mother involved in women's clubs or charities, the exemplary mother of
the 1920s was focused on her own children. Middle-class mothers were no
longer supposed to be active in maternal education or welfare work; they
were supposed to spend their time studying the latest theories on child care
so that they would be able to care for their own children. Indeed, the 1930
assertion of PTA president Minnie Bradford that child welfare and parent
education were one and the same negated the previous emphasis on social
change and reinforced the view that mothers, not poverty or the environment, were responsible for their children's problems.[67]

Despite the increasingly professional orientation of its national leaders,
the PTA remained a grassroots organization never fully accepted by psychologists or professionals in parent education. For example, the Child Study
Association of America, the most influential parent education group in the
1920s, worked closely with social and research scientists, but remained aloof
from the amateurish PTA. CSAA leader Sidonie Gruenberg considered the
PTA useful for disseminating materials on parent education, but incompatible with serious group work. Two surveys of school superintendents

also document their frustration with what they considered the lack of professionalism in the PTA. Administrators criticized PTA meetings for being too devoted to child welfare and entertainment. They objected that members overemphasized the defects in the school program, frequently supported teachers who were out of harmony with the school administration, and did not behave "professionally" or with appropriate deference to experts. Perhaps aggravated by politically active women whose interests sometimes conflicted with their own, male school administrators accused PTA members of making trouble and of being primarily interested in their own personal gain. They suggested that relations between the school staff and the PTA could be improved if mothers stayed out of politics and cooperated more closely with the schools. Like the authors of childrearing manuals in the same decade, professional educators considered mothers an impediment to their children's development.[68]

In the end, sentimental maternalism was partly a victim of its own success. Although club mothers played a key role in the initial development of parent education and social welfare programs, the professionalization of those fields limited the role that women at the grassroots could play in their administration. As academic conferences replaced mothers' study circles, health clinics and kindergartens — services often initiated by white and black organized mothers — were incorporated into public and private agencies and run by professionals. Rank-and-file PTA members were no longer considered unpaid professionals administering charities and welfare programs, but volunteers who assisted the professionals in their work.

Some of the social services initiated by clubs' mothers were run by the progressive reformers in the Children's Bureau network. Unlike sentimental maternalists, who disavowed the political nature of their work, and African American activists, who were unable to get the ear of white policymakers, progressive maternalists openly extended social motherhood into government, expanding state responsibility for child welfare while simultaneously creating professional opportunities for educated women. The maternalist ideology and activism of the Children's Bureau women was markedly different from that of the National Congress of Mothers, and it is the subject of the next chapter.

NOTES

1. Dorothy Canfield Fisher, *Mothers and Children* (New York: Henry Holt, 1914), 258–59.

2. Progressive-era maternalism had roots in the temperance, antislavery, and moral reform associations of the antebellum period. See Carroll Smith-Rosenberg, *Religion and the Rise of the City: the New York City Mission Movement, 1812–*

1870 (Ithaca, N.Y.: Cornell University Press, 1971); Mary P. Ryan, *Cradle of the Middle Class: Family and Community in Oneida County, New York, 1780–1865* (New York: Cambridge University Press, 1981); Barbara Epstein, *The Politics of Domesticity: Women, Evangelicalism, and Temperance in Nineteenth-Century America* (Middletown: Wesleyan University Press, 1981); Lori D. Ginzberg, *Women and the Work of Benevolence: Morality, Politics, and Class in the Nineteenth-Century United States* (New Haven: Yale University Press, 1990); Peggy Pascoe, *Relations of Rescue: The Search for Female Moral Authority in the American West, 1874–1939* (New York: Oxford University Press, 1990).

3. This is not to say that motherhood rhetoric ceased, only that it no longer had the ability to inspire a mass movement for welfare. Some progressive reformers in government continued to employ maternalist rhetoric. See Eileen Boris, "Regulating Industrial Homework: The Triumph of 'Sacred Motherhood,' " *Journal of American History* 71 (Mar. 1985): 745–63.

4. Historians have generally ignored the PTA, even though it is one of the largest and most influential women's organizations in the twentieth century. No organizational history has appeared since Harry and Bonaro Overstreets' *When Children Came First: A Study of the P.T.A. Idea* (Chicago: National Congress of Parents and Teachers, 1949). Theda Skocpol's *Protecting Soldiers and Mothers: The Politics of Social Provision in the United States, 1870s-1920s* (Cambridge: Harvard University Press, 1992), examines the contribution the National Congress of Mothers made to maternalist welfare reform, and Steven Schlossman discusses its role in the prewar child study movement in "Before Home Start: Notes toward a History of Parent Education in America, 1897–1929," *Harvard Education Review* 46 (Aug. 1976): 436–67. The Congress is also discussed briefly in Sheila M. Rothman, *Woman's Proper Place: A History of Changing Ideals and Practices, 1870–1930* (New York: Basic, 1978); and Deirdre English and Barbara Ehrenreich in *For Her Own Good: 150 Years of Advice to Women* (Garden City: Anchor, 1978).

5. The name of the National Congress of Mothers was changed to the National Congress of Mothers and Parent Teacher Associations in 1908 and to the National Congress of Parents and Teachers in 1924. In order to avoid confusion and repetition of the cumbersome name, I have referred to the organization as the Mothers' Congress or by its current colloquial name, the PTA, throughout the text. National Congress of Parents and Teachers, *Golden Jubilee History, 1897–1947* (Chicago: National Congress of Parents and Teachers, 1947), 72; Overstreet, *Where Children Come First*, 195–97, 203.

6. Overstreet, *Where Children Come First*, and the PTA's *Golden Jubilee History* provide the best summaries of the organization's activities. See also Julian Butterworth, *The Parent-Teacher Association and its Work* (New York: Macmillan, 1929).

7. "Message from the President," *National Congress of Mothers Magazine* 1 (Nov. 1906): 2; Hannah Kent Schoff, *The Wayward Child: A Study of the Causes of Crime* (Indianapolis: Bobbs-Merrill, 1915), 12.

8. The aims of the Congress were printed in every issue of the organization's

magazine. Additional aims included kindergartens; laws caring for neglected and dependent children; the juvenile court; probationary care in individual homes rather than institutions; parent education; "high ideals" of marriage; the nation's responsibility to childhood; and surrounding childhood with "loving, wise care . . . that will develop good citizens, instead of law-breakers and criminals." See, for example, *Child-Welfare Magazine* 8 (Apr. 1914).

9. Mrs. Theodore W. Birney, "Need for Organization," in Weeks, ed., *Parents and their Problems*, ed. Mary Harmon Weeks (New York: Ferd P. Kaiser Publishing, Co., 1914), 8:32.

10. On the Spider Web Chart, see J. Stanley Lemons, *The Woman Citizen: Social Feminism in the 1920s* (Urbana: University of Illinois Press, 1973), 209–27; Nancy F. Cott, *The Grounding of Modern Feminism* (New Haven, Conn.: Yale University Press, 1987), 242, 249–50.

11. National Congress of Mothers, *The Work and Words of the National Congress of Mothers: First Annual Session* (New York: D. Appleton, 1897), reprinted in *National Congress of Mothers: The First Conventions*, ed. David J. Rothman and Sheila M. Rothman (New York: Garland Publishing, 1987).

12. Mrs. Theodore W. Birney, "The Congress Origins," in Weeks, ed., *Parents and their Problems*, ed. Mary Harmon Weeks (New York: Ferd P. Kaiser Publishing Co., 1914), 8:25–27; PTA, *Golden Jubilee History*, 36–37; Mrs. Theodore W. Birney, "Official Call to Congress," in National Congress of Mothers, *Work and Words*, ix, 10.

13. Quoted in Schlossman, "Before Home Start," 442, and Susan Tiffin, *In Whose Best Interest? Child Welfare Reform in the Progressive Era* (Westport: Greenwood Press, 1982), 21. See Charles Strickland and Charles Burgess, eds. *Health, Growth and Heredity: G. Stanley Hall on Natural Education* (New York: Teachers College Press, Columbia University, 1965). For Hall's biography, see Dorothy Ross, *G. Stanley Hall, The Psychologist as Prophet* (Chicago: University of Chicago Press, 1972).

14. G. Stanley Hall, "New Ideals of Motherhood," in National Congress of Mothers, *The Child in Home, School, and State: Proceedings of the Annual Meeting* (Washington, D.C.: National Congress of Mothers, 1905), 27. For an interesting analysis of Hall's ideas about masculinity, see Gail Bederman, "Racial Pedagogy or the Big Stick? G. Stanley Hall, Theodore Roosevelt, and the Manly Quest to Civilize the Primitive" (Paper Presented to the Organization of American Historians, Chicago, 1992).

15. Milicent W. Shinn, *The Biography of a Baby* (Boston: Houghton Mifflin Co., 1900), 5–6; Hall quoted in Ross, *G. Stanley Hall*, 260.

16. Birney, "The Congress Origins," 29; PTA, *Golden Jubilee History*, 24–28; Edward T. James, Janet Wilson James, Paul S. Boyer, eds., *Notable American Women* (Cambridge: Belknap Press, 1971), 1:147–48.

17. PTA, *Golden Jubilee History*, 48–67; James, James, Boyer, eds, *Notable American Women*, 3:237–39.

18. PTA, *Golden Jubilee History*, 21; Frances Ellen Watkins Harper, "The Afro-American Mother," and "Appendix," in National Congress of Mothers, *Work and Words*, 67–70, 255.

19. "Miss Anthony's Advice to Mothers," *Woman's Journal* (Sept. 8, 1900): 285; "Mrs. Stanton to the Mothers' Congress," *Woman's Journal* (May 26, 1900): 162. Stanton wrote of the Mothers' Congress, "I deem this organization altogether the most important yet formed in any period or nation."

20. Hannah Kent Schoff, "The Childless Wife," *National Congress of Mothers' Magazine* 2 (Apr. 1908): 189; Theodore Roosevelt, "Address to Congress on the Welfare of Children," *National Congress of Mothers' Magazine* 2 (Apr. 1908): 174.

21. Helen Gardener, "The Moral Responsibility of Women in Heredity," in National Congress of Mothers, *Work and Words*, 135–36.

22. Alice Lee Moque, "Reproduction and Natural Law," in National Congress of Mothers, *Work and Words*, 125; "State News," *Child Welfare Magazine* 6 (Nov. 1911): 108. For a useful discussion of the intersection of race and gender in American welfare reform, see Gwendolyn Mink, "The Lady and the Tramp: Gender, Race, and the Origins of the American Welfare State," in *Women, the State, and Welfare*, ed. Linda Gordon (Madison: University of Wisconsin Press, 1990), 92–122.

23. Lucy Bainbridge, "Mothers of the Submerged World," in National Congress of Mothers, *Work and Words*, 49, 51; Frances Newton, "The Mother's Greatest Needs," in National Congress of Mothers, *Work and Words*, 153.

24. See Schlossman, "Before Home Start," 443–44.

25. Overstreet, *Where Children Come First*, 150; "State News," *Child-Welfare Magazine* 5 (May 1911): 175.

26. Mrs. Frederic Schoff, "Guardians of Childhood in Home and Nation," *National Congress of Mothers' Magazine* 3 (Apr. 1909): 231–32; "President's Desk," *Child-Welfare Magazine* 6 (Mar. 1912): 215.

27. Sybil Avery Perkins, "Child Hygiene in the Rhode Island Congress of Mothers," *Child-Welfare Magazine* 5 (May 1911): 164–65; "State News," *Child-Welfare Magazine* 8 (Dec. 1913): 148; "State News," *Child-Welfare Magazine* 9 (Nov. 1914): 103–5; *Child-Welfare Magazine* 11 (June 1917): 301. A PTA-sponsored Mothers' Education Center in Los Angeles reported a total of 14,097 cases. "Annual Report of Baby Week Extension Committee, Los Angeles Mothers' Education Center" enclosed in Louise C. Heilbron to Julia Lathrop, June 1, 1920, File 4–15–4–3, Children's Bureau Records, Central Files, 1914–50, Record Group 102, National Archives, Washington, D.C.

28. "State News," *Child-Welfare Magazine* 10 (Sept. 1915): 35.

29. U.S. Children's Bureau, *Prenatal Care* Publication No. 4 (Washington, D.C.: Government Printing Office, 1913), 5; idem, *The Promotion of the Welfare and Hygiene of Maternity and Infancy for the Fiscal Year Ending June 30, 1929* Publication No. 203 (Washington: Government Printing Office, 1931), 24; PTA, *Golden Jubilee History*, 97.

30. "State News," *Child-Welfare Magazine* 5 (May 1911): 175; Mrs. Frederic Schoff, "The National Congress of Mothers," *Club Woman* 10 (Mar. 1903): 241.

31. PTA, *Golden Jubilee History*, 28–30; Overstreet, *Where Children Come First*, 49; "Legislative Work for Kindergartens," *Child-Welfare Magazine* 10 (Aug. 1916): 444; Bessie Locke, "Kindergarten Extension," *Child-Welfare Magazine* 12 (May 1918): 173; "Parent-Teacher Associations of Erie Save Kindergarten System,"

Child-Welfare Magazine 7 (Dec. 1912): 116. On the kindergarten movement, see Michael Steven Shapiro, *Child's Garden: The Kindergarten Movement from Froebel to Dewey* (University Park: Pennsylvania State University Press, 1983); Elizabeth Dale Ross, *The Kindergarten Crusade: The Establishment of Preschool Education in the United States* (Athens: Ohio University Press, 1976); Karen Wolk Feinstein, "Kindergartens, Feminism, and the Professionalization of Motherhood," *International Journal of Women's Studies* 3 (Jan.-Feb. 1980): 28–3; Ann Taylor Allen, "'Let Us Live with Our Children': Kindergarten Movements in Germany and the United States, 1840–1914," *History of Education Quarterly* 28 (Spring 1988): 23–48.

32. Schoff, *Wayward Child,* 80–81.

33. Ben B. Lindsey, "Present Outlook for the Juvenile Court," *National Congress of Mothers' Magazine* 4 (Dec. 1909): 103; Schoff, *The Wayward Child,* 9, 12–13, 80. The history of the juvenile court has been well documented. See, for example, Anthony M. Platt, *The Child Savers: The Invention of Delinquency* (Chicago: University of Chicago Press, 1969), and Steven L. Schlossman, *Love and the American Delinquent: The Theory and Practice of "Progressive" Juvenile Justice, 1825–1920* (Chicago: University of Chicago Press, 1977.)

34. Schoff, *The Wayward Child,* 64–72.

35. "State News," *Child-Welfare Magazine* 11 (May 1917): 268.

36. "President's Desk," *Child-Welfare Magazine* 12 (May 1918): 162; "President's Desk," *Child-Welfare Magazine* 11 (June 1917): 277; Mrs. Frederic Schoff, "Some Vital Questions of the Hour for Mothers," *Child-Welfare Magazine* 11 (June 1917): 285–87; "State News," *Child-Welfare Magazine* 12 (May 1918): 184.

37. "State News," *Child-Welfare Magazine* 11 (Aug. 1917): 345; "President's Desk," *Child-Welfare Magazine* 12 (Mar. 1918): 114–15.

38. Quoted in PTA, *Golden Jubilee History,* 35.

39. Jacqueline Jones, *Labor of Love, Labor of Sorrow: Black Women, Work, and the Family from Slavery to the Present* (New York: Basic, 1900), 65–66.

40. Frances Ellen Watkins Harper, "The Afro-American Woman," in National Congress of Mothers, *Work and Words,* 67–71; Mrs. Anna Murray, "The Negro Children of America," in National Congress of Mothers, *The Child in Home, School, and State,* 174.

41. Dr. Samuel McCune Lindsay, "Children of Porto Rico," in National Congress of Mothers, *The Children in Home, School, and State,* 135.

42. "President's Desk," *Child-Welfare Magazine* 12 (May 1918): 163; U.S. Bureau of Education, *The Kindergarten as an Americanizer* (Washington, D.C.: Government Printing Office, 1919), 1–2; Mrs. Jeremiah Rhodes, "Department of Americanization," *Child-Welfare Magazine* 14 (Oct. 1919): 44.

43. Linda Gordon, "Family Violence, Feminism, and Social Control," *Feminist Studies* 12 (Fall 1986): 471.

44. Fisher, *Mothers and Children,* 280–81. The book was commended in the *Child-Welfare Magazine* 21 (Oct. 1926): 91.

45. Mary Mumford, "The Public School and the Immigrant," *Child-Welfare Magazine* 4 (Apr. 1910): 232.

46. PTA, *Golden Jubilee History*, 58, 101; Overstreet, *Where Children Come First*, 268–69.

47. "Report of National Chairman on Extension of Work Among Colored People," Box 11, Folder 224, Elizabeth Tilton Papers, Arthur and Elizabeth Schlesinger Library on the History of Women in America, Radcliffe College, Cambridge, Mass.

48. "President's Desk," *Child-Welfare Magazine* 10 (Mar. 1916): 230–31. See Mrs. Booker Washington, "Negro Women's Club Work," *Club Woman* 10 (May 1903): 297.

49. Paula Giddings, *When and Where I Enter: The Impact of Black Women on Race and Sex in America* (New York: Bantam, 1984), 94–95. On the National Association of Colored Women, see Wilson Moses, *The Golden Age of Black Nationalism, 1850–1925* (Hamden, Conn.: Archon, 1978), chap. five; Charles Harris Wesley, *The History of the National Association of Colored Women's Clubs: A Legacy of Service* (Washington, D.C.: NACWC, 1984); Elizabeth L. Davis, *Lifting as They Climb: The National Association of Colored Women* (Washington, D.C., 1933); Tullia K. Brown Hamilton, "The National Association of Colored Women, 1896 to 1920" (Ph.D. diss., Emory University, 1978).

50. For an analysis of the differences between black and white women's welfare activism that is not limited to these two organizations, see Linda Gordon, "Black and White Women's Welfare Activism," *Journal of American History* 78 (Sept. 1991): 559–90. Recent works on black women's reform activism include Dorothy Salem, *To Better Our World: Black Women in Organized Reform, 1890–1920* (Brooklyn, N.Y.: Carlson Publishing, 1990); Cynthia Neverdon-Morton, *Afro-American Women of the South and the Advancement of the Race, 1895–1925* (Knoxville: University of Tennessee Press, 1989); Jacqueline Rouse, *Lugenia Burns Hope: Black Southern Reformer* (Athens, Ga.: University of Georgia Press, 1989); Anne Firor Scott, "Most Invisible of All: Black Women's Voluntary Associations," *Journal of Southern History* 56 (Feb. 1990): 3–22; Darlene Clark Hine, "'We Specialize in the Wholly Impossible': The Philanthropic Work of Black Women," in *Lady Bountiful Revisited: Women, Philanthropy, and Power*, ed. Kathleen D. McCarthy (New Brunswick, N.J.: Rutgers University Press, 1990); Gerda Lerner, *The Majority Finds Its Past* (New York: Oxford University Press, 1979), chap. 6. See also the documents in Edyth L. Ross, ed. *Black Heritage in Social Welfare, 1860–1930* (Metuchen, N.J.: Scarecrow Press, 1978).

51. Hamilton, "The National Association of Colored Women," 39–51. In her comparison of black and white women activists, Linda Gordon found that 85 percent of the black women married, although many "led lives quite independent of their husbands." Gordon, "Black and White Visions of Welfare," 568.

52. Davis, *Lifting as They Climb*, 132–80. Biographical information on Terrell and Bethune can be found in Barbara Sicherman and Carol Hurd Green, eds., *Notable American Women: The Modern Period* (Cambridge: Belknap Press, 1980), 76–80, 678–80. See Dorothy Sterling, *Black Foremothers, Three Lives* (New York: Feminist Press, 1979), for information on Terrell and Ida B. Wells.

53. See Eileen Boris, "The Power of Motherhood: Black and White Activist

Women Redefine the 'Political,' " *Yale Journal of Law and Feminism* 2 (Fall 1989): 25–49.

54. Quoted in Salem, *To Better Our World,* 268n, 31.

55. Mary Church Terrell, "Greetings from the National Association of Colored Women," *The National Association Notes* 2 (Mar. 1899): 1. Eileen Boris notes that in the manuscript version, the word "weaker" is crossed out and "oppressed" scratched in above. Boris, "The Power of Motherhood," 36.

56. Quoted in Giddings, *When and Where I Enter,* 100.

57. Terrell quoted in Salem, *To Better Our World,* 31; Williams excerpted in Gerda Lerner, *Black Women in White America* (New York: Vintage, 1972), 575–76. See also Beverly W. Jones, "Mary Church Terrell and the National Association of Colored Women, 1896–1901," *Journal of Negro History* 67 (Spring 1982): 20–33; and Farah Jasmine Griffin, "'A Layin' on of Hands': Organizational Efforts Among Black American Women, 1790–1930," *Sage* (Student Supplement, 1988): 23–29.

58. "Home Influences Among Colored People," *National Association Notes* 1 (May 15, 1897).

59. *The Club Woman* 10 (Aug. 1904), 27; *National Association Notes* 8 (Oct. 1904).

60. Louie D. Shivery, "The History of the Gate City Free Kindergarten Association," excerpted in *Black Heritage in Social Welfare,* ed. Ross, 258–63; Lerner, *Majority Finds Its Past,* 88; Neverdon-Morton, *Afro-American Women,* 142–43.

61. See Jacqueline A. Rouse, *Lugenia Burns Hope,* and "Atlanta's African-American Women's Attack on Segregation, 1900–1920," in *Gender, Class, Race and Reform in the Progressive Era,* ed. Noralee Frankel and Nancy S. Dye (Lexington: University Press of Kentucky, 1991), 10–23; Louie D. Shivery, "The Neighborhood Union," in *Black Heritage in Social Welfare,* ed. Ross, 264–81; Ralph E. Luker, "Missions, Institutional Churches, and Settlement Houses: The Black Experience, 1885–1910," *Journal of Negro History* 69 (Summer/Fall 1984): 101–13.

62. Cott, *Grounding of Modern Feminism,* 249.

63. Florence Watkins to Elizabeth Tilton, Dec. 12, 1922, Mar. 21, 1923, and May 4, 1923, Folder 246, Elizabeth Tilton Papers, Schlesinger Library.

64. "The Vital Object of the Congress of Mothers," *Child-Welfare Magazine* 13 (June-July 1919): 281. See also James Killius, "What's the matter with the PTA Movement?" *Child-Welfare Magazine* 17 (Feb. 1923): 224–26, and the responses in March and May 1923.

65. PTA, *Golden Jubilee History,* 82–84; "1927 Resolutions," *Child-Welfare Magazine* 21 (Aug. 1927): 558.

66. PTA, *Golden Jubilee History,* 102, 109; Orville Brim, *Education for Child-rearing* (New York: Russell Sage Foundation, 1959), 330.

67. PTA, *Golden Jubilee History,* 119. According to Roberta Wollons, the Child Study Association of America, the major parent education organization in the 1920s, also retreated from social reform in the 1920s. Roberta L. Wollons, "Educating Mothers: Sidonie Matsner Gruenberg and the Child Study Association" (Ph.D. diss., University of Chicago, 1983), 311. See Steven L. Schlossman, "Phi-

lanthropy and the Gospel of Child Development," *History of Education Quarterly* 21 (Fall 1981): 275–99, and idem, "The Formative Era in American Parent Education: Overview and Interpretation," in *Parent Education and Public Policy,* ed. Ron Haskins and Diane Adams (Norwood, N.J.: Ablex, 1983), 7–39.

68. Wollons, "Educating Mothers," 245–46; Julian Butterworth, *The Parent-Teacher Association and Its Work* (New York: Macmillan, 1929), 40. The results of a questionnaire distributed by the PTA to school superintendents in Iowa were reported in "State News," *Child-Welfare Magazine* 14 (Apr. 1920): 251.

3

"The Welfare of Mothers and Babies Is a Dignified Subject of Political Discussion": Progressive Maternalism and the Children's Bureau

With the creation of the U.S. Children's Bureau in 1912, maternalists entered government, and women's work for child welfare gained a new legitimacy. "Work for infant welfare is coming to be regarded as more than a philanthropy or an expression of good will," Children's Bureau chief Julia Lathrop proclaimed in 1914. "It is a profoundly important public concern which tests the public spirit and the democracy of a community."[1]

The establishment of a national children's bureau underscored how thoroughly women's work of child care was politicized in early twentieth-century America. The Children's Bureau was the first federal agency headed and staffed primarily by women, and it owed its existence in large measure to the maternalist movement and, especially, the social settlements. The idea for the agency came from Lillian Wald, a nurse and founder of New York's Henry Street Settlement, and Florence Kelley, a Henry Street resident and director of the National Consumers' League. Its first two chiefs, Julia Lathrop (1912–21) and Grace Abbott (1921–34) were long-time residents of Hull-House, the famous Chicago settlement. Although maternalists and women activists engaged in child welfare work many years before the ccreation of the Children's Bureau, the federal agency coordinated the disparate activities of voluntary women's organizations into a powerful nationwide campaign. For almost two decades, the Bureau acted as the women's branch of the federal government; the spotlight it placed on maternal and child welfare made many women feel they had a stake in politics for the first time.

In many ways, the progressive maternalism of the Children's Bureau staff represents a halfway point between the sentimental maternalism of the National Congress of Mothers and the feminist position to be discussed in the next chapter. Like other maternalists, progressive women reformers assumed that women had a special capacity for nurture by virtue of being women, stressed women's political obligation to raise the nation's citizens, held privileged women responsible for all children's welfare, and insisted on the virtues of an Anglo-American family structure that defined men as breadwinners and kept women and children at home. Yet their ideology differed from that of club mothers in three important ways. For one thing, the Children's Bureau women openly asserted women's right and desire, as well as responsibility, to participate in the public world. For another, they combined motherhood rhetoric with appeals to justice and democracy, rather than to morality and social order. Finally, they rejected a sentimental view of motherhood and embraced science and professionalism as values equally available to women and men. Despite believing that women had a natural interest in child welfare because they were female, progressive maternalists staked their claim to authority in welfare administration not on their feminine capacity for nurture but on their professional expertise. Thus, while the leaders of the Mothers' Congress welcomed men as purveyors of science and professionalism onto their advisory board, women in the Children's Bureau network fought fiercely for female professionals to control child welfare programs. Eventually they were willing to sacrifice federal funding for maternal and infant health services rather than allow the administration of those services to be handed over to men.

Progressive maternalism must also be distinguished from feminism, for maternalists understood the universe in terms of social relations and obligations, rather than political and economic independence and individual rights. Unlike feminists, who strived for equality in the public sphere, they deplored the labor-force participation of married women and made the protection of mothers and children their political priority. "If a declaration of independence were to be written today," the Bureau wrote in 1923, "American women would ask that in the enumeration of the objects for which governments are instituted the welfare of children should head the list."[2] The Children's Bureau women thought in terms of relationship and compromise, not individualism and conflict, and they envisioned a maternalist society in which educated women such as themselves could both find self-fulfillment and help others by expanding the social welfare services of the state. Progressive maternalists, convinced that all women had a disposition for child welfare, were far more sensitive to class and ethnic differences than either club mothers or feminists. Nevertheless, they believed that scientific childrearing methods and the Anglo-American family structure afforded the best protection for children, and never recognized the power relations embedded in their cultural conflicts over child care.

The contradictory nature of maternalist welfare policy is evident in the two major Progressive-era campaigns of the Children's Bureau: infant health and child labor reform. In the first, the Bureau's strategy of publicizing "scientific" information on childrearing and on the prevention of infant mortality sparked a broad-based women's movement for child health. Grass-roots mothers welcomed government intervention into their "private" health concerns because of their fears for their children's health. In the second Children's Bureau campaign, however, maternalist efforts to protect children functioned in an entirely different way. Unlike the federal baby-saving campaign, which made maternal and child health a mass political concern, child labor reform took place mostly in an administrative (and therefore apolitical) setting. Although Bureau officials administered a federal child labor law that they believed protected children, many mothers found the law intrusive because it ignored economic realities and operated from alien ideas about family life. When working to prevent child labor, Children's Bureau maternalists operated not as political advocates in tune with grassroots women's wants and desires, but as social workers attending to working-class needs as they defined them. Yet policies designed and implemented without the input of the mothers affected by them were inevitably controlling. The tension between the democratic and administrative goals of progressive women reformers characterized the history of the Children's Bureau — and of maternalist welfare reform.

The Creation of the Children's Bureau

Florence Kelley and Lillian Wald came up with the idea of a federal children's bureau at breakfast one morning in 1903. As the story goes, they were reading the morning newspaper when they noticed a letter from a Boston woman concerned about the large number of infant deaths in summer and a news article about a trip the Secretary of Agriculture was making to investigate damage done by the boll weevil to southern cotton fields. Wald purportedly mused, "If the Government can have a department to take such an interest in the cotton crop, why can't it have a bureau to look after the nation's child crop?" Kelley is said to have taken Wald's idea to Edward Devine, general secretary of the New York Charity Organization Society. They in turn presented it to President Roosevelt.[3]

Although the drive to create a federal children's bureau was vigorously supported by settlement residents and club women (though not National Congress of Mothers president Schoff), the main organization behind it was not a women's group, but the National Child Labor Committee (NCLC). The NCLC had been organized in 1904 to investigate child labor and lobby for stronger laws against it, and Kelley, Wald, and Jane Addams were charter members. Columbia University professor Samuel Lindsay, the NCLC's first secretary, drafted the first children's bureau bill, which was introduced in

Congress in 1906 but died in committee. It eventually took eleven bills to get the Children's Bureau signed into law.[4] The idea of a federal agency for children received a major boost with the endorsement of President Theodore Roosevelt and participants at the 1909 White House Conference on the Care of Dependent Children, a gathering of two hundred prominent welfare workers, including Kelley, Wald, Devine, and Homer Folks of the New York Charities Aid Association. The conference was important as a symbol of the federal government's willingness to play a role in matters of child welfare. Although some delegates objected to government interference in what were thought to be matters for private agencies, conference participants overwhelmingly adopted resolutions supporting mothers' pensions and a federal Children's Bureau. Still, the final resolutions represented a compromise between private charity officials and advocates, like Wald, of an activist government agency. The Conference called for the creation of a federal children's agency to do research and a private organization to serve as its activist arm.

The White House Conference brought new attention to the children's bureau bill then pending in Congress. Addams, Kelley, and Wald testified in congressional hearings, as did Devine, Folks, Alexander McKelway and Owen Lovejoy of the National Child Labor Committee, juvenile court judges Ben B. Lindsey of Denver and Julian Mack of Chicago, and a representative of the General Federation of Women's Clubs. Proponents of the Children's Bureau pointed out the irony that Congress appropriated federal funds to protect crops and livestock, but not children. Opponents objected that a federal children's bureau was a violation of states' rights, a waste of money since it duplicated existing work done in the states, and an unwarranted intrusion into private family life. On April 9, 1912—six years after the first Children's Bureau bill was introduced in Congress—President William Howard Taft signed the Children's Bureau into law.[5]

The creation of the Children's Bureau was an important sign of federal interest in child welfare, but its limited budget of $25,640 and small staff of fifteen suggest that Congress intended it to be merely symbolic. Housed in the Department of Commerce and Labor, the Children's Bureau was conceived as a research agency designed to "investigate and report . . . upon all matters pertaining to the welfare of children and child life among all classes of our people." The law specifically mentioned infant mortality, employment, juvenile courts, "dangerous occupations," "accidents and diseases," and legislation affecting children. Congress deleted "illegitimacy" and "juvenile delinquency," and added a clause forbidding Bureau agents to enter any home "over the objection of the head of the family."[6]

For women activists, the appointment of long-time Hull-House resident Julia Lathrop as Children's Bureau chief was a triumph equal to the creation of the Bureau itself. Although well qualified for the position, Lathrop was appointed less for her personal ability than because of her position in the progressive women's movement. Women reformers lobbied hard behind the scenes for the appointment of a woman as Bureau chief, and Lathrop's appointment as the first woman head of a federal agency was both a recognition of women's efforts in the formation of the Bureau and an acknowledgment of their special concern for child welfare. That President Taft appointed and Congress approved a woman to direct the new federal agency — eight years before the Nineteenth Amendment gave them the right to vote — suggests both the power of dominant beliefs in women's responsibility for child welfare and the lack of importance politicians attached to the new agency.

"The first appropriation was small," Lillian Wald remarked, "but the first appointment was big." Like others who worked with the Children's Bureau, Wald credited Julia Lathrop with its early success. Born in Rockford, Illinois, in 1858, Lathrop grew up in a politically active Republican family. Her father served in the state senate and U.S. Congress. Her mother, a suffragist, was in the first graduating class of Rockford Seminary. Lathrop attended Rockford for a year, and then transferred to Vassar. After graduation she worked in her father's law office for ten years. She moved to Hull-House in 1890 and quickly joined its inner circle.[7]

Julia Lathrop lived at Hull-House for more than twenty years, and the child welfare policy she developed and administered as Children's Bureau chief was based on settlement philosophy. For example, Lathrop probably acquired what one colleague called her "staunch belief in the importance of social research as a sound means of social reform" at Hull-House.[8] She contributed a chapter to the 1895 book, *Hull House Maps and Papers,* which was based on an innovative house-to-house survey of working and living conditions in the Hull-House neighborhood, and she modeled the Children's Bureau investigations into infant mortality on the same method. Furthermore, the settlement interest in the physical, psychological, and economic well-being of the "whole" child was reflected in the range of Children's Bureau studies on child labor, juvenile delinquency, and child health.

There is little information on Lathrop's personal development at Hull-House, but it is likely that her politics, like those of her fellow residents, moved from cultural benevolence to social welfare in the 1890s. She ran a discussion group called the Plato Club in the House's early days, but by 1893 had become interested in social welfare. During the depression of that year, Lathrop was a volunteer county visitor, investigating relief applicants in the Hull-House district. Appointed the first woman on the Illinois Board of Charities in 1893, she began a lifelong crusade against political patronage in the social services and for civil service reform. Lathrop was convinced that state agencies could not serve the public welfare unless they were run efficiently and staffed by qualified personnel, and so she advocated the training of social workers and the standardization of employment procedures. She saw the professionalization of social work as a way to simultaneously improve social services and provide rewarding jobs for educated women.[9]

Despite her genuine respect and sympathy for the poor, Lathrop's interest in reform was motivated more by her belief in the responsibility of privilege than by any personal identification with their troubles. "The justice of today is born of yesterday's pity," she remarked, combining the parlance of charity with that of human rights.[10] Indeed, the language of progressive maternalists often betrayed their matronizing attitudes toward cultures different from their own. For example, when Jane Addams described the settlement's intention "to preserve and keep [for immigrants] whatever of value their past life contained," she implied that Hull-House's mostly Anglo-American residents were best able to determine which immigrant traditions held value in the United States.[11]

Although progressive maternalists were more sensitive to immigrant customs than other Anglo-Americans of their time, their tolerance of diversity generally stopped short at matters affecting children. Maternalism was, after all, about raising American citizens. Thus, while Hull-House residents encouraged immigrants to preserve their traditions through pageants, festivals, and folk art, they objected to the preservation of daily customs they feared might harm children. For example, the Hull-House infant health clinic tried to stop mothers from relying on traditional healing to cure sick children, while the public kitchen encouraged immigrants to replace their spicy food with simple, less expensive, and supposedly healthier "American" fare.[12]

An incident early in Lathrop's Hull-House career illustrates the intolerance of maternalists when immigrants did not share their assimilationist values. Despite being deeply moved by the problems of Russian Jews fleeing for their lives, Lathrop could not understand their efforts to maintain their religious practices in the United States. Jane Addams explained: "One of the few occasions on which I saw Julia Lathrop display real indignation was when a group of the forlornest refugees came with an interpreter to complain . . . that it had been discovered that the soup given to them . . . was made of loaves of bread boiled in hot water which had first been saturated with lard. I heard Julia Lathrop who cared for no ritual herself exclaim: 'Of course you would rather starve!' "[13] Lathrop's humanitarian work was rooted in a secular and peculiarly American faith in science and progress, and it was difficult for her to understand or appreciate religious and cultural traditions different from her own.

Several historians have pointed out the irony that the women of Hull-

House and the Children's Bureau were able to develop careers and escape
the nuclear family while promoting stay-at-home motherhood for the rest.[14]
Lathrop herself never married or had children, but she insisted that motherhood was the "most universal and essential of employments." Like her
mentor Jane Addams, she justified sweeping social reforms and new careers
for middle-class women by insisting that modern social conditions required
mothers to extend their traditional work of child care into the community.
As Lillian Wald shrewdly proclaimed, "It was an awakening for me to
realize that when I was working in the interests of those babies . . . I was
really in politics."[15]

Like club mothers, progressive women reformers believed that women's
status would be enhanced and children's lives improved if motherhood had
"the status of a profession." Lathrop insisted that "the first and simplest
duty of women is to safeguard the lives of mothers and babies, to develop
the professional dignity of all motherhood, as motherhood has too long
suffered from sheer sentimentality, which always rests on its oars." Yet
despite their common goal of professionalizing motherhood, the maternalism
of the Children's Bureau differed from that of the National Congress of
Mothers in two ways. First, while sentimental maternalists wanted to raise
the status of motherhood so that women would be more content to stay
at home, progressives wanted women to be able to choose with dignity
between marriage or career. (They did not think women could choose both.)
Second, although leaders of the Mothers' Congress idealized the patriarchal
family system of the past, Lathrop in typical progressive fashion embraced
the "new order," in which "partnership" between men and women supplanted "ownership." Lathrop assumed most married women would choose
to stay home with their children, but she believed that all women should
have the "fullest scope for earning and for just treatment as individuals"
before marriage and when "family cares permit." She stressed women's need
for higher education and "freedom for individual development," but did
not question the division of labor — or "partnership" — in the family, where
men and women were "equally responsible, the father for the support of
the home, the mother for the wise comfort and peace within it."[16]

Like Jane Addams, Lathrop was a pragmatic reformer who operated
successfully in the male political world by stressing women's special role
in child welfare. Turning to advantage the meager funding of the Children's
Bureau and its lack of administrative power, the mostly female Bureau staff
presented themselves as government outsiders, as women engaged in their
traditional work of child care. Lathrop's continuous insistence that motherhood was "the most important calling in the world" and her denial of
female career ambition allowed the Children's Bureau women to extend
their political influence without appearing to do so. The progressive ma-

ternalism of the Bureau staff thus facilitated women's entrance into politics, although it confined them to traditionally feminine concerns such as child welfare.

Lathrop's use of motherhood rhetoric was at least in part a response to the widespread objections to women in public life. As a visible, if not powerful, woman in a high government position, she had to contend with congressional opponents — and even some Children's Bureau friends — who doubted women's administrative abilities. Called unwomanly, "mannish," and "bespectacled and sharp nosed spinsters," women in government insisted that child welfare reform was simply an extension of the mothering work women traditionally did in the home. Lillian Wald sarcastically responded to critics, describing the "new and mannish venture" of the Children's Bureau chief in this way: "She rouses the nation, or tries to rouse it, to the needs of the baby. She takes the baby out of the obscure, so often neglected and hidden crib, into the full light of publicity. . . . That is one of the things that women do when they function in public life. They exercise their intelligence for the preservation of the things that are important to them and have always been and always will be."[17]

Lathrop and her supporters did not only emphasize her empathy and femininity, however. They also described her in seemingly masculine terms, such as statesmanlike and judicious. Their need to use opposing traits reflects the contradictory position of the Children's Bureau itself. The Bureau was both political and nonpolitical; it was a public agency addressing private family concerns that depended primarily on private organizations (such as settlement houses and women's clubs) for support. The Bureau owed its very existence to politicians' and club mothers' idealized view of motherhood, yet its staff rejected such sentimentality in favor of professionalism and science. Lathrop herself had long dismissed the idea that women were naturally more empathic than men. "I am sure that we [women] do not monopolize any of the finer qualities of human nature," she told the Illinois Board of Charities in the 1890s. "The power of tenderness and sympathy and adaptation are those that belong to choice individuals, and not to man or woman as such."[18]

The Politics of Baby Saving

The practical political education Lathrop acquired at Hull-House was evident in the strategy she designed for the Children's Bureau: a strategy intended both to protect children and safeguard women's role in government. Anxious to defend the Bureau from its detractors and to justify its expansion, Lathrop decided that the Bureau's initial activity should avoid controversy while building public support for the new agency. Thus, although the movement to establish the Bureau was originally identified with child labor reform, Lathrop astutely determined to make the agency's first focus infant health. Building on the pure-milk campaigns, child health clinics, and instructional programs already being run by private charities and women's clubs, Lathrop placed the Children's Bureau at the center of a burgeoning baby-saving campaign. Within a few years the Children's Bureau was the nation's major child health organization.[19]

The decision to focus on infant mortality reflects not only Lathrop's political acumen, but also the deep personal feelings members of the Children's Bureau network had about maternal and child mortality. As we have seen, few families were spared the suffering that resulted from the high death rates among women and children in the early twentieth century. Julia Lathrop, who was named for an aunt who had died as a child, had a grandmother who died in childbirth. Florence Kelley was one of eight children, all but three of whom died in infancy and early childhood; her daughter died when only nineteen years old. Jane Addams, the eighth of nine children, was just two years old when her mother and a new baby died from complications of childbirth. Three other Addams children had already died, two of them before their first birthdays. Dorothy Reed Mendenhall, one of the few married women on the Children's Bureau staff, lost two young children and suffered permanent injury as a result of bad obstetrics. Her grandmother had died in childbirth. "Undoubtedly," Mendenhall later reflected, "the tragic death of my first child . . . was the dominant factor in my interest in the chief function of women, 'the bearing and rearing of children.' Most of my work came out of my agony and grief. . . . *A mother never forgets.*"[20]

Their experiences as settlement residents also left women reformers with daily reminders of the need for maternal and child health care. Lillian Wald observed that when poor women were asked what type of social service they valued most, they usually replied, "The nurse who comes when the baby comes." Addams and Lathrop helped mothers with health care in their neighborhood and delivered at least one baby — to an unmarried woman who had no doctor and no neighbors willing to help her. The baby, named Julius John after the women who brought him into the world, died when he was four months old.[21]

Aware of the suffering caused by infant mortality, and convinced that educating mothers would reduce the number of deaths, Lathrop made the publication and distribution of childrearing literature one of the Bureau's first priorities. Written in a friendly, accessible style, *Prenatal Care* (1913) and *Infant Care* (1914) made the medical advice familiar to middle-class readers of such popular works as Dr. Luther Emmett Holt's *The Care and Feeding of Children* available to a wider audience. The bulletins combined scientific facts on nutrition and disease with sample menus and practical suggestions on making baby clothes and designing the nursery. Their blend of medical information, practical advice, and time-saving tips — and the fact that author Mary Mills West was a widowed mother of five and not a physician — reflected Lathrop's perception that infant health and welfare depended on much more than medicine.[22]

The Children's Bureau bulletins reflected the Progressive era faith in social science, efficiency, and reform. Lathrop and West believed that women up-to-date in their knowledge of child care would demand better health care, food and housing, and, in turn, that improved social conditions would enable more women to raise their children in the "proper" way. Thus the pamphlets railed against "superstition" and asserted the authority of modern science over tradition. Holding up white middle-class childrearing norms as the ideal, they stressed the importance of feeding by the clock and the dangers of cuddling and spoiling the baby. At the same time, the bulletins contained useful information that tried to take most women's limited budgets into account, and called for social and economic reform. By beginning *Infant Care* with a discussion of living conditions — and pointing out that the advice in *Prenatal Care* was based on the assumption that families had access to pure milk, adequate health care, and a "standard of life . . . high enough to permit a woman to conserve her strength for her family" — West hoped to persuade mothers to demand these things for their children, and to convince policymakers of the need for reform.[23]

If G. Stanley Hall's child study literature idealized motherhood but paid little attention to mothers' work, the Children's Bureau bulletins revealed progressive maternalists' deep respect for women's domestic labor. West was aware of the arduous conditions under which most mothers labored, and her advice was intended to safeguard the child's health and reduce the mother's workload. She encouraged mothers to protect themselves from overwork by arranging children's meals and naptimes to fit around their household chores. "The care of a baby is readily reduced to a system unless he is sick," she wrote. "Such a system is not only one of the greatest factors in keeping the baby well and in training him in a way which will be of value to him all through life, but reduces the work of the mother to the minimum and provides for her certain assured periods of rest and recreation."[24]

The Children's Bureau bulletins treated mothers as colleagues, not subordinates, of physicians. In keeping with the ideology of progressive maternalism, the Bureau staff took for granted women's responsibility for childrearing, but rejected a sentimental view of motherhood. Instead, Bureau literature portrayed motherhood as a profession demanding education and scientific knowledge. "Baby care is a great art and a great science," West wrote in the 1921 edition of *Infant Care;* "it is also the most important task any woman ever undertakes, and she should apply to this work the same diligence, intelligence, and sustained effort that she would give to the most exacting profession. It will only be when the profession of parenthood is thus dignified that children will come into their full inheritance of health, efficiency, and happiness."[25]

Perhaps because West imparted kind words and sympathy for overworked mothers along with the scientific advice, the Children's Bureau child care bulletins quickly became government best-sellers. In 1914, a year after *Prenatal Care* was published, Lathrop noted that demand "exceeded all expectations." Approximately 63,000 copies of *Infant Care* were distributed within six months of its publication, and almost 1.5 million copies were distributed between 1914 and 1921. Congressmen sent the bulletins to constituents, and women shared them with friends and relatives. Every year tens of thousands of mothers wrote the Bureau to request literature or ask for further advice.[26]

Lathrop envisioned the Children's Bureau much as Addams described Hull-House, as an "information and interpretation bureau" that served as an advocate for poor families and a mediator between mothers and child welfare institutions, and she tried to fashion the federal agency into a sort of national social settlement.[27] Obviously, the Bureau staff could not have the daily contact that settlement residents had with working people; nevertheless, they developed surprisingly personal relationships with mothers all across the country by working closely with local women's clubs, talking with mothers at health conferences, and responding personally to every one of the thousands of letters the Bureau received each year. Lathrop was particularly adept at using the mail to provide the advice, emotional support and practical assistance that, as a settlement worker, she had offered in person to women in their neighborhood. She and her staff sent advice, encouragement, and, occasionally, money out of their own pockets, to mothers who wrote them, and they frequently prevailed upon local charities, women's clubs, and the Red Cross to donate layettes, food, money, and nursing care to women in need. Offering sympathy and even material assistance from afar, the Progressive-era Children's Bureau functioned more as a distant relative or friend than a government bureaucracy.

The Bureau's unusually close interaction with grassroots women benefited its employees as well as the mothers. Middle-class staff members found meaningful work and got an education about the poverty, ill health, and concerns of most American mothers. Just as Hull-House residents "filled with admiration" for the "heroic" women of their neighborhood, Children's Bureau officials were frequently moved by the courage and determination of the mothers who wrote them. Lathrop was particularly impressed by a

Wyoming mother expecting her third child who lived sixty-five miles from a doctor and was "filled with perfect horror at the prospects ahead." The two women had a lengthy correspondence, and Lathrop made a personal contribution to the mother's layette and sent a public health doctor to visit. Appealing to her reform network, she raised $157.61 for the woman's hospital and medical fees and for her room and board in town.[28]

Lathrop's 1916 correspondence with an Idaho mother exemplifies her effort to build a bond with her constituents. Pregnant with her fifth child, Mrs. M. R. lived twenty-five miles from a doctor, was burdened by overwork and poverty, and feared she would die. "Talk about better babys," she wrote bitterly, "when a mother must be like some cow or mare when a babys come. If she lives, all wright, and if not, Just the same." Lathrop wrote back with a "great deal of sympathy" and expressed her hope that some day "our country will be so organized that there will be a doctor and nurse stationed so that no one can be twenty five miles from a physician." She enclosed the Bureau's infant care bulletins and explained that their author was herself the mother of five. "They were all very young when she was left a widow and had to begin to earn a living for them and for herself. That took courage, and I can see plainly that your life requires great courage too." Most women responded warmly to such compassionate words, and the Bureau files contain many letters from women who felt they had benefited from their personal encounters with the Bureau staff and associates. One young woman, whose own mother was dead, wrote a staff physician that "words cannot express what I feel for you in my heart. I can only write that I thank you infinitely for your kindness towards helping me with my baby."[29]

The personal allegiance grassroots women felt for the Children's Bureau was crucial to the success of two other early projects, a birth registration campaign and a series of investigations into the causes of infant mortality. Lathrop considered birth registration a precondition for all other child welfare work, for accurate information about infant mortality could not be obtained without birth statistics, and child labor and compulsory education laws could not be enforced if children's ages were unknown. However, in 1912, only eight states met the requirement for inclusion in the Census Bureau's birth registration area by registering 90 percent of their births.[30]

The Children's Bureau birth registration drive relied upon progressive maternalist strategies of coalition building and scientific research. Bureau staff members enlisted community support to gather and publicize information about the appalling lack of birth statistics, and they worked with community groups to convince legislators and public health officials of the need for reform. Lathrop enlisted experts from the American Medical Association, American Public Health Association, and Bureau of the Census to draft a model birth registration statute, and got the General Federation of Women's Clubs to launch a nationwide campaign. Over three thousand club women participated in birth registration drives in 1915. They conducted house-to-house surveys of infants in a given neighborhood and then compared their count to the official record of registered births. As the public record was usually deficient, women activists then lobbied state legislatures for better laws. By the end of 1919, fifteen states had been added to the birth registration area, bringing the total to twenty-three. Ten years later, forty-six states were included in the area.[31] In the process of gathering birth statistics, the Children's Bureau raised public awareness about the deficiencies of the system and organized a disparate women's health movement into a unified campaign. Even Hannah Schoff, the conservative president of the National Congress of Mothers, overcame her ideological differences with the more progressive Children's Bureau leaders — and her resentment over what she considered their failure to recognize her organization's special place in the child welfare movement — and cooperated fully with the Bureau's baby-saving campaign.[32]

The Children's Bureau's studies of infant mortality also combined social research with a useful organizing tool. In keeping with the Bureau's dual commitment to social science and reform, the goal of the studies was not to "conduct investigations for the sake of investigations but to conduct investigations which will aid in the improvement of the condition of children," assistant Bureau chief Lewis Merriam explained. The first study, conducted in 1913 in Johnstown, Pennsylvania, a steel town with a large immigrant population, was followed by six other investigations.[33] The Bureau's innovative use of interviews with mothers about their living children, instead of death records, shifted the discussion of infant death from the etiology of disease to the "whole" child. It also may have given Bureau agents a more sympathetic view of mothers than previous infant mortality investigators and brought grassroots mothers into the federal baby-saving campaign.

Lathrop recognized that the success of the Children's Bureau infant mortality studies depended upon the sympathy and support of local women, and Bureau agents worked closely with women's clubs, parent-teacher associations, the clergy, and the press to develop contacts in each community. The Bureau was convinced that almost every mother would be willing to help if she knew "her testimony may be helpful to other mothers rearing children," and it instructed investigators to appeal to women "on the ground that the Bureau recognizes mothers and that it plans to build its future work to a considerable extent on their advice, testimony, and cooperation." Conscious of the need to win women's support but aware that some might resent the government's inquiry into their private concerns, the Bureau employed only women investigators. Interviewers were told not to ask about illegitimate births or about income from boarders or private charities if doing so would offend or injure the reputation of any woman.[34]

The Children's Bureau infant mortality studies, like most writings of progressive maternalists, combined concern about poverty and the environment with a cultural bias in favor of middle-class family life. Interviewers focused on issues both economic and cultural, such as housing conditions, maternal employment, the father's income, nutrition, and access to medical care. They omitted questions about alcoholism and venereal disease, which conservatives considered leading causes of infant deaths, but asked about "superstitious" health practices and cultural variations in diet.

The most dramatic finding of the Children's Bureau studies — if not a surprising one, given the progressive emphasis on the environment — was the sharp correlation between poverty and infant mortality. (That the Bureau measured poverty by the father's income reveals the family wage assumptions embedded in the agency's economic critique.) According to the Bureau, a child whose father earned less than $550 per year was more than twice as likely to die as one whose father earned over $1,250. As the author of the Waterbury report explained, "The medical cause of death is the immediate cause only. Correctly speaking, it is not only a cause, but also a result — the result of improper economic and social conditions." To Children's Bureau chief Julia Lathrop, these statistics were a clarion call for social and economic reform. Summing up the results of the Bureau's first investigation, she declared: "The Johnstown report shows a coincidence of underpaid fathers, overworked and ignorant mothers, and those hazards to the life of the offspring which individual parents cannot avoid or control because they must be remedied by community action. All this points toward the imperative need of ascertaining a standard of life for the American family, a standard which must rest upon such betterment of conditions of work and pay as will permit parents to safeguard infants within the household."[35]

In emphasizing the social and economic causes of infant mortality, the Children's Bureau departed from most other investigators and from sentimental maternalists, such as Hannah Schoff, who tended to blame heredity and poor mothering for infant deaths. For example, a study for the Russell Sage Foundation prepared by Henry Hibbs used literacy and ability to speak English as "indices of intelligence." Noting the high infant mortality rates among the illiterate and foreign-born, Hibbs concluded that "the real underlying factor of infant mortality and the chief consideration in the health and welfare of babies is the strength, character, health, and intelligence of the mother." Infant mortality, then, was "mainly a question of motherhood." Progressive women reformers had a far more positive assessment of the mother's role, perhaps because they had more contact with working-class and farm women than other researchers and health professionals. Although agreeing that infant mortality often resulted from "preventable ignorance," Lillian Wald insisted that the "intelligent reaction of the tenement-house mother has been remarkably evidenced. In the last analysis babies of the poor are kept alive through the intelligence of the mothers."[36]

Nevertheless, the Children's Bureau staff was convinced that scientific methods of childrearing and an "American" family life were essential to children's health and well-being. Staff researchers, appalled by the spicy diet and seemingly casual table manners of many ethnic groups, devoted considerable attention to children's diet; the Bureau's infant mortality studies described in lurid detail the diets of immigrant children. Maternalists' concern with nutrition was justified; as many as one third of infant deaths were caused by gastric and intestinal diseases. However, their obsession with bland foods and a milk diet affirmed their middle-class values of moderation, simplicity and control. For Anglo-Americans raised to value moderation in expressions of love as well as in diet, the informal atmosphere of immigrant mealtime seemed to symbolize immorality and loss of control. When a Bureau investigator deplored the tendency of immigrant women to "express maternal love by sharing with the baby whatever they themselves especially liked to eat or drink," she revealed her misgivings about the sensuousness of their mother-child bond as well as about their diet.[37]

Nor did the Children's Bureau studies transcend the ethnic stereotyping of their time. Bureau investigators held a respectful, though somewhat romantic, view of immigrant mothers who seemed to share their cultural values regarding children. They approved of Jews because they placed a high priority on children's health even though they were poor, and they praised Italians for being "devoted to their children.... Though the homes were often dirty the babies seldom looked neglected." In contrast, Bureau investigators deplored Lithuanians' "striking lack of knowledge" and "fatalistic acceptance" of infant mortality, and they blamed "dirty" and "superstitious" African American midwives for numerous infant deaths.[38]

Like maternalism itself, the Children's Bureau baby-saving strategy was two-pronged, aimed at both the individual and the community. Lathrop and her staff worked simultaneously to raise the childrearing "standards" of individual mothers and to eliminate the social and economic conditions leading to infant deaths. "Poverty usually means low standards and ignorance on the part of the mother," wrote the author of the Manchester infant mortality report, "while ample income makes possible the attainment of higher standards, better medical attention, and greater knowledge in the care of the baby."[39] Lathrop and her staff hoped that educating women about the new scientific thinking on child care would convince them that infant deaths were preventable and lead them to demand health and welfare services.

It apparently did. Women responded enthusiastically to the Children's Bureau investigations; only two of the 1,553 mothers visited in Johnstown refused to be interviewed. In fact, many women complained because the visitors had not brought along childrearing information and because they were interested only in babies born in 1911, and not their other children. Furthermore, infant welfare activity in Johnstown increased even before the results of the study were published: local women organized an infant welfare exhibit, a baby welfare station, and little mothers' classes for older children.[40] The Bureau's door-to-door investigation into infant mortality had succeeded in turning the private grief shared among friends and family into a public — and political — issue.

The infant mortality studies, together with the scientific childrearing information distributed by the Bureau, raised countless mothers' expectations for health care, convinced them that their private worries were of national significance, and inspired many of them to support the federal baby-saving campaign. "It seems strange that conditions . . . year after year . . . have been perfectly needless," one mother wrote Lathrop. "It is only necessary to make the people realize that their conditions are not normal. And I am certa[i]nly glad if I can help in any way." Activist women worked for child welfare through their local clubs and PTAs, and the Children's Bureau coordinated their activities into a unified campaign. In 1916, the federal Bureau and the General Federation of Women's Clubs organized National Baby Week to synchronize the many local Baby Weeks already being run by women's clubs and private charities.[41]

The national baby-saving campaign reached its peak during World War I and the early 1920s, ironically just as Jane Addams and other progressive women reformers were coming under attack for their pacifism and progressive politics. Lathrop, who kept quiet about her personal opposition to the war, took advantage of the anxiety generated by large numbers of young men failing army physicals to build up the federal child health campaign. As chair of the Child Welfare Department of the Woman's Committee of the Council of National Defense, Lathrop obtained for the Bureau a special appropriation of $150,000. Officials designated 1918, the second year of war, as Children's Year. During that year, Children's Bureau physicians and nurses, assisted by volunteers across the country, publicized a standard of normal child development by weighing and measuring 6.5 million preschool children in more than 16,500 cities, towns, and villages. Many communities established permanent health clinics as a result of the publicity. However, because the clinics were funded and administered by local governments, and not the federal Children's Bureau, Bureau staffers retained the appearance of being reform-minded political outsiders, rather than administrators of a government bureaucracy.[42]

By the end of Children's Year, the Bureau's campaign to improve women's and children's health had altered the political landscape. Approximately 11 million women participated in the baby-saving movement that year. Moreover, between 1908—when physician S. Josephine Baker was appointed director of the New York City Bureau of Child Hygiene, the nation's first tax-supported child health agency — and 1920, thirty-five states established permanent child health bureaus. Most of them were headed by women. Lathrop acknowledged the political significance of these developments in a story about a politician, originally a Bureau supporter, who was distressed by the agency's "fussing over" mothers and babies. "He had become acquainted with the policy of protecting children from labor," Lathrop explained, "but was still embarrassed when asked to take seriously as a public matter, the [physical] welfare of young children and their mothers. Yet the fussing has gone on and the welfare of mothers and babies is near to becoming, as the prevention of child labor has been for years, a dignified subject of political discussion."[43]

Optimism reigned at the 1919 White House Conference on the Minimum Standards of Child Welfare. Organized ten years after the White House Conference on the Care of Dependent Children at which the Children's Bureau was born, the 1919 conference showed how far discussions of child welfare had come in a decade. While delegates at the first conference were divided over the question of public responsibility for child welfare, those at the 1919 meeting took it for granted. The conference made recommendations on the "minimum standards" for child welfare in three areas: child labor and education, maternal and child health, and children in need of special care. All the recommendations reflected maternalists' dual commitment to professional expertise and economic reform. Thus the conference called for instruction on hygiene throughout pregnancy, and for publicly funded maternity centers so that any woman who did not have a private physician could receive prenatal, childbirth, and postnatal care from a physician or other qualified attendant. At the same time, it recommended that all new mothers should have ten days rest after childbirth, household help for at least four weeks, and an "adequate income" to allow them to remain at home throughout the nursing period. According to the conference summary, "It was recognized that an adequate wage for the father, wholesome and pleasant housing and living conditions, and the abolition of racial discrimination are fundamentals to the realization of any child welfare program."[44]

Progressive maternalists thus affirmed their commitment to the family wage system and promoted culturally specific guidelines for child welfare even as they acknowledged the role of poverty and racial discrimination in infant mortality and disease. "Let us not deceive ourselves," Lathrop said in another speech the same year. "The power to maintain a decent family living standard is the primary essential of child welfare. This means a living wage and wholesome working life for the man, a good and skillful mother at home to keep the house and comfort all within it. Society can afford no less and can afford no exceptions. This is a universal need."[45]

The Administration of Child Labor Reform

The popular and highly politicized campaign the Children's Bureau waged to protect infant health presents a marked contrast to its administrative regulation of child labor. Unlike the federal baby-saving campaign, Bureau efforts at child labor reform neither grew out of, nor led to, broad-based support among grassroots mothers. Although many mothers welcomed government "protection" of children's health, those who depended on the earnings of their offspring seem to have considered the "protection" of children from wage labor an unwarranted intrusion into their private affairs. Many wanted government assistance with child care, but they wanted it on their own terms: they wanted to retain control of their mothering work. Yet while infant health reform promised to ease the mother's burden, legal restrictions on child labor generally deprived poor families of much-needed income without providing them with a viable substitute for lost wages. That meant more work for mothers, who had to increase their economic contribution to the household without reducing their housework load. Because they tended to add to mothers' work, child labor laws never achieved the popularity of public health programs among working-class mothers.

The twin goals of the Children's Bureau, improving infant health and abolishing child labor, were two sides of a coherent maternalist ideology, which was founded on new "scientific" findings about the importance of physical health and play to wholesome child development. Both operated from a cultural perspective often at odds with working-class and farm mothers. Maternalist ideas about medicine and hygiene often clashed with folk childrearing practices, and maternalist views on child labor challenged traditional thinking about the needs of children and the importance of work. However, while many working-class women welcomed federal involvement in health care out of fear for their children's lives, mothers' needs and reformers' goals did not converge in the case of child labor reform. Maternalist ideas about child welfare and protection were the same in both cases. What was different was the effect of maternalist child welfare policy on working-class mothers — and therefore mothers' response.

Maternalist reformers were right to be horrified by child labor. At the turn of the century, an estimated 2 million children under fifteen were gainfully employed.[46] They labored in coal mines, textile mills, and canning factories, and toiled with their families in agricultural and domestic labor and in industrial homework. Reform-minded investigators found seven-year-olds in canneries, thirteen-year-olds working eight hours a day in coal mines, and twelve-year-olds struggling to work a six-hour "half" day in a factory while they attended school. Children as young as four years old worked full-time in canneries and fields. Furthermore, the evidence suggested that child labor posed a real danger to children's health. Long hours of repetitive labor in damp, dark, or dusty surroundings stunted growth; tuberculosis, curvature of the spine and industrial accidents were common among child workers. A study of children who worked in factories while attending school found that 27 percent were hearing impaired and that 37 percent had vision problems, compared to only 4 percent hearing and 6 percent vision problems among children who did no factory work. Two-thirds of child laborers in the Colorado beet fields were found to have orthopedic defects, a fact the Children's Bureau attributed to "undue strain on immature muscles."[47]

Working-class parents surely abhorred these conditions, but they did not necessarily share reformers' ideas about the remedy. In contrast to Anglo-American maternalists, who took for granted the dependence of wives and children on male breadwinners, many families of child earners came from rural traditions where everyone was expected to contribute to the family maintenance. Even after migrating to urban industrial areas, they faced low wages and periodic unemployment that made it impossible to survive on adult labor alone. Child labor was essential to family survival and, in the eyes of many, a positive alternative to truancy and gangs. Furthermore, many children were anxious to earn their own wages, either because they wanted to be more independent or because they wanted to help contribute to the family's support. An informal study of five hundred Chicago child factory workers found that 82 percent would rather work than go to school.[48]

The disparity between working-class women's reaction to baby saving and to child labor reform is strikingly evident in the Children's Bureau studies of child labor. While most mothers willingly told Bureau field workers about their infants who died, child labor investigators found that "parents were often afraid to admit that their children worked." Many women lied to Bureau agents because they were afraid of being fined or of having their children's wages taken away. For example, one woman, apparently not recognizing the Children's Bureau field worker as such, boasted that her seven-year-old son could "make more money than any of them picking shrimp," but later denied that any of her children worked. "Lots of children do work [in canneries], and when the inspector comes they run and hide," another mother explained. "They're on to him, and run whenever they see a stranger. They can get away into places where you'd never think of looking." Some parents were open in their approval of children's wage-work, however. "The great majority of mothers visited considered child labor as a matter of course," the Children's Bureau reported, "and it was not uncommon for them to boast of the skill of very small children in shucking oysters and picking shrimp."[49]

Given working-class women's enthusiasm for publicly funded maternal and infant care and grievances with child labor regulations, it is ironic that the Children's Bureau's first venture into administration came when the Department of Labor assigned it responsibility for enforcing the 1916 Keating-Owen Act, the first federal child labor law. The enactment of Keating-Owen was a victory for maternalists because it marked a new level of state commitment to protecting children and because it gave women in the federal government real administrative authority for the first time. Drafted by the National Child Labor Committee, the child labor bill used the interstate commerce clause to prohibit children under fourteen from working in mills, factories or canneries and to prevent those under sixteen from working in mines or quarries. Children under sixteen years old were prohibited from night work and from laboring more than eight hours a day. The $150,000 allocated for the bill's enforcement surpassed all previous appropriations to the Children's Bureau and enabled Lathrop to bring in fellow Hull-House resident Grace Abbott to direct its new Child Labor Division.[50]

Lathrop had long tried to bring Grace Abbott into the Children's Bureau. Although twenty years younger than Lathrop and Addams, Abbott was nonetheless a trusted member of the Hull-House inner circle. Like her mentors, she was from a prominent midwestern Republican family; her father was Nebraska's first lieutenant governor. Abbott and her sister Edith moved to Hull-House in 1908; Edith became a prominent social work educator and Grace worked with the Immigrants' Protective League, which assisted new arrivals to Chicago and sought to liberalize immigration laws. She resisted Lathrop's requests that she work for the Children's Bureau until 1917, when the reduced flow of immigrants and the new administrative authority of the Children's Bureau made the offer seem attractive for the first time. Abbott returned to Chicago after Keating-Owen was declared unconstitutional, but went back to Washington in 1921 when she was appointed Lathrop's successor. She presided over the Children's Bureau during the Sheppard-Towner years and fought hard but unsuccessfully for a child labor amendment to the Constitution. Although retiring from the Bureau in 1934, Abbott helped draft the children's sections of the Social Security Act.[51]

While significant as the first federal child labor law, the Keating-Owen

Act was a modest bill. The minimum standard of protection fixed by federal law was weaker than that established under many state child labor laws. For example, while New York set minimum standards for children's health and level of education, no such provisions were in the federal law. Moreover, the federal bill covered only about 150,000 workers, and made no provision for the majority of child wage earners, who worked in agriculture, domestic work, industrial homework, and the street trades. It thus provided no protection for some of the most vulnerable child workers, a disproportionate number of whom were children of color. Still, Lathrop and Abbott expected the child labor law to be a stepping stone to further reform. Their hopes were dashed when the Keating-Owen Act was declared unconstitutional after only nine months of operation.[52]

Enforcement of the Keating-Owen Act was a difficult task, and Abbott directed most of the Bureau's resources to southern states with child labor standards below the federal law. She hired federal agents to inspect working conditions in factories and to issue employment certificates to child wage earners. Because birth registration statistics were inadequate, however, the job of verifying children's ages for work permits was nearly impossible. In North and South Carolina, for example, less than 1 percent of young applicants for work permits had birth certificates. As a result, Bureau agents were overwhelmed with the difficult task of determining children's ages, and often looked with suspicion on parents of child wage earners who they believed would lie to obtain work permits for their children.[53] Most of the relatively small number of letters concerning the Keating-Owen Act from the parents of child earners asked the Bureau to circumvent the rules by allowing documentation of a child's age that had been found unacceptable or by granting a work permit to an underage youth.[54]

The sympathy and respect for poor mothers that marked the Children's Bureau correspondence on baby saving are lacking in its correspondence on the child labor law. During the same period that staff members in the Bureau's Maternity and Infancy Division helped poor mothers obtain money, clothing, and nursing care, those in the Child Labor Division rejected child workers' proof of age and denied their families' requests for assistance. Despite expressing sympathy for parents who lost income as a result of the child labor law, the Bureau staff tersely stated that the agency had no "discretion" in individual cases. They did not contact local agencies to help poor families and suggested no other means of assistance. Instead of acting as political advocates of poor mothers and helping them find other means of support—as they did when women wrote them about health care— Bureau officials acted as bureaucrats and maintained there was nothing they could do for individual families. Compassionate and friendly to poor mothers

who shared their cultural values regarding childrearing, progressive maternalists remained aloof from those who did not.[55]

Remarkably, some women who were angry about the child labor law
continued to see the Children's Bureau as a friend. Perhaps this reflects the
strength of the agency's reputation as women's advocate or shows mothers'
regret over the harsh conditions of their children's labor. One South Carolina
woman wrote Abbott that she believed her to be "sincere" but ignorant of
the impact of the law. Pointing out that families depended on children's
wages because men did not earn enough to support them, she warned that
the bill would force mothers to leave their children at home alone while
they went out to work. The woman's letters show her resentment of
lawmakers who believed that parents of child earners were motivated by
greed and her objection to government intervention into what she considered
private family matters. Insisting that cotton mill workers were not "ig-
noran[t] heartless unfeeling brutes totally unfit to manage their own affairs,"
she implored Abbott to "Try to place your self in our place, and think how
you would like for some one to take the most sacred thing in the world
from you — the privilege of governing your own children and being allowed
to make an honest living." Still, the woman's long letters to Grace Abbott
and their friendly closings (i.e., "I am your friend and well wisher") suggest
that, despite her opposition to the Keating-Owen Act, she felt that she had
an ally in the Children's Bureau.[56]

Progressive maternalists were well aware of the hardship caused by the
child labor law, and they strongly supported economic reforms, such as
mothers' pensions and higher wages for male workers, that they thought
would make child earning unnecessary. However, they believed that child
labor was too big an evil to be tolerated until those other reforms could be
won. As a result, the Children's Bureau settled for half a loaf and supported
an inadequate child labor law that did not cover most young workers and
that made no provision for lost income. For families whose survival depended
on children's wages, however, half a loaf seemed worse than none.

The June 1918 Supreme Court decision declaring the Keating-Owen Act
to be unconstitutional was a bitter blow for child labor reformers and the
Children's Bureau staff. According to Lathrop, the Bureau was "embarrassed"
by the Court's 5–4 decision that Keating-Owen was an invasion of states'
rights and an unlawful extension of the interstate commerce clause. Nevertheless, progressive women reformers were encouraged by Oliver Wendell
Holmes' vigorous dissent, and they continued to agitate for child labor
reform. One month after the Supreme Court decision, the War Labor Policies
board voted to make the standards of the child labor law a condition of
federal contracts. The Children's Bureau played an instrumental role in
securing a second federal child labor law, passed in 1919 but declared un-

constitutional three years later, and it lobbied vigorously for a child labor amendment to the constitution. In the 1920s, Grace Abbott and her staff publicized the extent of child labor and the inadequacy of existing laws — in 1923, only thirteen states had standards that measured up to the original child labor law — and they struggled to sustain the diverse coalition supporting the children's amendment.[57]

The progressive women's reform network threw all its weight behind the child labor amendment. Initially, reformers were optimistic about the amendment's chances; it was strongly supported by the National Child Labor Committee and the American Federation of Labor, and it had the endorsement of Presidents Warren G. Harding and, later, Calvin Coolidge. The Women's Joint Congressional Committee, comprised of representatives from most major women's organizations — including the National Congress of Mothers (its legislative work now directed by liberals Elizabeth Tilton and Florence Watkins), League of Women Voters, General Federation of Women's Clubs, National Consumers' League, and Women's Trade Union League — staunchly supported the measure, which easily passed both houses of Congress in June 1924.[58]

Few women reformers were prepared for what happened next. (Retired Bureau chief Lathrop, noting "how much sentiment exists against central control," was an important exception.) Anticommunists organized a bitter propaganda campaign against the child labor amendment, personally attacking its supporters and misrepresenting its terms. Led by the far-right Sentinels of the Republic and the staunchly antiunion National Association of Manufacturers, opponents of the amendment accused the "Kelley-Abbott gang" of being communists under direct order from Moscow. They charged that the child labor amendment violated states' rights, represented a frightening expansion of federal bureaucracy and state power, and forced parents to give up control of their children to the federal government. "It seeks to substitute national control, directed from Washington, for local and parental control, to bring about the nationalization of the children, and to make the child the ward of the Nation," the Sentinels claimed. "It is a highly socialistic measure — an assault against individual liberty." By early 1925, six states had refused the amendment and only three states had ratified it. Reformers and maternalists tried to keep the movement alive; they formed a committee called Organizations Associated for Ratification of the Child Labor Amendment, with PTA secretary Florence Watkins as chair and former Children's Bureau chief Lathrop as vice-chair. But it was to no avail. By 1930, only six states had accepted the proposed amendment, and the child labor amendment was lost.[59]

The failure of the child labor amendment, along with the defeat of the Sheppard-Towner Act to be discussed in chapter six, signaled the end of the maternalist movement. The anticommunist attacks and red-baiting of key leaders such as Abbott, Lathrop, and Florence Kelley seriously weakened the maternalist coalition. We have already seen the dissension the Red Scare caused within the PTA; similar disagreements led to the 1928 withdrawal of the General Federation of Women's Clubs from the Women's Joint Congressional Committee and to the increasing reluctance of organizations such as the League of Women Voters to take a stand on social legislation.[60] In addition, the bitter struggle between progressive women reformers and feminists over the Equal Rights Amendment (to be examined in the next chapter) further exposed the fact that maternalists did not speak for all women, thereby weakening their claim to authority over child welfare and their coalition for reform.

Although members of the Children's Bureau network sustained their reform principles through the 1920s (when work for welfare was unpopular) and into the 1930s, their reform vision was increasingly administrative and apolitical. Progressive maternalists had long maintained that children's care and welfare needs could best be determined by trained experts, though they stressed the importance of combining professionalism with grassroots women's activism, and of joining expertise with democracy. However, by the mid-1920s, the conservative backlash against feminism and reform, and the searing critique of mother-love by childrearing experts like John Watson, had weakened both the maternalist movement and professional women's claim to child welfare. Ironically, the movement's decline was exacerbated by the contradictions within progressive maternalism itself — especially its appeal to both maternal and scientific authority on the one hand, and its melding of political and administrative child welfare strategies on the other. When Bureau officials claimed authority in social welfare matters on the basis of their professional expertise, not their nurturing qualities, they undermined the maternalist claim to a uniquely feminine perspective on social issues — and to women's special authority in matters of child welfare. When they professionalized social services and made them a matter of public policy, they reduced the role women at the grassroots could play in welfare administration and reform. And when they created employment opportunities in social work and welfare bureaucracies for educated women, they weakened the hold of the prevailing idea that middle-class women's place was in the home. Ironically, by succeeding at their goal of getting the government to assume responsibility for child welfare, progressive maternalists contributed to the depoliticization of mother-work.

In the end, progressive maternalists improved conditions for some poor mothers and created new careers for educated women, but they failed to make real and long-lasting changes in mothers' work and status. As long as they were maternalists, wedded to nineteenth-century ideas about women's special aptitude for child care and men's singular role as providers, they could not have done otherwise. Unfortunately, as the next chapter shows, feminists who challenged maternalist ideas about gender difference and that family wage also failed to sustain a political strategy empowering to mothers.

NOTES

Portions of this chapter previously appeared in my article, "Hull House Goes to Washington: Women and the Children's Bureau," in *Gender, Class, Race and Reform in the Progressive Era*, ed. Noralee Frankel and Nancy S. Dye (Lexington: University Press of Kentucky, 1991).

1. U.S. Children's Bureau, *Second Annual Report* (Washington, D.C.: Government Printing Office, 1914), 8.

2. U.S. Children's Bureau, *Eleventh Annual Report* (Washington, D.C.: Government Printing Office, 1923).

3. Dorothy E. Bradbury, "The Children's Advocate: The Story of the United States Children's Bureau, 1903–1946," n.d., pp. 1–2, Grace and Edith Abbott Papers, Regenstein Library, University of Chicago.

4. Schoff publicly supported the idea of a children's bureau, but argued that it should be placed in the Bureau of Education. "President's Desk," *Child-Welfare Magazine* 6 (Mar. 1912): 215. NCLC secretary Owen Lovejoy complained privately that Schoff opposed the Children's Bureau bill, "first on one ground and than [*sic*] on another." Owen Lovejoy to Miss Wald, Feb. 13, 1912, Box 38, Folder 2, Abbott Papers. On the origins and early years of the Children's Bureau, see Robyn L. Muncy, *Creating a Female Dominion in American Reform, 1890–1935* (New York: Oxford University Press, 1991), 38–65; Nancy Pottishman Weiss, "Save the Children: A History of the Children's Bureau, 1903–1918" (Ph.D. diss., University of California-Los Angeles, 1974); Louis J. Covotsos, "Child Welfare and Social Progress: A History of the United States Children's Bureau, 1912–1935" (Ph.D. diss., University of Chicago, 1976).

5. James Johnson, "The Role of Women in the Founding of the U.S. Children's Bureau," in *"Remember the Ladies": New Perspectives on Women in American History*, ed. Carol V. R. George (Syracuse, N.Y.: Syracuse University Press, 1975), 185; House Committee on Labor, *Hearings on H.R. 4694, A bill to establish in the Department of Commerce and Labor a Bureau to be known as the Children's Bureau*, 62nd Congress, 1st Session, May 12, 1911.

6. Law establishing the Children's Bureau, quoted in U.S. Children's Bureau, *Prenatal Care*, Publication No. 4 (Washington, D.C.: Government Printing Office, 1913), 2; Weiss, "Save the Children," 84.

7. Quoted in Bradbury, "The Children's Advocate," 58. On Lathrop's early years, see Jane Addams, *My Friend, Julia Lathrop* (New York: Macmillan, 1935).

8. Edith Abbott quoted in Addams, *My Friend*, 161.

9. Addams, *My Friend*; Jane Addams, *Twenty Years at Hull-House* (Urbana: University of Illinois Press, 1990; orig. 1910), 181. On the relationship between professionalization and social welfare reform, see Muncy, *Creating a Female Do-*

minion, and Elizabeth K. Hartley, "Social Work and Social Reform: Selected Women Social Workers and Child Welfare Reforms, 1877–1932" (Ph.D. diss., University of Pennsylvania, 1985).

10. Quoted in Bradbury, "The Children's Advocate," 65.

11. Addams, *Twenty Years at Hull-House,* 136.

12. Barbara Sicherman, *Alice Hamilton: A Life in Letters* (Cambridge: Harvard University Press, 1984), 119; Addams, *Twenty Years at Hull-House,* 78, 147–48. Also see Hilda Satt Polachek, *I Came a Stranger: The Story of a Hull-House Girl* (Urbana: University of Illinois Press, 1989), and Rivka Shpak Lissak, *Pluralism and Progressives: Hull House and the New Immigrants, 1890–1919* (Chicago: University of Chicago Press, 1989).

13. Addams, *My Friend,* 51.

14. Muncy, *Creating a Female Dominion,* 122; Jill Conway, "Women Reformers and American Culture, 1870–1930," *Journal of Social History* 5 (Winter 1971–72), 164–277.

15. Julia Lathrop, "Highest Education for Women," *Journal of Home Economics* 8 (Jan. 1916): 2; R. L. Duffus, *Lillian Wald, Neighbor and Crusader* (1938), quoted in *Notable American Women,* vol. 3, ed. Edward T. James, Janet Wilson James, and Paul S. Boyer (Cambridge: Harvard University Press, 1971), 528.

16. Addams, *My Friend,* 40–41; Julia Lathrop, Speech before the International Congress of Working Women, Nov. 3, 1919, Box 60, Folder 10, Abbott Papers.

17. *Congressional Record,* vol. 61, 67th Cong., 1st Sess., June 29, 1921, 8759; Wald quoted in Weiss, "Save the Children," 124. Alexander McKelway of the National Child Labor Committee was one Children's Bureau supporter who doubted women's administrative abilities. See Lela B. Costin, *Two Sisters for Social Justice: A Biography of Grace and Edith Abbott* (Urbana: University of Illinois Press, 1983), 105–6.

18. Weiss, "Save the Children," 174; Lathrop quoted in Costin, *Two Sisters,* viii.

19. The Children's Bureau soon supplanted the American Association for the Study and Prevention of Infant Mortality as the nation's major child health organization. On the history of the AASPIM, see Richard A. Meckel, *Save the Babies: American Public Health Reform and the Prevention of Infant Mortality, 1850–1929* (Baltimore: Johns Hopkins University Press, 1990), 109–23. See also Alisa Klaus, "Women's Organizations and the Infant Health Movement in France and the United States, 1890–1920," in *Lady Bountiful Revisited: Women, Philanthropy, and Power,* ed. Kathleen D. McCarthy (New Brunswick, N.J.: Rutgers University Press, 1990).

20. Addams, *My Friend,* 4; Kathryn Kish Sklar, ed. *Autobiography of Florence Kelley: Notes of Sixty Years* (Chicago: Charles H. Kerr, 1986), 30–31; Allen Davis, *American Heroine: The Life and Legend of Jane Addams* (New York: Oxford University Press, 1973), 5; Dorothy Reed Mendenhall, Unpublished Autobiography, Typescript, Box 3, Folder J, p. 19–20, Dorothy Reed Mendenhall Papers, Sophia Smith Collection, Smith College.

21. Lillian Wald, *Windows on Henry Street* (Boston: Little, Brown & Co., 1934), 86; Addams, *My Friend,* 52–53.

22. U.S. Children's Bureau, *Prenatal Care,* Publication No. 4 (Washington, D.C.: Government Printing Office, 1913); idem, *Infant Care,* Publication No. 8 (Washington, D.C.: Government Printing Office, 1914). L. Emmett Holt's *The Care and Feeding of Children: A Catechism for the Use of Mothers and Children* (New York: D. Appleton & Company, 1894) went through twenty-eight editions from its publication until the mid 1920s. See U.S. Children's Bureau, *The Story of Infant Care* (1965), in File 8–6–8 C 437(1), Children's Bureau Records, Central Files, 1914–50, Record Group 102, National Archives, Washington, D.C. (hereafter cited as CB).

23. Children's Bureau, *Prenatal Care,* 6.

24. Children's Bureau, *Infant Care,* 59.

25. U.S. Children's Bureau, *Infant Care* rev. ed. (Washington, D.C.: Government Printing Office, 1921), 42.

26. Julia Lathrop to William B. Wilson, Jan. 12, 1914, File 6007, CB; U.S. Children's Bureau, *Third Annual Report* (Washington, D.C.: Government Printing Office, 1915), 11. The Bureau received 120,760 letters in 1927. U.S. Children's Bureau, *Fifteenth Annual Report* (Washington, D.C.: Government Printing Office, 1927), 42.

27. Addams, *Twenty Years at Hull-House,* 99.

28. Ibid., 102; Mrs. A. P., Wyoming, to Miss Lathrop, Oct. 19, 1916 and Nov. 21, 1916, reprinted in Ladd-Taylor, *Raising a Baby the Government Way: Mothers' Letters to the Children's Bureau* (New Brunswick, N.J.: Rutgers University Press, 1986), 49–51. Julia Lathrop to Mrs. W. F. Dummer, June 16, 1917, Box 59 Folder 4, Abbott Papers. Copies of the correspondence between Lathrop and Mrs. A. P. are in the Abbott Papers.

29. Mrs. M. R., Idaho, Jan. 4, 1916; Lathrop to Mrs. M. R.; Mrs. F. D., Quebec, Dec. 18, 1921, reprinted in Ladd-Taylor, *Raising a Baby,* 133–34, 111.

30. See Jacqueline K. Parker and Edward M. Carpenter, "Julia Lathrop and the Children's Bureau: The Emergence of an Institution," *Social Service Review* (Mar. 1981): 67–70.

31. Parker and Carpenter, "Julia Lathrop," 69; U.S. Children's Bureau, *The Promotion of the Welfare and Hygiene of Maternity and Infancy for the Fiscal Year Ending June 30, 1929,* Publication No. 203 (Washington, D.C.: Government Printing Office, 1931), 21. Only South Dakota, Texas, and the Territory of Hawaii remained outside the birth registration area at the end of 1929.

32. On the tension between Schoff and the Children's Bureau staff, see W. F. Bigelow to Harriet Anderson, Mar. 25, 1920, and the correspondence between Schoff and Anna Rude, all in File 10,406, CB.

33. Merriam quoted in Weiss, "Save the Children," 185. The seven cities were Johnstown, Pennsylvania; Manchester, New Hampshire; Waterbury, Connecticut; Brockton, Massachusetts; Saginaw, Michigan; New Bedford, Massachusetts; Akron, Ohio. Investigations of infant mortality were also conducted in Montclair, New Jersey, and Baltimore, Maryland. Despite listing different authors, the Children's Bureau infant mortality studies can be considered representative of Children's Bureau philosophy. The booklets were heavily edited by the central office to reflect

the agency's perspective. For a summary of the Bureau findings, see U.S. Children's Bureau, *Causal Factors in Infant Mortality: A Statistical Study Based on Investigations in Eight Cities*, Publication No. 142 (Washington, D.C.: Government Printing Office, 1925).

34. "Instructions to Agents" [for Manchester], n.d., File 11-312-1, CB; "Memorandum for Field Agents," Mar. 27, 1913, File 11-421, CB; Jessamine Whitney to Lewis Meriam, Apr. 16, 1915, File 11-312-2, CB. See also Theresa S. Haley to Lewis Meriam, May 21, 1915, File 11-483, CB. In reality, Children's Bureau investigators were not always so open-minded. A field worker in Manchester, complaining that one woman did not take her interview seriously, suggested that similar cases may have "crept in especially among the unscrupulous women of the lower classes." Herbert Grant, "Investigation — Infant Mortality, Case Reports," July 13, 1915, File 11-433, CB. For a different perspective on the Bureau's hiring only women investigators, see Muncy, *Creating a Female Dominion*, 52.

35. Julia Lathrop, "Income and Infant Mortality," *American Journal of Public Health* 9 (Apr. 1919): 270-74; U.S. Children's Bureau, *Infant Mortality: Results of a Field Study in Waterbury, Ct., Based on Births in One Year*, Publication No. 29 (Washington, D.C.: Government Printing Office, 1918), 26; idem, *Infant Mortality: Results of a Field Study in Johnstown, Pa., Based on Births in One Calendar Year*, Publication No. 9 (Washington, D.C.: Government Printing Office, 191), 8.

36. Henry H. Hibbs, Jr., *Infant Mortality: Its Relation to Social and Industrial Conditions* (New York: Russell Sage Foundation, 1916), 100, 60, 58, 61; Wald, *The House on Henry Street* (New York: Henry Holt & Co., 1915), 55. Hibbs was more sympathetic to economic factors than many other writers. Paul Popenoe and Roswell Johnson cite Hibbs as an example of a misguided emphasis on poverty and the environment in *Applied Eugenics* (New York: Macmillan, 1917), 411.

37. Children's Bureau, *Infant Mortality in Waterbury*, 26-28; idem, *Infant Mortality: Results of a Field Study in Akron, Ohio, Based on Births in One Year, 1920*, Publication No. 72 (Washington, D.C.: Government Printing Office, 1920), 35-36.

38. Children's Bureau, *Infant Mortality in Johnstown*, 29-30; idem, *Infant Morality in Akron*, 19; idem, *Infant Mortality in Waterbury*, 32; idem, *Maternity and Child Care in Selected Rural Areas of Mississippi*, Publication No. 88 (Washington, D.C.: Government Printing Office, 1921), 21-22.

39. U.S. Children's Bureau, *Infant Mortality: Results of a Field Study in Manchester, N.H., Based on Births in One Year*, Publication No. 20 (Washington, D.C.: Government Printing Office, 1917), 71.

40. Children's Bureau, *Infant Mortality in Johnstown*, 6; Weiss, "Save the Children," 191; "Report of Infant Welfare Work Carried on in Johnstown, Pa. During the Summer of 1914 by the Associated Charities," File 11-419, CB.

41. Mrs. A. P. Nov. 21, 1916, reprinted in Ladd-Taylor, *Raising a Baby*, 51; Grace Abbott, "Ten Years' Work for Children," *North American Review* 218 (Aug. 1923): 189-200.

42. Abbott, "Ten Years Work," 199.

43. Ibid., 199; Muncy, *Creating a Female Dominion*, 100; Julia Lathrop, Address

given before the National Suffrage Association, Mar. 28, 1919, Box 60, Folder 10, Abbott Papers.

44. U.S. Children's Bureau, *Minimum Standards for Child Welfare Adopted by the Washington and Regional Conferences on Child Welfare, 1919,* Publication No. 62 (Washington, D.C.: Government Printing Office, 1919), 2, 6–7, 15.

45. Julia Lathrop, "Child Welfare Standards a Test of Democracy," Presidential Address before the National Conference of Social Work, June 1, 1919, Box 60, Folder 10, Abbott Papers.

46. Walter I. Trattner, *Crusade for the Children: A History of the National Child Labor Committee and Child Labor Reform in America* (New York: Quadrangle, 1970), remains the best history of child labor reform. For statistics about the extent of the problem, see pp. 40–41.

47. Edna D. Bullock, ed. *Selected Articles on Child Labor* (White Plains, N.Y.: H. W. Wilson, 1915), 84, 121, 136–38; U.S. Children's Bureau, *Child Labor and the Work of Mothers in Oyster and Shrimp Canning Communities on the Gulf Coast,* Publication No. 98 (Washington, D.C.: Government Printing Office, 1922), 14; idem, *Child Labor and the Work of Mothers in the Beet Fields of Colorado and Michigan,* Publication No. 115 (Washington, D.C.: Government Printing Office, 1923), 77.

48. Children's Bureau, *Child Labor and the Work of Mothers in Oyster and Shrimp Canning Communities,* 18. Helen Todd, article in Bullock, ed., *Selected Articles on Child-Labor,* 216. For an insightful discussion of the Children's Bureau's position on child labor, see Weiss, "Save the Children," 243–54.

49. Children's Bureau, *Child Labor and the Work of Mothers in Oyster and Shrimp Canning Communities,* 11–12.

50. "An Act to Prevent Interstate Commerce in the Products of Child Labor, and For Other Purposes," reprinted in U.S. Children's Bureau, *Administration of the First Federal Child-Labor Law,* Publication No. 78 (Washington, D.C.: Government Printing Office, 1921), 174–76.

51. See Costin's fine biography, *Two Sisters.*

52. See Children's Bureau, *Administration of the First Federal Child-Labor Law;* Costin, *Two Sisters,* 103–12; Trattner, *Crusade for the Children,* 128–32. For an earlier survey of state laws, see U.S. Children's Bureau, *Child Labor Legislation in the United States,* Publication No. 10 (Washington, D.C.: Government Printing Office, 1915).

53. Weiss, "Save the Children," 263; and the correspondence between the federal Children's Bureau officials and field agents in file group 25-4-1, CB. Also see "Experiences in Child-Labor Law Administration," typescript of radio release, Jan. 30, 1923, Box 40, Abbott Papers.

54. For example, see Mrs. C. K., Texas, to Grace Abbott, rec'd. Sept. 1917, File 25-2-1-1, CB; Mrs. J. A., Georgia, to Children's Bureau, Mar. 8, 1918, File 25-4-1-1, CB; Mr. S. H., South Carolina, to Labor Department, rec'd. Sept. 1917, File 25-4-1-1, CB.

55. See Grace Abbott to S. H., Sept. 26, 1917, File 25-4-1-1, CB; W. H. S. to

Richard E. Byrd, Dec. 20, 1917, File 25-2-1-1, CB; and other letters in those file groups.

56. Mrs. C. N., South Carolina, to Grace Abbott, June 3, 1917, June 18, 1917, July 17, 1917, File 25-2-1-1, CB.

57. Julia Lathrop to Mrs. James Rae Arneill, June 29, 1918, File 6011, CB; Trattner, *Crusade for the Children*, 134–42; Costin, *Two Sisters*, 110–15, 150–58.

58. All member organizations of the WJCC endorsed the children's amendment. Annual Report of the Secretary, Nov. 19, 1923, Reel 3, Women's Joint Congresssional Committee Records, Library of Congress.

59. Costin, *Two Sisters*, 151, 155; Lemons, *Woman Citizen*, 220, 146–47. See also Trattner, *Crusade for the Children*, 163–86.

60. J. Stanley Lemons, *Woman Citizen: Social Feminism in the 1920s* (Urbana: University of Illinois Press, 1973), 146–47.

4

"How Cruelly Unjust
to Handicap All Women":
Feminism and the Abandonment
of Motherhood Rhetoric

While maternalists accented women's duty to care for their families, feminists insisted on their self-fulfillment as individuals. While maternalists presupposed and perhaps even strengthened married women's economic dependence on men, feminists held economic freedom as one of their most cherished principles. Yet maternalism and feminism coexisted, if somewhat uneasily, in the women's movement of the Progressive era; it was only in the 1920s, when activist women had to face the question of "what next" after suffrage, that the alliance fell apart. The debate over the Equal Rights Amendment (ERA) represents the first systematic feminist challenge to motherhood rhetoric and maternalist ideology. Before the ERA's introduction, however, feminists frequently used the rhetoric of motherhood to critique the patriarchal family. It was not until the mid 1920s that most of those who called themselves feminists abandoned the language of sexual difference to focus almost exclusively on attaining equal rights in the public sphere. Despite the extraordinary power of motherhood as an organizing device during the Progressive era, by the late 1920s it had come to be seen as "at odds" with feminism and female autonomy.[1]

Feminists' move away from motherhood rhetoric was due in large measure to the influence of the equal rights–oriented National Woman's Party (NWP) and its charismatic leader, Alice Paul. The NWP was the organizational center of feminism in the 1910s and 1920s. Established in 1913 as the Congressional Union, a militant suffrage group that split off from the moderate National American Woman Suffrage Association (NAWSA), it became the Woman's Party in 1917. The NWP's flamboyant style and neutral position during World War I attracted socialists and pacifists, such as Crystal Eastman and Florence Kelley, even as it antagonized NAWSA leaders and most other members of the Children's Bureau network. Feminists further irritated maternalists and moderate suffragists by challenging the ideology of womanly service then dominating the women's movement, insisting instead on women's right to self-expression in work, personal relations, and life-style. Many feminists combined the individualist goal of personal emancipation with a socialist challenge to the economic system. According to the historian Nancy Cott, "Feminism was full of double aims, joining the concept of women's equality with men to the concept of women's sexual difference, joining the aim of antinomian individual release with concerted social action, endorsing the 'human sex' while deploying political solidarity among women."[2]

Progressive-era feminists used maternal metaphors less frequently than maternalists, but they did not reject motherhood rhetoric entirely. Most still assumed that women were more sensitive to children's needs than men, and they tried to raise public awareness about the value of mothers' and housewives' work. Some experimented with cooperative living arrangements designed to emancipate mothers, and many worked with maternalists for suffrage, peace, and social welfare reform. It was only in the 1920s, when there was no longer a suffrage issue to hold diverse groups of women activists together, that feminism and maternalism clearly diverged. The debate over the effect of the Equal Rights Amendment on welfare services and protective labor laws brought fundamental differences in ideology and political style to a head. Feminists, who made individual women's right to equal opportunity in the public sphere a political priority, fought with maternalists, who strove first of all to protect women in their family role. Since the reasoning of the first group depended on the language of gender sameness and equality, maternalists — needing to sharpen the distinctions between the two sides — had to stress women's difference from men. The result, a simplified understanding of women's nature and a polarized movement that shattered illusions of gender solidarity, was a loss to both sides.

Feminists' abandonment of motherhood rhetoric both reflected and reinforced the broader societal trends away from politicized motherhood in the 1920s. We have already examined the PTA's turn away from reform and the Children's Bureau's increasingly administrative outlook. The feminist rebellions of the Progressive era were also reoriented in the 1920s. Postwar disillusionment and the Red Scare, combined with a rapidly expanding consumer economy, encouraged women (and men) to turn inward — rather than to radical political movements — to find individual fulfillment and personal independence. Films and popular magazines celebrated women as fun-loving flappers, wives, and companions, rather than mothers and social reformers, and presented consumerism as the key to domestic happiness and personal fulfillment. Childrearing experts discussed the dangers of mother-love. Although some feminists remained committed to a broad vision of social change, most focused on individual economic opportunity as the key to women's emancipation; there was surprisingly little feminist analysis of childrearing or the home. Except for several books and a handful of articles on motherhood in the NWP magazine *Equal Rights,* family and welfare issues were not addressed in the feminist program, and conflicts between wagework and family were resolved in private. It was a legacy that has only recently begun to change.[3]

Feminism and Motherhood before the 1920S: Charlotte Perkins Gilman and Ellen Key

Feminism and maternalism were joined before 1920, even though they were constructed on different views of women's rights and nature. As we have seen, maternalists generally understood women's rights and responsibilities through the lens of motherhood. They based their political work on gender difference and (when they supported suffrage) justified women's right to vote primarily on the grounds that it was necessary to protect their families. "If woman would fulfill her traditional responsibility to children," explained Jane Addams, "then she must bring herself to the use of the ballot."[4] American feminists, by contrast, insisted that women's primary relationship to the state be as citizens and workers, not as mothers. While maternalists assumed that most women would find fulfillment by staying home with their children, feminists asserted women's desire to combine marriage with career. While progressive reformers and club mothers spoke of social service and ministering to women's needs, feminists conceived their activism in terms of individual human rights. At a time when most people saw women only within a web of family relations, they asserted women's individual autonomy, challenged the idea of the family wage, and demanded economic — as well as legal and political — independence from men.

In part the difference between feminists and maternalists was generational. With several important exceptions, including Charlotte Perkins Gilman and Harriot Stanton Blatch, most American feminists reached young adulthood in the twentieth century. Crystal Eastman, for example, was born in 1881, making her some twenty years younger than Birney, Schoff, Addams, and Lathrop. Moreover, her life story would not have been possible a generation earlier. The child of two Congregationalist ministers, she was a lawyer who conducted a major investigation of industrial accidents and was instrumental in the passage of New York's workers' compensation law. A socialist, peace activist, journalist, and mother, she was twice married and once divorced. She kept her maiden name, advocated legalized birth control, and wrote about alternative living arrangements in articles such as "Marriage under Two Roofs."[5]

Yet until the 1920s, even feminists like Eastman utilized the rhetoric of motherhood. They saw no conflict between gender equality and difference; in Katharine Anthony's words, feminists advocated "the emancipation of woman both as a human-being and a sex-being." "The program of feminism is not the mere imitation of masculine gestures and motions," Anthony explained in her 1915 book, *Feminism in Germany and Scandinavia.* "The program of feminism is the development of a new science of womanhood. It is true that an important part of the program is the reinstatement of woman as a human being. . . . But there is every need that women should not follow blindly in the path of their brothers but should test the way ahead of them as they go." Like maternalists, feminists of the 1910s rejected the idea of motherhood as a "private" concern, and argued that reproduction and childrearing were—and should be—of concern to the entire community. Unlike maternalists, they acknowledged potential conflict between women's desire for freedom and self-fulfillment and the demands of their children. Admitting that, in Henrietta Rodman's words, "the care of the baby is the weak point in feminism," feminists tried to transform the family.[6]

Many American feminists, following the influential theorist Charlotte Perkins Gilman, believed that the root of women's subordinate status was their economic dependence and isolation in the home. In contrast to maternalists, who wanted to protect the private home, Gilman portrayed it as wasteful, inefficient, and oppressive to women. Insisting that the private home had outgrown its usefulness and that women should seek fulfillment in paid employment, she advocated the socialization of household chores such as cooking, laundry, and even childcare. Gilman's work was very popular among Progressive-era intellectuals and reformers, despite its variance from the maternalist view of the home. Jane Addams and Florence Kelley applauded her work, and Gilman was a frequent visitor at Hull-House.[7]

As Gilman was a leading architect of the American feminist critique of motherhood, it is significant that she did not entirely reject maternal thinking. She believed that men and women were more similar than different, but assumed nevertheless that women's capacity to mother shaped their nature. "The constructive tendency is essentially feminine; the destructive masculine," she wrote in *The Home.* "Male energy tends to scatter and destroy, female to gather and construct." Still, Gilman condemned "matriolatry," the blind worship of mothers, and was (for the pre–World War I era) unusually harsh in her assessment of the abilities of the average mother. Criticizing the "beloved dogma" that maternal instinct naturally fitted women for childrearing, she quipped, "You may observe mother instinct at its height in a fond hen sitting on china eggs—instinct, but no brains."[8]

The lively debate between Gilman and Swedish feminist Ellen Key over the politics of motherhood and direction of the women's movement illustrates the broad range of opinion in feminist writings on motherhood. Unlike Gilman, who wanted to dismantle the traditional home so that mothers could find fulfilling work and become productive members of society, Key was a romantic individualist who believed that childrearing was itself a productive social contribution and women's ultimate fulfillment. Idealizing the bond between mother and child, she proposed a "new morality" that would allow mothers, whether or not they were married, to raise their children in their own homes. In contrast, Gilman argued that private homes were destructive for both women and children, and called on the state to take over childrearing tasks that previously had been performed at home. While Key would preserve the biological differences between men and women, Gilman stressed the "human qualities" men and women shared. Unlike the Swedish feminist, she thought that most women had neither the talent nor the inclination for full-time childrearing.[9]

Both writers were well known among American women activists. Although Key did not have a large following in the United States—no doubt because of her radical views on love and marriage—both maternalists and feminists followed her writings with interest. Her books sold well and her theories were widely discussed in liberal magazines such as the *Atlantic Monthly*. Moreover, Key was extremely influential in Europe; her theories on state-supported motherhood and free love were incorporated into the important German Bund für Mutterschutz, which was established in 1904 to strengthen married women's legal rights, legalize "free unions" and birth control, and provide financial support for unmarried mothers.[10]

Despite the many differences between them, both Key and Gilman centered their feminist politics on motherhood. Both assumed women's responsibility for childrearing, and considered women's economic and psychological dependence on men to be harmful to children as well as to their mothers. And both envisioned a matriarchal state that had peace, the education of children, and the eugenic perfection of the race as its central goals. Like many well-known reformers and intellectuals of their time, both Key and Gilman embraced evolutionary theory and the new "science" of eugenics. They belonged to what historian Daniel J. Kevles called the "social-radical" wing of the eugenics movement and used eugenic arguments to "prove" that women's oppression was damaging to the "race."[11] Although differing with conservative, or "mainline," eugenicists on the question of women's place, both writers were optimistic about the possibility of improving human society through selective breeding—and quite unconcerned by the controlling aspects of eugenic thought. Yet despite their similarities, the solutions each feminist advanced to the problems of women's oppression—paying mothers to stay at home on Key's part, and socializing child care on Gilman's—reflected their contrasting ideas about motherhood. While the Swedish writer idealized mother-love and hoped to empower women as mothers, Gilman wanted to develop women's human qualities and free them from the home.

Throughout her work, Key emphasized the preservation and reinforcement of the "ineradicable differences" between men and women. "The man's work is to *kindle* the fire on the hearth, the woman's is to *maintain* it," she wrote; "it is man's, to *defend* the lives of those belonging to him; woman's, to *care* for them." Unlike traditionalists, however, Key did not exalt maternal sacrifice or place men's work on a higher plane. Instead, she romanticized motherhood as the "most perfect human state," a "natural balance between the happiness of the individual and of the whole, between self-assertion and self-devotion, between sensuousness and soulfulness." The Swedish feminist also departed from traditionalists in her insistence on the sensuousness of motherhood. Her "New Morality," which held that love and parental responsibility were more significant than legal institutions, rejected the desexualized maternal ideal of the Anglo-American Victorian era, and posed a challenge to those maternalists (and feminists like Gilman) who held on to the passionless ideal. Key was, according to one American critic, both more radical and more conservative than American feminists. While her ideas about love and marriage were revolutionary, she had a reactionary concept of motherhood. She challenged the male-headed family, but idealized the mother-child bond. Moreover, the critic complained, she virtually ignored men, rendering motherliness "almost a religious cult, with a subordinate paternity."[12]

Key was a romantic individualist who (like G. Stanley Hall and the sentimental maternalists) had a nostalgic view of the past and feared that modern industrial conditions were eroding mother love. Like maternalists, she worried that women who toiled at household chores and labored outside the home were too exhausted to adequately care for their families, making motherhood a burden and not the fulfilling vocation it ought to be. Yet Key did not condemn women (like herself) who chose not to have children; instead, she blamed the declining birth rate on women's economic dependence on men. She therefore proposed that the government pay mothers a "money-wage" to dignify their work in the home and to compensate them for lost wages. Convinced that woman's soul was "filled by the child, just as the man of science is possessed by his investigations," Key believed that it was natural for mothers to stay at home when their children were small. Only when mothering was economically valued like other work would they stop seeking self-respect in work outside the home.[13]

Just as Key's views on free love and economic independence distinguished her from maternalists, her romantic ideas about the mother-child bond put her in sharp conflict with feminists like Gilman. She condemned the selfishness of "amaternal" feminists, who she believed wanted to "free" women for jobs outside the home by having the state take over childrearing. In Key's view, amaternal feminists accepted the "faulty premises" of a society that was turning away from mother love. Emulating the male model of success, they confused human qualities with male ones, equal rights with similar functions, and denied the female side of themselves. Key worried that a feminism that minimized sexual difference would antagonize men and upset the sexual balance society required. The woman movement should emancipate motherliness, not erode it, she wrote; it was in order that motherliness should "penetrate all spheres of life that woman's liberation is required."[14]

Gilman responded to Key's critique in witty articles in her journal, *The Forerunner.* Although she shared the Swedish writer's desire for a child-oriented society, she rejected Key's idealized view of the all-wise mother and insisted that children needed the additional care of "specialists in child culture." "Motherhood is a common possession of every female creature; a joy, a pride, a nobly useful function," she wrote in an earlier book. "Teach-erhood is a profession, a specialized social function, no more common to mothers than to fathers, maids or bachelors. The ceaseless, anxious strain to do what only an experienced nurse and teacher can do, is an injury to the real uses of motherhood."[15]

According to Gilman, the entire society suffered because women were expected to educate their own children in their own homes. Constant contact between mother and child led to strain between them; even the "motherliest mother" could breathe a little more freely when the baby was asleep or at school. "Every normal woman should be a mother," she wrote, but only one woman in twenty had a "genius for child care." Thus, she proposed that children live in "baby-gardens" where they would be raised by profes-sionals, "born educators" who had both the natural talent and training necessary for childrearing.[16]

Gilman's ideas about motherhood reflected her own experience. Born in 1860 to a prominent New England family, she grew up poor because her father deserted the family when she was a child. Her early experiences taught her the need for women to be self-supporting and economically independent. After her first marriage and the birth of her daughter, Gilman had a nervous breakdown, which she fictionalized in "The Yellow Wall-Paper." She was put on doctor S. Weir Mitchell's famous rest cure, which prohibited reading, writing, and exercising, but only became more depressed. She recovered only when she left her family and traveled alone to California. Gilman relinquished custody of her child to her husband and supported herself by writing, lecturing, and managing a boarding house. Though she loved her daughter, Gilman had been frustrated as a full-time mother.

Personally oppressed by women's economic and psychological dependence on men in the nuclear family, she developed a theory that would free middle-class women from full-time childrearing and allow them to be "productive" members of society.[17]

In distinguishing between "mere childbearing" and "the unlimited processes of child-rearing," Gilman took American feminist theory an important step forward. Nevertheless, she did not fully develop her insight and continued to extol motherhood. Like many of her contemporaries, Gilman believed that mother-love was the "main current of race-preservation," the basis of all human affection and social progress. In her utopian novel *Herland,* she described a civilization of women in which social planning was centered around the needs of children and mother love was "raised to its highest power" in order to create a society of peace, order, and cooperation. Though not every woman in the utopian country of Herland bore children, all were "Conscious Makers of People," mothers in the metaphoric sense. In Gilman's view, it was precisely because society valued children so highly that they did not live with their mothers, but in baby-gardens that were especially constructed to be safe places for children to play. Mothers lived near the nursery and breastfed their babies, but they left their education to trained professionals.[18]

Mother-love in Herland was "National, Racial, Human." Childbearing was considered too important to leave to chance or individual whim, and thus was eugenically regulated to breed out defective traits and to create a perfect race. As a result, Gilman explained, children in Herland were "the most perfectly cultivated, richly developed roses," not the "tumbleweeds" of American society. Most women in Herland had only one child, and those considered unfit were not allowed even that, but no one in Gilman's utopia contested such social control. "Mother-love has more than one channel of expression," one inhabitant explained; "I think the reason our children are so — so fully loved, by all of us, is that we never — any of us — have enough of our own." Like most people of her time, Gilman framed issues of reproduction and child care in terms of national welfare and race progress, not individual choice. "We [Americans] are commonly willing to 'lay down our lives' for our country," she wrote, "but they [women in Herland] had to forego motherhood for their country — and it was precisely the hardest thing for them to do."[19] Although Gilman challenged the male-breadwinner/ female-homemaker family structure, she did not believe, as most feminists do today, that individual women had an unequivocal right to control their reproduction.

Feminist ideas about motherhood must be distinguished from those of traditionalists, however. In contrast to conservative and even maternalist ideas about home and motherhood, which assumed that mothers should stay at home and approved women's economic dependence on men, the feminist ideology of motherhood bound women together not as helpmates or dependents of men, but as their makers. Both Key and Gilman saw mothers as powerful creators of life who commanded respect and authority. Motherhood did not signify subordination to men; indeed, there were no men at all in Gilman's utopia! Instead, it signified creativity, power, and autonomy. If "motherliness" were woman's nature, it did not depend on having biological children, and thus implied no relation to or dependence on men.

By associating motherhood with all women, whether or not they bore and raised children, Progressive-era feminists — like maternalists — posited a gender consciousness that could potentially reach across class and national boundaries. Unlike the concept of sisterhood, which was based on equality, the ideology of motherhood united women of different generations, enabling older, experienced women to act as mentors and teachers of the young and allowing the growth and maturation of every individual in the culture. At the same time, the feminist ideology of motherhood was rooted in the cultural presumptions of the Anglo-American middle class. It took for granted that some mothers (e.g., those who followed modern scientific childrearing advice) knew best how to educate and discipline children. And while maternalism aimed to uplift mothers deemed inadequate and assimilate them and their children into "American" culture, individualist feminist theory tended to render the poor and "unfit" invisible — even, in Gilman's eugenic utopia, unborn.[20]

Economic Independence for Mothers: Cooperative Housekeeping or the Endowment of Motherhood?

Convinced that women's economic independence was a precondition of their liberation, Progressive-era feminists put forth two main strategies to win economic freedom for mothers. The first, and the one most prominent in the United States, was Gilman's idea of socializing housework to free women to work in the public sphere. The second, which had a greater influence on the women's and labor movements in Europe than in America, was in line with Key's proposal of motherhood endowment, or state wages for motherhood. Both strategies (they were not mutually exclusive) challenged the idea that women and children should be dependent on men's wages for financial support. Both also assumed that child welfare was the responsibility of the entire society, not just individual mothers, although neither questioned women's primary responsibility for childrearing. Not surprisingly, given their challenge to the ideal of dependent womanhood and the system of the family wage, both feminist strategies for liberating mothers operated more on the level of discourse than policy.

Most American feminists, following Gilman, equated wagework with financial independence and made seeking equality in the public sphere their priority. In this, they are to be distinguished from club mothers, who emphasized woman's place in the home, and from progressive women reformers, who acknowledged women's need for meaningful work, but saw paid employment as an alternative to marriage and expressed little concern about women's economic independence. In contrast to maternalists, who saw married women less as individuals than as family members, feminists regarded women as individuals first. Speaking of women's wants as well as their needs, they insisted on the right to combine wagework with marriage. The "modern woman" was dissatisfied with a "purely domestic career," feminist lawyer and activist Crystal Eastman declared. "She wants money of her own. She wants work of her own. She wants some means of self-expression, perhaps, some way of satisfying her personal ambitions. But she wants a husband, home and children, too. How to reconcile these two desires in real life, that is the question."[21]

Many feminists considered housework to be one of the biggest obstacles to married women's self-fulfillment and equality in the public sphere. Although ready-to-wear clothing, canned food, and other purchasable commodities had reduced the physical labor of housewives who could afford them, they felt that the hours still spent each day on housework afforded women little time for themselves and not enough opportunity to spend time with their children. "Motherhood can never be the incidental thing that fatherhood is," editorialized the radical magazine *The Freeman*. "But on the other hand it is hardly necessary that motherhood and a business or professional career shall be mutually exclusive. If society wants such of its women as are editors and bank presidents to be mothers as well, it must cease to demand that they also be housewives."[22]

Growing numbers of middle-class women in the early twentieth century wanted a (volunteer, if not paid) life outside the home, and they did not want their lives to be consumed by housework. Many, perhaps most, continued to rely on domestic help, but as manufacturing jobs increased, the number of servants willing to live in declined. Another solution to the housework problem had to be found, and in the 1910s and early 1920s many people sought it in cooperative or socialized housekeeping.[23] The idea of cooperative housekeeping was not new in the 1910s, for working-class (and some middle-class) housewives had long engaged in informal and formal cooperatives and shared responsibility for domestic chores with neighbors and female kin. However, the idea of socializing housework with the intention of liberating mothers from housework, rather than simply easing their workload, was an innovative and controversial idea.[24]

The foremost example of socialized housework in the Progressive era is the unsuccessful attempt by Henrietta Rodman to build a twelve-story feminist apartment house in New York City. Rodman, a mother and high school English teacher who was well known for her successful campaign to win maternity leave for New York City teachers, was a dynamic leader well suited to the project. Like Gilman, Rodman's principal concern was women's economic independence and equality in the public sphere; her Feminist Alliance developed an early version of the equal rights amendment in 1914. Also like Gilman, Rodman believed that the home had to be restructured before professional women could successfully combine wage-work and family. (She thought poor women already had the "most fundamental right . . . to continue their career after marriage.")[25]

Rodman's feminist apartment house was based on Gilman's idea that the private home was an evolutionary anachronism. She argued that it was in the interest of progress to mechanize and socialize the four "primitive" industries remaining in the home: food preparation, household cleaning, clothing, and child care. The plan provided for trained professionals working in the building's basement to cook, sew, wash dishes, and do the laundry for each family, who would dine on professionally prepared meals served either at home or in a common dining hall. Trained professionals would also care for the children, who beginning at age two would attend a rooftop Montessori school, where they could dance, play sports, and run around freely. Round corners and built-in bathtubs would reduce the work of the "specialist corps" who cleaned individual apartments.[26]

Rodman responded to conservative objections that the feminist apartment house was antimotherhood in a lengthy interview in the *New York Times*. Affirming her belief in women's natural maternal role, she warranted that most women needed children as well as a career in order to find fulfillment. "The baby is the great problem of the woman who attempts to carry the responsibilities of wage earning and citizenship," she explained. "We must have babies for our own happiness, and we must give them the best of ourselves — not only for their own good, not only for the welfare of society, but for our own self-expression." Although few professional women could individually afford to employ an acceptable nurse, Rodman observed, many more could do so if they did it cooperatively. Furthermore, the mother "emancipated" from domestic servitude would develop an "intimate spiritual relation" to her child. "The mother of the past has been so busy with her children that she hasn't had time to enjoy them," Rodman declared in an early version of the modern concept of quality time. "The point is not how long but how intensely a mother does it."[27]

Like Gilman, Rodman believed that women and men were both different and the same. She emphasized the need for women to develop their human characteristics, but supposed that there were immutable differences between the sexes because of women's capacity for motherhood. Thus, although she advised a gender-neutral education in a coeducational Montessori school to develop human qualities in girls, Rodman had little to say about the education of boys. She told the *New York Times* that men were probably not "naturally fitted" for infant care. "On the whole, I believe that mothercraft would remain largely the study and work of women," she said.[28]

Although Rodman claimed that women would be happier and the entire society more productive if wives could contribute to the family's support, she did not consider how the mostly female workers the apartment house planned to employ would combine their own "careers" with housekeeping and motherhood. As one historian pointed out, she "had no analysis of the conflicts of either gender or economic class involved in reorganizing domestic work."[29] Like most American feminists of her time, she wanted to hire other women to do the housework, but she never imagined splitting household responsibilities with men or sharing the chores with women of her class.

After plans for the feminist apartment house collapsed, largely as a result of disagreements among supporters and wartime difficulties in obtaining funding, public discussion of strategies to liberate mothers subsided for a time. It returned a few years later, when socialist feminists pondered the direction feminism should take after suffrage had been won. Crystal Eastman rejected "cooperative schemes" as the solution to women's economic dependence because they could not entirely eliminate housework. "As far as we can see ahead people will always want homes," she wrote, "and a happy home cannot be had without a certain amount of rather monotonous work and responsibility." Moreover, Eastman observed, even though growing numbers of married women worked outside the home, housekeeping had changed little. "But these bread-winning wives have not yet developed home-making husbands," she lamented. From factory workers to businesswomen, the responsibility for housework rested on women, who coordinated and supervised the household help even if they did not do all the actual tasks themselves. In Eastman's view, the goal of feminism should be to "change the nature of man so that he will honorably share that work and responsibility." And that, she believed, required a political approach.[30]

Eastman's feminist program combined personal strategies, such as cooperative housekeeping and raising "feminist sons," with sweeping changes in public policy. She endorsed "voluntary motherhood," or legal birth control, the rewriting of marriage, divorce, and illegitimacy laws, the elimination of all barriers to equality in the public sphere, and the endowment of motherhood—so that childrearing would be "recognized by the world as work, requiring a definite economic reward and not merely entitling the performer to be dependent on some man." In her view, only an "adequate economic reward" from the government for mothers' work of childrearing would free women in a capitalist society. "It is idle to talk of real economic independence for women unless this principle is established."[31]

Significantly, Eastman advocated both motherhood endowment and the Equal Rights Amendment. In contrast to Gilman, she saw mothering as work that benefited society, and she recognized that many women found it more fulfilling than wage earning. Unlike Key, she understood that motherhood was not women's only (or even major) means of self-expression. Instead, Eastman saw motherhood endowment as an option, not incompatible with equal rights in employment, that would improve the financial situation of working-class families and make it easier for mothers *who wanted to* to stay at home with their children. For Eastman, there was no contradiction between defending motherhood and asserting equality. Indeed, she declared, once women achieved their feminist goals—which included motherhood endowment as well as legal equality—"there is no reason why woman should not become almost a human thing."[32]

Yet Eastman's views were unconventional, and serious discussion of a salary paid directly to mothers from the government made little headway in the United States. However, motherhood endowment was a major issue in the German women's movement and a topic of heated debate in England between 1917 and 1925. The product of British Labor and socialist politics, motherhood endowment was endorsed by prominent socialists H. G. Wells and Beatrice and Sidney Webb, by the working-class Women's Cooperative Guild, and by the middle-class socialist Fabian Women's Group. Eleanor Rathbone, an elite Liverpool social worker, feminist, and future member of Parliament, was the prime mover behind the reform. A champion of what was called the "new feminism," Rathbone insisted that real equality for women had to take their special experiences and needs into account. "New feminists" made the state-funded economic independence of mothers a principal goal; they combined equal-rights goals (such as equal pay for equal work) with difference-based ones (such as motherhood endowment and protective labor laws). In this way, "new feminism" can be seen as an attempt to unite the feminist and maternalist perspectives. It combined the feminist challenge to the family wage system with the maternalist regard for mothers' work. Still, Rathbone's "new feminism" did not question the traditional assumptions that women were responsible for childrearing or that children should be raised in the nuclear family home.[33]

Given the strong European interest in the issue, it is not surprising that the chief advocates of motherhood endowment in the United States were (with the exception of economist Paul Douglas) socialist feminists who had close ties to the European women's movement. Eastman and Harriot Stanton Blatch, Elizabeth Cady Stanton's daughter and a leader of the National Woman's Party, lived for a time in England. Katharine Anthony, author of the American introduction to the 1918 report of Rathbone's Family Endowment Committee, had published a book on feminism in Germany and Scandinavia.[34]

Public discussion of the state endowment of motherhood in England and the United States received a boost during World War I, when the wives of English and Canadian servicemen received small pensions directly from the government as compensation for their husbands' lost wages. British "separation allowances" for the wives and children of servicemen were universal and paid entirely from state funds; the Canadian system, by contrast, combined compulsory allotments paid out of servicemen's wages with money from the government. Although the allowances in both countries were inadequate to meet families' entire subsistence needs, observers in Britain remarked that women and children were healthier, better fed, and better clothed during the war than they had been in peacetime. Moreover, separation allowances appeared to give many wives a degree of economic independence and a "sense of security, of ease, of dignity... for the first time in their lives."[35] Although the United States made no provision for soldiers' families, Children's Bureau chief Julia Lathrop tried unsuccessfully to pass a bill modeled on the Canadian plan, which would have provided allotments or allowances to the families of American servicemen during World War I. However, she and other American maternalists considered state allowances to mothers inappropriate for peacetime.[36]

In the 1920s, British feminists divided just as bitterly over the questions of equal rights versus motherhood endowment and protective legislation as Americans did over protective labor legislation alone. Rathbone and the "new" feminists were bitterly challenged by "equal-rights" feminists, such as Millicent Garrett Fawcett, who worried that laws giving special recognition to women as mothers would undercut their claims to equality with men. In contrast to new feminists, who assumed that improving women's position in the family would lead to equality in the public sphere, equal-rights feminists thought just the opposite: that eliminating public discriminations would empower women at home. Neither seemed to recognize that the conditions of women's work in the home and the exploitation of wageworkers outside it were inseparable and needed to be attacked simultaneously.

In contrast to the way in which British feminists divided on the question, the most outspoken American proponents of motherhood endowment were members of the equal-rights oriented National Woman's Party and vigorous opponents of protective labor laws. Crystal Eastman and Harriot Stanton

Blatch both supported the Equal Rights Amendment but placed motherhood endowment high on their feminist agenda, at least rhetorically. Blatch, when asked "What Next?" after suffrage, wrote: "The most important item in the woman's program [is] the endowment of motherhood. Every woman, whether the wife of a millionaire or a day laborer, will in the world built by women, be made to feel that society honors motherhood sufficiently to raise it above sordid dependence."[37] Yet despite the endorsement of some members and a sprinkling of articles on the subject in its journal *Equal Rights,* the National Woman's Party rejected Crystal Eastman's proposals for motherhood endowment and birth control at its 1921 convention and focused instead on removing legal discriminations against women. Without a strong Socialist or Labor Party tradition behind it, motherhood endowment never took hold in the United States.[38]

Although feminist efforts to politicize motherhood continued through the early 1920s, by the end of the decade public discussion of the economic independence and emancipation of mothers had all but disappeared, even among feminists.[39] In part this is because attention was focused on another question: the issue of (white) married women's employment. Despite their relatively small numbers — fewer than one-tenth of all wives worked outside the home in 1920 — wage-earning wives were the subject of a spirited public debate. The proportion of married women in the labor force doubled between 1900 and 1930, rising six times as fast as that of unmarried women workers.[40] While traditionalists saw this as a threat to the home, and maternalists considered it an indication of economic desperation, feminists welcomed wives' wagework as a step toward their emancipation. The feminist defense of married women's right to work outside the home regardless of motherhood or their husbands' financial status directly challenged the family wage ideal. However, the majority of feminists in the 1920s presupposed a conventional family life in most other respects. Most accepted the ideology of the companionate family and argued that both marriage and fulfilling wagework were necessary for women's happiness; neither alone was enough. While this viewpoint was an advance in some ways, it subsumed motherhood and personal fulfillment in heterosexual relations in a way that progressive maternalism and the older feminism of Charlotte Perkins Gilman did not.[41]

Even the most imaginative efforts to move beyond an individualist approach to the career-marriage issue in the 1920s did not confront the male-headed family structure. The work of Ethel Puffer Howes, the principal supporter of socialized housework in that decade, is illustrative. Howes, a mother of two and a psychologist who taught at Harvard and Wellesley, agreed with Gilman and Rodman that women should not have to choose between wagework and motherhood. However, she was more concerned with helping women balance career and family than with enabling them to compete as equals in the public sphere. In a series of articles that appeared in the *Woman's Home Companion* in 1923, Howes advocated a combination of part-time careers and professionally-run services for cooking, cleaning, and child care. She used the language of maternal responsibility to free women from domestic chores, arguing that cooperative housekeeping would enable mothers to "keep fresh the family wellspring of love" and enjoy precious time with their children. Yet in contrast to maternalists, who thought of married women primarily in terms of their family responsibilities, Howes stressed the need to "integrate the woman's normal family life with a genuine continuous intellectual interest" outside the home. Combining maternal rhetoric with a recognition of women's individuality and citizenship, she argued that women could not "wash and iron and scrub and cook and garden and can and sweep, and still be the mothers and wives *and citizens* we ought to be." "It is the duty of the women of this country to free themselves from irrational drudgery for the sake of their higher duties as wives and mothers, *and as individuals*" (my emphasis in both places).[42]

Between 1925 and 1931 Howes put her ideas into practice at the Smith College Institute for the Coordination of Women's Interests. Funded by the Laura Spelman Rockefeller Memorial Foundation, the Institute issued studies of cooperative laundries and food services, helped college graduates find part-time careers, and established a dinner kitchen and a cooperative nursery school for employed mothers. Although a laudable effort to move beyond private solutions to the career-family dilemma, Howes's Institute provided services only to the most economically and educationally privileged women. Nor did it pose a real challenge to the family wage system or the private home. Howes's acknowledgment that part-time careers would keep women on what we now call a "mommy track" at the margins of their professions reveals her assumption that husbands were the primary breadwinners and women the primary caregivers. Howes was concerned less with married women's right to economic independence than with their need for fulfillment in both professional and family life.[43]

Despite its limitations, Howes's effort to make the career-family dilemma a matter of public concern ran counter to the times, and the Institute folded in 1931 because of lack of support. Many Smith students and faculty apparently considered the Institute's emphasis on domestic problems unacademic and feared that it would undermine society's acceptance of women with careers. More and more, the difficulties of combining career and family were presented as personal problems to be solved individually, not collectively, with the help of sympathetic husbands, domestic help, consumer goods, and the new scientific information on family psychology.[44]

The principle of wages for motherhood also took a private turn in the mid 1920s. As we have seen, most American feminists at that time saw paid employment outside the home as the answer to the problem of married women's economic dependence. Even those who addressed the dependence of full-time homemakers generally did so in a private way: husbands—and not the state—should pay their wives an allowance. For example, NWP leader Doris Stevens argued in *The Nation* that homemaking should be recognized as a "joint, cooperative enterprise" with a "flexible contract of mutual support" in which husbands would agree to support their wives. What women should do if their husbands could or would not pay them— much less what mothers should do if they had no husbands—Stevens did not say.[45]

The discussion of wages for wives, rather than mothers, in American popular magazines reflects the depoliticization of motherhood in the 1920s. Psychology and consumerism rather than cooperative housekeeping and motherhood endowment, and personality adjustment rather than social reform, were presented as solutions to the problems of the modern family. According to one proponent of working wives, combining marriage and work outside the home was an "individual dilemma which each woman must, perforce work out in the way that best fits her individual situation." Women who had domestic help, who used labor-saving appliances, or who followed Lillian Gilbreth and applied principles of time engineering to household chores, could combine housework with a career; cooperative housekeeping was unnecessary.[46]

By the mid 1920s, the idea that college-educated women could combine career and marriage (if not motherhood) had become acceptable in some liberal middle-class circles. Even the staid *New York Times* commented that forcing educated women to choose between marriage and career resulted in a "certain impoverishment of life" for women and "serious losses to society."[47] Advocates of career mothers could point to new psychological theories which emphasized the dangers of mother-love, and to the fact that two-income families could provide more material advantages for children. Yet the ideology of the companionate marriage and the growing acceptance of employed wives in the 1920s put women in a new double bind. Even though most people still thought that mothers should stay home while their children were young, full-time homemakers were often dismissed as unproductive and even dangerous to their children because they did not have enough to do and did not contribute to the family's support. Thus, the growing acceptance of wage-earning wives—accompanied as it was by the depoliticization of motherhood—heightened the divisions between career women and stay-at-home mothers, leading some women in each group to attribute their difficulties not to discrimination or the privatized family, but to each other. Household efficiency expert Lillian Gilbreth reflected this unfortunate development when she declared that the "greatest obstacle faced by women who wanted to combine career and family" was not household or family responsibilities, nor job discrimination, nor men, but the "college-trained women . . . who boasts that she gives all of her time to her family."[48]

Motherhood Depoliticized: The Equal Rights Amendment Debate

Feminism was both a victim and cause of motherhood's depoliticization, for the emphasis the National Woman's Party placed on achieving equality in the public sphere reinforced as well as reflected the idea that child care was a secondary, private concern. The decision of NWP leaders to focus exclusively on the Equal Rights Amendment was a direct challenge to progressive maternalism; the debate may have been especially bitter because members of the two groups had long worked together in social settlement work and for peace, woman suffrage, and welfare reform. By contrast, sentimental maternalists had not often formed alliances with feminists (no doubt because of their differences over woman suffrage), and they did not take a strong stand against the ERA. This may be because the ERA debate came at a time of internal dissension within the PTA or because of the organization's lesser commitment to protective labor legislation.[49]

The decision to focus on the Equal Rights Amendment was made largely by National Woman's Party leader Alice Paul. Paul, a Swarthmore graduate with a Ph.D. in sociology from the University of Pennsylvania, was inspired by the militance of British suffragettes while a student in England and had worked briefly in the suffrage movement there. She was frustrated by the slow, state-by-state strategy of the National American Woman Suffrage Association, and formed the militant Congressional Committee within NAWSA. Paul's aggressive political style clashed with NAWSA's more moderate approach, and she soon broke with the older organization, forming the rival Congressional Union in 1913. The CU, which became the National Woman's Party in 1917, disagreed with NAWSA over its emphasis on a suffrage amendment to the constitution (rather than state referenda), over its flamboyant tactics and picketing of the White House, and over its strategy of punishing the "party in power," even during World War I. The unconventional style and single-minded devotion of NWP members breathed new life into the suffrage movement even as they alienated NAWSA leaders.[50]

The ratification of the Nineteenth Amendment in August 1920 posed the question of "what next" after suffrage, and NWP members met to decide the issue at their February 1921 convention. At the behest of the NWP's inner circle, delegates rejected proposals that the group focus on disarmament, work for the voting rights of black women, or adopt Crystal Eastman's proposal for a six-point feminist program that included birth control and motherhood endowment. Instead, they voted in favor of the majority resolution of the National Executive Committee. They disbanded the old NWP and immediately reconvened under the same name, making the removal of women's legal disabilities their sole purpose. The decision to focus exclusively on equal rights, and the way it was made, alienated a number of delegates, some of whom left the organization. Crystal Eastman, for example, objected that the leadership had allowed too little time for discussion and had railroaded the majority resolution through the convention. Yet despite her disappointment at its failure to take up her program, Eastman remained with the NWP. Florence Kelley, a member of the NWP's National Executive Committee but a devoted champion of protective labor laws and other welfare legislation, was one who broke with the Party.[51]

The differences between feminism and maternalism exploded in the conflict over the Equal Rights Amendment. Before 1920, most maternalists and feminists, including Paul, supported sex-based labor laws—although some sentimental maternalists, such as Schoff, opposed too-stringent government regulations, and some feminists, such as Blatch, opposed any legal "protection" for adult women.[52] NWP leaders tried at first to reconcile the idea of an equal rights amendment with welfare and protective labor legislation. In 1921, they passed a bill in Wisconsin that granted equal rights to men and women unless doing so would "deny to females the special protection and privileges they now enjoy for the general welfare." However, neither opponents nor supporters of the ERA were satisfied by the clause, and Paul soon concluded that all sex-based legislation was an obstacle for women seeking equality in employment. In December 1923, the Equal Rights Amendment was introduced into Congress.[53]

Fearful of the ERA's effect on the welfare and protective labor laws that had long been their political priority, progressive maternalists such as Kelley vigorously opposed the blanket amendment even before it was finalized. They objected that the ERA would overturn hard-won minimum-wage and maximum-hours laws for women workers, mothers' pension legislation, and the Sheppard-Towner Act, which Kelley described as "an inequality by reason of sex, in favor of women—maternity not applying alike to both sexes." Kelley insisted that women needed special protection from the government, since the excessive work of mothers was a major cause of infant and maternal death and women's working conditions were so often worse than men's. Unlike feminist ERA supporters, who considered all employment for women a step toward economic independence, Kelley saw wage earning primarily as an additional burden on overworked mothers.[54]

Most progressive maternalists hoped that government protection would eventually be extended to men. Nevertheless, they promoted laws directed to women—both because the Supreme Court ruled protection for male workers unconstitutional, and because they believed that women, as potential mothers, were more physically vulnerable than men. The association between motherhood and biological weakness was legally established in *Muller v. Oregon*, the 1908 Supreme Court case that upheld an Oregon law limiting to ten hours the work day of women employed in factories, laundries, or mechanical establishments. Oregon's attorney Louis Brandeis presented the Court with the famous Brandeis brief (written largely by the attorney's sister-in-law Josephine Goldmark, of the National Consumers' League), which relied not on legal precedent but on evidence that long hours were dangerous to women's health. Convinced by Brandeis and Goldmark that women were "fundamentally weaker" than men, the Court upheld special labor laws for women, even though it rejected protection for men as interfering with freedom of contract. "Woman's physical structure and the performance of maternal functions place her at a disadvantage," the decision read. "This is especially true when the burdens of motherhood are upon her. . . . As healthy mothers are essential to vigorous offspring, the physical well-being of woman becomes an object of public interest and care in order to preserve the strength and vigor of the race."[55] By 1925, all but four states limited women's working hours, usually to nine or ten hours a day; eighteen regulated rest periods and meal times; sixteen prohibited night work, and thirteen states had a minimum wage for women workers.[56]

Although committed to women's equality in public life, progressive women reformers battled the ERA by emphasizing the permanence of sexual differences and women's responsibility for motherhood. "The great mass of women . . . believe that the most important function of woman in the world is motherhood," editorialized the *Woman Citizen*, "that the welfare of the child should be the first consideration, and that because of their maternal functions women should be protected against undue strain." "Women need a kind of protection which men do not need . . . to safeguard the future physical well-being of the race," declared National League of Women Voters president Maud Wood Park. The differences between men and women were "so far reaching, so fundamental, that it is grotesque to ignore them," Florence Kelley wrote. "Women cannot be made men by act of the legislature or by amendment of the Federal Constitution. . . . The inherent differences are permanent. Women will always need many laws different from those needed by men."[57]

In stressing the vulnerability of motherhood, progressive maternalists did not necessarily mean to imply that childbearing made women weaker than men. "That does not mean that women are inferior or superior to men," insisted Clara Beyer, but "refusal to recognize the biological differences between men and women does not make for equality." Like other reformers, Beyer attributed the high sickness and death rates of wage-earning mothers and their children to their double burden and to excessive fatigue and strain in the childbearing years. "These actualities may not be pleasant to our feminist friends, but they will not be removed by playing ostrich."[58]

For their part, NWP feminists had three principle objections to protective labor laws. The first was that special laws classed women with children as a group in need of protection, rather than treating them as adult citizens in their own right. The second was that the laws did not actually protect mothers, and even increased their hardship. Compulsory maternity leave and restrictions against night work were considered particularly onerous, since unpaid maternity leave deprived families of an important source of income, and night work not only paid better than day jobs but enabled mothers to spend time with their children during the day. Moreover, feminists contended, advocates of sex-based labor laws were not really interested in protecting women from arduous work, since they let women perform the "unpaid labor of the world" with no protest that it was beyond their strength. They might have added (but significantly did not) that protective labor laws did not even apply to agricultural and domestic labor, the largest and most backbreaking employment categories for women, and the ones in which women of color were most likely to be employed.[59]

The third, and, for the purposes of this study, most significant feminist argument against protective legislation, was the objection to the idea that motherhood was a "constant corollary for womanhood." As Mary Murray of the NWP Industrial Council observed, "Motherhood is the most glorious advantage women can enjoy, but all women do not enjoy this privilege. . . . There are women who never marry, women beyond the childbearing age. How cruelly unjust to handicap all women at all times under the guise of protecting motherhood."[60]

The NWP's response to maternalist objections that the Equal Rights Amendment would overturn "mothers' legislation" shows both the Party's determination to separate "motherhood" from "womanhood" and the political difficulty of doing so in the early 1920s. To anti-ERA claims that mothers' pensions and the Sheppard-Towner Act would be invalidated by the amendment, NWP leaders responded that special laws for mothers would not be affected since they, like military pensions, applied not to all women but only to a "special group of women who have performed a service for their country." According to Doris Stevens, maternity legislation was intended to assist "a special group of women under special circumstances. It is not special legislation for *women*; it is for *mothers*. All women are not mothers. All mothers are not in constant need of maternity protection." NWP feminists supported government responsibility for children's welfare, but not for adult women's. Thus they ostensibly approved mothers' pensions because aid was not granted to "mothers as such," but was designed "to benefit poor children" living at home. However, they favored legislation such as a Colorado statute that granted allowances to either parent.[61]

The ERA debate also exposed fundamental differences between feminists and maternalists over political priorities and style. On one side, NWP leaders saw gender oppression as primary and placed the goal to achieve equal rights for women above other political commitments. They pointed to persisting discriminations against women — many states did not allow women to serve on juries, grant them equal guardianship of children, or permit married women to sign contracts without their husbands' consent — and argued that the ERA would erase in one fell swoop the many laws that put women at a disadvantage. Other issues, such as birth control, peace, and racial justice, were seen as diversions. (For example, they considered the disfranchisement of southern black women after the Nineteenth Amendment to be a racial issue not properly taken up by a feminist organization.) On the other side, maternalists placed a greater priority on specific humanitarian reforms than on feminism and on what they considered the abstract principle of equal rights. They argued that discriminatory laws should be dealt with on a case-by-case basis.

Feminists also challenged the ideas about women's responsibility for social service and child welfare that maternalists held dear, insisting that women needed to be free themselves before they could truly provide for their children. Crystal Eastman explained this position in the NWP journal *The Suffragist*: "If we cling to these women's reform organizations we but perpetuate the old separation, 'charity and church work for women, politics for men,'. . . Certainly a Woman's International which includes peace, education and child welfare among its objectives cannot be said to be consciously feminist in outlook. . . . [A] genuine feminist . . . knows that woman's battle for her own freedom must be kept clear of entangling alliances."[62] Another feminist put it even more forcefully: "I was made perfectly sick by hearing all of this stuff from the woman's clubs about devoting ourselves to service, and all the rest of it," she declared after hearing representatives from other women's groups speak before the 1921 NWP convention. "Before you can serve you must have power — must have power before we can think about service."[63]

The battle over the ERA permanently altered the feminist understanding of motherhood. In a positive vein, it challenged the common assumption that women's and children's interests were always the same, and it exposed the maternalist self-deception that women were united on the grounds of motherhood. More negatively, it contributed to the narrowing of feminist thinking about childrearing and about maternal and child welfare. With few exceptions, neither advocates nor opponents of the ERA in the 1920s actively supported cooperative housekeeping, motherhood endowment, or even unionization as an alternative way to ease the dilemma of working-class and wage-earning mothers. Although their emphasis on women's right to wagework provided a necessary challenge to the concepts of the male provider and family wage, most feminists assumed, erroneously, that elim-inating legal discrimination in the public sphere would change the balance of power at home. Their almost exclusive focus on equal rights in the 1920s left unexplored the implications of women's responsibility for child care on their status in society and on their relationship to men and children in the family.

The debate over the Equal Rights Amendment was not, of course, the only reason for the narrowing of feminist thinking about motherhood in the 1920s; the conservative political climate and consumer economy set the context for the feminist response. Still, by framing strategies in terms of *either* equality *or* difference, the ERA debate obscured the complex realities of women's working lives in and outside the home, and of the power relations within the family. While maternalists embraced dominant cultural assumptions about women's self-sacrifice, responsibility for child care, and dependence on men, feminists tried to escape being defined by motherhood by seeking equality in the public sphere and leaving behind the world at home. Rather than try to change society to accommodate mothers, as some of their foremothers had done (and as Eastman and a handful of others still wanted to do), they equated wage earning with freedom and concentrated on removing the legal obstacles to work outside the home.

By the end of the 1920s, issues of childrearing and of maternal and child welfare were near the bottom of the NWP's feminist agenda. The absence of discussion about motherhood endowment, cooperative housekeeping, and collectivized child care informed the directions of both feminism and welfare policy in the 1920s and beyond. The narrow feminist focus on equal rights led some women who had other political priorities (such as peace, racial justice, or child welfare reform) to reject the label of feminism, and it led those who thought the elimination of gender inequality more urgent than other issues to distrust laws or social services directed specifically toward mothers. As a result, there was little feminist interest in maternal and child welfare policy. Motherhood was depoliticized and the care of children con-sidered a private concern.

In the 1910s, however, these developments were as yet unknown, and some feminists worked with maternalists in a campaign to get the govern-ment to assume responsibility for the health and well-being of mothers and children. The next two chapters examine the biggest successes of the ma-ternal and child welfare movement: mothers' pensions and the Sheppard-

Towner Maternity and Infancy Act. They explore the reform efforts — and interactions — of sentimental maternalists, progressive maternalists, feminists, and grassroots mothers; and they assess the impact of health and welfare policy on mothers' work. The histories of these two campaigns illuminate both the possibilities and the limitations of maternalist welfare reform.

NOTES

1. The phrase is from Carl Degler, *At Odds: Women and the Family from the Revolution to the Present* (New York: Oxford University Press, 1980).

2. Nancy F. Cott, *The Grounding of Modern Feminism* (New Haven: Yale University Press, 1987), 50, also 35–39, 75–77.

3. Exceptions include Alice Beal Parsons, *Woman's Dilemma* (New York: Thomas Y. Crowell Co., 1926); Suzanne La Follette, *Concerning Women* (New York: Arno Press, 1972, orig. 1926); Blanche Wiesen Cook, ed., *Crystal Eastman on Women and Revolution* (New York: Oxford University Press, 1978); editorial, "Who Supports the Family?" *Equal Rights* 13 (Feb. 13, 1926): 4; editorial, "Too Expensive," *Equal Rights* 13 (Mar. 13, 1926): 36; Mrs. Emilie Berliner, "The Work of Homemakers," *Equal Rights* (Nov. 1, 1930): 310. For a more optimistic interpretation of this history, see Wendy Sarvasy, "Beyond the Difference Versus Equality Policy Debate: Post-Suffrage Feminism, Citizenship, and the Quest for a Feminist Welfare State," *Signs* 17 (Winter 1992): 329–62.

4. Jane Addams, "Why Women Should Vote," *Ladies' Home Journal* (1910), reprinted in *The Social Thought of Jane Addams,* ed. Christopher Lasch (New York: Bobbs-Merrill, 1965), 144–51.

5. Cook, ed. *Crystal Eastman,* 1–36, 76–83.

6. Katharine Anthony, *Feminism in Germany and Scandinavia* (New York: Henry Holt & Co., 1915), 6, 251; *New York Times,* Jan. 24, 1915, V: 9.

7. Charlotte Perkins Gilman, *Women and Economics* (New York: Harper & Row, 1966, orig. 1898); idem, *The Home: Its Work and Influence* (Urbana: University of Illinois Press, 1972, orig. 1903); idem, *The Living of Charlotte Perkins Gilman, An Autobiography* (New York: D. Appleton, 1935).

8. Gilman, *The Home,* 87, 60, 55.

9. See especially Ellen Key, *The Woman Movement* (New York: G. P. Putnam's Sons, 1912); "Ellen Key's Reply to her Critics," *Current Literature* 52 (March 1912): 317–19; Charlotte Perkins Gilman, "On Ellen Key and the Woman Movement," *The Forerunner* 4 (February 1913): 35–38; idem, "Education for Motherhood," *The Forerunner* 4 (October 1913): 259–62.

10. Among Key's most important books and articles appearing in the United States were Ellen Key, *The Century of the Child* (New York: Arno Press, 1972, orig. 1909); idem, *Love and Marriage* (New York: G. P. Putnam's Sons, 1911); idem, "Motherliness," *Atlantic Monthly* 110 (Oct. 1912): 562–70; idem, "Education for Motherhood," *Atlantic Monthly* 112 (July 1913), 48–56, (Aug. 1913): 191–97. See Cott, *Grounding,* esp. 41–49, on the Gilman-Key debate, and Mari Jo Buhle, *Women and American Socialism, 1870–1920* (Urbana: University of Illinois Press,

1983), 292–94, on Key's influence on American socialists. On Key and the Mutterschutz movement, see Kay Goodman, "Motherhood and Work: The Concept of the Misuse of Women's Energy, 1895–1905," in *German Women in the Eighteenth and Nineteenth Centuries: A Social and Literary History,* ed. Ruth-Ellen B. Joeres and Mary Jo Maynes (Bloomington: Indiana University Press, 1986), 110–27; Ann Taylor Allen, "Mothers of the New Generation: Adele Schreiber, Helene Stöcker, and the Evolution of a German Idea of Motherhood," *Signs* 10 (Spring 1985): 418–38; idem, *Feminism and Motherhood in Germany, 1800–1914* (New Brunswick, N.J.: Rutgers University Press, 1991); and Richard Evans, *The Feminist Movement in Germany, 1894–1933* (Beverly Hills: Sage, 1976), 120–39.

11. Daniel J. Kevles, *In the Name of Eugenics: Genetics and the Uses of Human Heredity* (New York: Knopf, 1985).

12. Key, *Woman Movement,* 58–59; idem, "Motherliness," 564; "Ellen Key's Attack on 'Amaternal' Feminism," *Current Opinion* 54 (Feb. 1913): 138. See also Ellen Key, *The Renaissance of Motherhood* (G. P. Putnam's Sons, 1916); and Cheri Register, "Motherhood at Center: Ellen Key's Social Vision," *Women's Studies International Forum* 5 (1982): 599–610.

13. Ellen Key, *Love and Marriage* (New York: G. P. Putnam's Sons, 1911), 101, 380.

14. Key, *Love and Marriage,* 211; idem, *Woman Movement,* 222–23; idem, *Renaissance of Motherhood,* 109.

15. Gilman, "On Ellen Key," 37; idem, *The Home,* 328.

16. Gilman, "Education for Motherhood," 260. See also idem, "Teaching the Mothers," *The Forerunner* 3 (Mar. 1912): 73–75; and idem, *Concerning Children* (Boston: Small, Maynard & Co., 1901).

17. See Gilman, *Living;* Ann J. Lane, *To Herland and Beyond: The Life and Work of Charlotte Perkins Gilman* (New York: Pantheon, 1990); Mary A. Hill, *Charlotte Perkins Gilman: The Making of a Radical Feminist, 1860–1896* (Philadelphia: Temple University Press, 1980).

18. Charlotte Perkins Gilman, "Paid Motherhood," *The Independent* 61 (Jan. 1907): 76; idem, *Concerning Children,* 193; idem, *Herland,* ed. Ann J. Lane (New York: Pantheon, 1978, orig. 1915), 57, 68.

19. Gilman, *Herland,* 69–72.

20. See Susan S. Lanser's provocative rereading of Gilman's "The Yellow Wall Paper," in "Feminist Criticism, 'The Yellow Wallpaper,' and the Politics of Color in America," *Feminist Studies* 15 (Fall 1989): 415–41.

21. Quoted in Elaine Showalter, *These Modern Women, Autobiographical Essays from the Twenties* (Old Westbury, N.Y.: Feminist Press, 1978), 5. By the late 1910s, working-class feminists also asserted women's right to work for personal independence and satisfaction. Maurine Weiner Greenwald, "Working-Class Feminism and the Family Wage Ideal: The Seattle Debate on Married Women's Right to Work, 1914–1920," *Journal of American History* 76 (June 1989): 118–49.

22. "An Economic Phase of Feminism," *The Freeman* 1 (Apr. 7, 1920): 81.

23. Phyllis Palmer points out that servants, more than labor-saving devices, made it possible for middle-class women to engage in paid work and social service

activities outside the home. Phyllis Palmer, *Domesticity and Dirt: Housewives and Domestic Servants in the United States, 1920–1945* (Philadelphia: Temple University Press, 1989).

24. On older and especially working-class cooperative housekeeping ventures, see Dolores Hayden, *The Grand Domestic Revolution: A History of Feminist Designs for American Homes, Neighborhoods, and Cities* (Cambridge, Mass.: MIT Press, 1981), and the series of articles by Ethel Puffer Howes in *Woman's Home Companion* in 1923.

25. George MacAdam, "Feminist Apartment House to Solve Baby Problem," *New York Times*, Jan. 24, 1915, 9:1. On Rodman's career, see June Sochen, *Movers and Shakers: American Women Thinkers and Activists, 1900–1970* (New York: Quadrangle, 1973), 37–41.

26. MacAdam, "Feminist Apartment House."

27. Ibid.

28. Ibid.

29. Hayden, *Grand Domestic Revolution*, 202.

30. Crystal Eastman, "Now We Can Begin," orig. 1920, reprinted in Cook, *Crystal Eastman*, 52–57.

31. Ibid. According to Maurine Greenwald, working-class feminists in Seattle also combined a call for cooperative housekeeping with the economic independence of mothers. See Greenwald, "Working-Class Feminism," 137–38, 143.

32. Eastman, "Now We Can Begin," 57.

33. Susan Pedersen calls Rathbone's politics "maternalist feminism." See "The Failure of Feminism in the Making of the British Welfare State," *Radical History Review* 43 (1989): 86–110. My understanding of the British debate over motherhood endowment is indebted to Pederson and to Jane Lewis, especially "Beyond Suffrage: English Feminism in the 1920s," *Maryland Historian* 6 (Spring 1975): 1–17, and *The Politics of Motherhood: Child and Maternal Welfare in England, 1900–1939*. See also Hilary Land, "The Family Wage," *Feminist Review* 6 (1980): 55–77; and Carol Dyhouse, *Feminism and the Family in England, 1880–1939* (London: Basil Blackwell, 1989).

34. See Paul Douglas, *Wages and the Family* (Chicago: University of Chicago Press, 1926); Katharine Anthony, ed., *The Endowment of Motherhood* (New York: B. W. Huebsch, 1920); Harriot Stanton Blatch, *Challenging Years* (New York: G. P. Putnam's Sons, 1940).

35. Rathbone quoted in Susan Pedersen, "Gender, Welfare, and Citizenship in Britain during the Great War," *American Historical Review* 95 (Oct. 1990): 1003. A different perspective is in Suzie Fleming's introduction to Eleanor Rathbone, *The Disinherited Family* (Bristol, England: Falling Wall Press, 1986, orig. 1924).

36. Julia C. Lathrop, "Provision for the Care of the Families and Dependents of Soldiers and Sailors," *Proceedings of the Academy of Political Science* 7 (Feb. 1918): 796–807; Julia Lathrop to Mary O'Neill, Jan. 27, 1919, File 10–471–21, Children's Bureau Records, Central Files 1914–50, Record Group 102, National Archives, Washington, D.C.

37. Harriot Stanton Blatch, "What Next?" *The Suffragist* 8 (Oct. 1920): 235.

38. Crystal Eastman, "Alice Paul's Convention," in Cook, *Crystal Eastman*, 57–63. See also the Transcript of National Woman's Party Convention, Feb. 18–21, 1921, Box 21, Folder 318, Alice Paul Papers, Arthur and Elizabeth M. Schlesinger Library on the History of Women in America, Radcliffe College, Cambridge. Mass.

39. There were some notable exceptions, especially the remarkable book by Alice Beal Parsons, *Woman's Dilemma* (New York: Crowell, 1926).

40. Cott, *Grounding*, 129; Lynn Y. Weiner, *From Working Girl to Working Mother: the Female Labor Force in the United States, 1820–1860* (Chapel Hill: University of North Carolina Press, 1985), 6, 101.

41. See, for example, Virginia MacMakin Collier, *Marriage and Careers, a Study of One Hundred Women who are Wives, Mothers, Homemakers, and Professional Workers* (New York: Bureau of Vocational Information, 1926). Cott, *Grounding*, 179–211, contains an insightful analysis of the debate over married women's employment. Greenwald, "Working-Class Feminism," examines the debate in working-class Seattle.

42. Ethel Puffer Howes and Myra Reed Richardson, "Getting Together," *Woman's Home Companion* 50 (June 1923): 30; Ethel Puffer Howes, "The Progress of the Institute for the Coordination of Women's Interests," Oct. 12, 1928, Folder 26, Institute for the Coordination of Women's Interests Records, Sophia Smith Collection, Smith College; Ethel Puffer Howes, "True and Substantial Happiness," *Woman's Home Companion* 50 (Sept. 1923): 75. Also see C. Todd Stephenson, "'Integrating the Carol Kennicotts': Ethel Puffer Howes and the Institute for the Coordination of Women's Interests," *Journal of Women's History* 4 (Spring 1992): 89–113.

43. For a contemporary critique of the Smith Institute, see Parsons, *Woman's Dilemma*, 211–12. Also see Cott, *Grounding*, 202–4, and Hayden, *Grand Domestic Revolution*, 271–77.

44. Hayden, *Grand Domestic Revolution*, 276–77.

45. Doris Stevens, "The Home as a Joint-Stock Company," *The Nation* 122 (Jan. 27, 1926): 81. See also William Johnston, "Should Wives Be Paid Wages," *Good Housekeeping* 80 (Mar. 1925): 30–31; Hugh Black, "Money and Marriage," *Delineator* 98 (June 1921): 2; Beatrice Barmby, "Wages for Wives," *Delineator* 118 (Mar. 1931).

46. Quoted in Lois Scharf, *To Work and to Wed: Employment, Feminism, and the Great Depression* (Westport, Conn.: Greenwood Press, 1980), 35. See *New York Times*, July 29, 1926, 21:4, and July 30, 1926, 15:5, for Lillian Gilbreth's views on working wives.

47. *New York Times*, Sept. 7, 1926, 20:5, and July 30, 1926, 15:5. The acceptance of married women's employment was short-lived, for the Depression increased hostility to working wives even as the number of married women workers continued to grow. See William H. Chafe, *The American Woman: Her Changing Social, Economic, and Political Roles, 1920–1970* (New York: Oxford University Press, 1972), and Scharf, *To Work and to Wed*.

48. *New York Times*, Aug. 3, 1926, 11:2.

49. It is possible that the relatively conservative leaders of the National Congress of Mothers were reluctant to support protective labor legislation because they did not want to acknowledge women as permanent (if secondary) members of the work force. In addition, some Congress leaders opposed what they considered government regulations and paternalism in the matter of child labor, and it is reasonable to assume that they held a similar position on the government regulation of women workers. According to Florence Watkins, executive secretary of the National PTA and recording secretary of the Women's Joint Congressional Committee (and an ERA opponent), PTA Legislative Chair Elizabeth Tilton was the only woman at a December 1921 WJCC meeting not to take a stand against the "Blanket Amendment." Tilton apparently "did not feel she had sufficient data from which to reach a conclusion." Annual Minutes of the Women's Joint Congressional Committee, Dec. 5, 1921, Reel 3, Women's Joint Congressional Committee Records, Library of Congress. See Hannah Kent Schoff, *The Wayward Child* (Indianapolis: Bobbs-Merrill Co., 1915); also Theda Skocpol, *Protecting Soldiers and Mothers: The Politics of Social Provision in the United States, 1870s-1920s,* (Cambridge: Harvard University, Press, 1992), chap. 6.

50. See Cott, *Grounding,* 53–81; Christine A. Lunardini, *From Equal Suffrage to Equal Rights: Alice Paul and the National Woman's Party, 1910–1928* (New York: New York University Press, 1986).

51. NWP Convention Transcript, Feb. 15–18, 1921, pp. 129–34; Eastman, "Alice Paul's Convention," 58–59; Nancy F. Cott, "Feminist Politics in the 1920s: The National Woman's Party," *Journal of American History* 71 (June 1984): 43–68; idem, *Grounding,* 66–81.

52. Hannah Kent Schoff may have opposed some protective laws for women workers on the same grounds that she opposed stringent child labor laws: that they were paternalistic and interfered with freedom of contract. See editorial in *Child-Welfare Magazine* 8 (May 1914): 250, cited in Skocpol, *Protecting Soldiers and Mothers.*

53. Quoted in J. Stanley Lemons, *The Woman Citizen: Social Feminism in the 1920s* (Urbana: University of Illinois Press, 1973), 187. See Cott, *Grounding,* 117–42.

54. Florence Kelley, "Twenty Questions About the Federal Amendment Proposed by the NWP," National Consumers' League pamphlet, Jan. 1922, Reel 1, Women's Joint Congressional Committee Records, Library of Congress.

55. Quoted in Elizabeth Faulkner Baker, *Protective Labor Legislation With Special Reference to Women in the State of New York, Columbia University Studies in History, Economics and Public Law,* vol. 116, no. 2 (New York: AMS Press, 1969, orig. 1925), 68.

56. Edward Clark Lukens, "Shall Women Throw Away Their Advantages?" *American Bar Association Journal* (Oct. 1925), clipping, Woman's Rights Collection 744, Schlesinger Library. Among the most useful works on the history of protective labor legislation are Susan Lehrer, *Origins of Protective Labor Legislation for Women, 1905–1925* (Albany: SUNY Press, 1987); Judith Baer, *The Chains of Protection* (Westport, Conn.: Greenwood Press, 1978); Alice Kessler-Harris, *Out*

To Work: A History of Wage-Earning Women in the United States (New York: Oxford University Press, 1982), 180–214; Ann Corinne Hill, "Protection of Women Workers and the Courts: A Legal Case History," *Feminist Studies* 5 (Summer 1979): 247–73.

57. Gertrude Foster Brown, "Editorially Speaking," *Woman Citizen* (July 1926): 24; National League of Women Voters, "Specific Bills for Specific Ills" (1924), leaflet, Woman's Rights Collection 744, Schlesinger Library; Florence Kelley, "Shall Women Be Equal Before the Law? No!" *The Nation* 114 (Apr. 12, 1922): 421. A somewhat different interpretation can be found in Sybil Lipschutz, "Social Feminism and Legal Discourse: 1908–1923," *Yale Journal of Law and Feminism* 2 (Fall 1989): esp. 133–42. Focusing on minimum wage laws, Lipschutz argues that in the 1920s "social feminists" (or progressive maternalists, to use my term) stopped using arguments based on biological difference, and justified protective laws on the grounds of economic and social differences.

58. Clara Beyer, "What is Equality?" *The Nation* 116 (Jan. 31, 1923): 116.

59. Jane Norman Smith, "Protective Legislation for Women," *International Woman Suffrage News* (June 1924), clipping, Woman's Rights Collection 744, Schlesinger Library. See Alma Lutz, "Should Woman's Work Be Regulated by Law? *Atlantic Monthly* (Sept. 1930), clipping, Woman's Rights Collection 1088, Schlesinger Library.

60. Quoted in Sheila M. Rothman, *Woman's Proper Place: A History of Changing Ideals and Practices, 1870–1930* (New York: Basic, 1978), 157.

61. "Equal Rights by National Amendment," *Equal Rights* 14 (June 11, 1927): 143; Doris Stevens, "The 'Blanket' Amendment — A Debate. I. Suffrage Does Not Give Equality," *Forum* 72 (Aug. 1924): 145–52. For a slightly different interpretation, see Sarvasy, "Beyond the Difference Versus Equality Policy Debate."

62. Crystal Eastman, "What Next?" *Suffragist* 8 (Nov. 1920): 278.

63. "Transcript of the National Woman's Party Convention," 60.

PART THREE

Mothers and the State

God help the poor mothers of today. . . . Men in long service receive their pension. Mothers deserving receiv[e] nothing.

— Mrs. H. B., reprinted in Ladd-Taylor,
Raising a Baby the Government Way

Lonely ranches in Arizona and Idaho and slum dwellers in the most congested cities are increasingly able to command resources for safety of their young children, undreamed of by women of my mother's generation. . . . My own modest share in this life-saving measure [the Sheppard-Towner Act] is an abiding happy memory.

— Florence Kelley, *The Autobiography of Florence Kelley*

Everything that counts in the common life is political.

— Mary Ritter Beard, "Mothercraft"

5

"Every Mother Has a Right":
The Movement
for Mothers' Pensions

Comparing the European and American feminist movements in 1915, Katharine Anthony delineated two distinct branches of the women's movement. German feminists, influenced by Ellen Key, rallied around "Mutterschutz" (the protection of mothers), while Americans mobilized for "Votes for Women" and the campaign for political rights. In Anthony's view, women's emancipation ultimately depended on both issues. There was "no real conflict" between the mother-protection movement and the campaign for equality, she insisted; both "function together like the right eye and the left eye in a single act of vision." Anthony's optimism about combining the two feminist perspectives may seem far-fetched today, but it was not entirely unwarranted at the time. In the early 1910s, perhaps just as her book was going to press, maternalist appeals for mother-protection and feminist demands for economic independence seemed to come together in a new movement for mothers' pensions.[1]

The mothers' pensions movement was one of the most successful reforms of the early twentieth-century United States. Also known as widows' pensions or mothers' aid, these laws spread like "wildfire" in the 1910s, achieving more rapid legislative success than any other social justice reform of the Progressive era. The first direct provision of mothers' aid was instituted by Juvenile court judge E. E. Porterfield in Kansas City, Missouri, in 1911; the first statewide mothers' pension law was enacted in Illinois the same year. Mothers' pension laws, which empowered local governments to make payments to poor mothers so their children would not have to be placed in institutions, were endorsed by a broad alliance of maternalists, feminists, juvenile court judges, social workers, trade unionists, and politicians. They were vigorously promoted by liberal journals and women's magazines, especially the *Delineator*. Virtually the only opposition to the laws came from

private charity workers who objected to public aid. Within eight years of
the enactment of the first law, thirty-nine states, mostly in the north and
west, provided some form of mothers' aid. In 1935 the Social Security Act
nationalized the program, then called Aid to Dependent Children.[2]

Women in all three groups examined in this study were active supporters
of state-funded mothers' pensions in the 1910s and 1920s, although they
advocated them for different reasons and in different ways. Sentimental
maternalists saw mothers' pensions as a means to preserve maternal dignity,
to help "deserving" poor women fulfill their traditional childrearing responsibilities, and to prevent juvenile delinquency by ensuring that impoverished children had good homes. The National Congress of Mothers made
the campaign for mothers' aid a cornerstone of its maternalist welfare policy.
By contrast, progressive maternalists saw mothers' aid more as a practical
way of ameliorating women's and children's poverty. Although they agreed
with club mothers that children needed a home and mother-love, they
described pensions not in the sentimental parlance of the Mothers' Congress,
but in the language of social work and progressive reform. They placed
mothers' aid alongside other reforms that they hoped would eliminate the
structural causes of women's poverty, such as protecting the male bread-
winner from industrial accidents and raising his wages. The third group in
the study, feminists, were less active in the mothers' pension movement
than maternalists. Nevertheless, some feminists, no doubt inspired by the
European feminist Mutterschutz movement, regularly joined local legislative
campaigns for state aid. Unlike maternalists, who endorsed publicly funded
mothers' allowances only for families who did not have the support of a
male breadwinner, they saw mothers' pensions as a step toward the remuneration — and liberation — of all mothers.

The swift passage of mothers' pension laws owed much to the idealized
images of home and motherhood that pervaded early twentieth-century
American culture. Many middle-class Anglo-Americans, worried about class
conflict and urban poverty — and convinced by G. Stanley Hall's "science"
of child study that children belonged in their own homes — feared that
youth who did not grow up under their mothers' care might turn to a life
of crime or pauperism. They saw mothers' pensions as a way to make sure
that impoverished children received the "proper" care and supervision of a
mother, and thus to prevent social disorder. To these concerns maternalists
added another, more progressive, objective. Pointing to the contrast between
politicians' idealized depiction of motherhood and the economic vulnerability of real mothers and children, who through no fault of their own
might be thrown into poverty upon the desertion or death of a father, they
urged the enactment of mothers' pension laws to honor the mother and
acknowledge her service to the state.[3]

The belief that states should pay poor single mothers to raise their children at home, rather than place them in an institution, represented a significant break from the child protection practices of the past. The ideology of scientific charity that dominated welfare policy in the late nineteenth century opposed all public assistance to the poor in their own homes. Hostile to single-mother households and to childrearing practices that differed from middle-class norms, child-saving and charity organization societies generally removed children from economically unstable households and from families thought to be lacking in discipline and morality. They placed children in private orphanages or public asylums instead. However, by the turn of the century, publicity about the abysmal conditions of children's asylums, along with concern about their high cost and new ideas about child development, led to a growing consensus against institutionalization. Even traditional child-saving agencies, such as the Society for the Prevention of Cruelty to Children, reversed their earlier position and provided home aid to "deserving" widowed mothers. Still, most charity officials were afraid that poor mothers would come to think of public aid as their right, and they remained vigorously opposed to publicly funded allowances (as opposed to private charity) to mothers in their own homes.[4]

The principle of providing aid to mothers and children in their own homes received a national hearing at the 1909 White House Conference on the Care of Dependent Children, the same conference that endorsed the idea of a federal Children's Bureau. Although there was no consensus on the role of the government — most delegates actually opposed public funding for mothers' pensions — the White House conference helped legitimate the view that child welfare was a public responsibility. The widely quoted conference resolution reflected participants' idealized view of "home life" and their misgivings about its cultural variations.

> Home life is the highest and finest product of civilization. It is the great molding force of mind and of character. Children should not be deprived of it except for urgent and compelling reasons. Children of parents of worthy character, suffering from temporary misfortune and children of reasonably efficient and deserving mothers who are without the support of the normal breadwinner, should, as a rule, be kept with their parents, such aid being given as may be necessary to maintain suitable homes for the rearing of the children. This aid should be given by such methods and from such sources as may be determined by the general relief policy of each community, preferably in the form of private charity rather than of public relief. Except in unusual circumstances, the home should not be broken up for reasons of poverty, but only for considerations of inefficiency or immorality.[5]

As the White House Conference resolution makes clear, the debate over mothers' pensions was structured to a great extent by the concerns of the private charities. Conference delegates assumed that "inefficiency" and immorality were compelling reasons for breaking up the home and expressed a preference for private charity over public aid. Nevertheless, the Conference spurred on the drive for state-funded mothers'pensions and served as the basis for resolutions in favor of public aid by organizations such as the National Congress of Mothers.[6]

Inspired by the White House Conference and moved by the sentimental appeals to motherhood, activist women and reformers campaigned vigorously for mothers' aid. Within two years after Illinois passed the first statewide mothers' pension bill, eighteen states enacted similar laws. Yet despite the broad-based campaign for its passage, the actual administration of mothers' aid was invariably left to social workers, and its subsequent history was one of bureaucratization. Of the three groups studied here, only the Children's Bureau women sustained more than a passing interest in mothers' pensions—and they operated not as reformers seeking to dignify motherhood, but as administrators trying to improve child welfare standards. The reframing of the dialogue on mothers' pensions (in the 1920s called aid to dependent children) in terms of a social work discourse on the "standards" of public aid, rather than a feminist or maternalist discussion about mothers' work and dignity, both reflected and furthered the depoliticization of motherwork.

Private charities lost their struggle against state aid for poor mothers, but the doctrine of scientific charity governed the implementation of aid nonetheless. Despite initial claims that the pension was a recognition of maternal service to the nation, most states severely limited those eligible for aid. Every state provided grants to widows, and some gave allowances to deserted wives and to mothers whose husbands were imprisoned or were mentally or physically incapacitated. However, most states had strict residency, nationality, and property requirements. Few states pensioned homeowners, even if they had no income, and some states required recipients to be U.S. citizens. Furthermore, following the doctrine of scientific charity, most states had a "suitable home" provision that held recipients up to certain behavioral standards. Aid was limited to "deserving" women who did not have illegitimate children or take in male boarders, and who were willing to follow "proper" (Anglo-American) methods of housekeeping and childcare.[7]

Mothers' pensions were also marked by taxpayer stinginess and the long-standing American resentment of public dependency. Indeed, a major argument in favor of mothers' aid—and, perhaps, a factor in the negligible opposition of right-wing groups—was its relative economy. Providing aid to mothers in their own homes was less expensive than placing children in institutions, especially since most pension programs were (under)funded from local revenues. As late as 1931, one-third of the administrative units authorized to grant mothers' pensions dispensed no aid at all.[8]

Mothers' pension administration did depart from private charity organization and relief giving in two important ways, however. For one thing, most states distributed aid through local juvenile courts rather than county welfare boards, both because they wanted to distinguish mothers' pensions from relief and because they perceived a connection between "broken homes" and juvenile crime. For another, many states specifically required that women be appointed to the investigatory commissions or agencies that administered the pensions. Taking advantage of the maternalist assumption that women had a special sensitivity to the needs of mothers and children, aid-to-mothers laws expanded employment opportunities for educated women in the expanding welfare system.

The story of mothers' pensions in the 1910s and 1920s illuminates the tension within maternalism between the rhetoric joining all women on the basis of motherhood on the one hand, and the design and implementation of social services only for needy mothers on the other. It shows not only how women activists shaped the U.S. welfare system; it also shows how American welfare politics shaped women's activism and their politics of motherhood.

Mothers' Pensions and the Women's Movement

Maternalist women's groups, such as the National Congress of Mothers and Parent-Teacher Associations and the General Federation of Women's Clubs, were the driving force behind the campaign for mothers' pensions. Progressive women reformers—such as Jane Addams, Julia Lathrop, Grace Abbott, Lillian Wald, and Mary Simkhovitch—also played a critical role, as did poor mothers, whose persistent demands for economic assistance from private charities, social settlements, and the federal Children's Bureau surely influenced middle-class reformers. Feminists such as Helen Todd and Inez Milholland also spoke out in favor of state-funded mothers' aid. Although the political views of female pension supporters varied, all believed that women raising children contributed as much or more to society as those working outside the home. Maternalists and feminists alike endorsed mothers' aid because it provided a home life for children, recognized mothers' service to society, and expanded women's rights to child custody. Although most saw mothers' aid only as a last resort for poor women who did not have the support of a man, some feminists and socialists considered it an "entering wedge" to motherhood endowment and economic independence.[9]

Mothers' pensions campaigns brought together a wide array of women's groups, prompting feminist historian Mary Ritter Beard to remark that "more women have agreed on the wisdom of mothers' pensions than on any other single piece of social legislation."[10] The moderate pro-suffrage *Woman's Journal* contained numerous articles on the subject. Grassroots Mothers' Pension Leagues, led by Henry Neil, the self-proclaimed "father" of mothers' pensions, sprang up all over the country, their popularity probably due partly to the fact that women were paid five dollars for every ten members (and ten dollars of dues) they signed up.[11] In Kansas, the National Congress of Mothers, the State Federation of Women's Clubs, the Woman's Christian Temperance Union, and the Good Citizenship League lobbied successfully for a mothers' pension law, which became the first bill passed after women in the state won the vote. In New York, the City and State Federations of Women's Clubs, the League of Mothers' Clubs, the National Women's Republican Association, the Association of Neighborhood Workers, and the National Federation of Settlements joined forces to secure an aid-to-mothers law.[12]

Yet despite the broad support for mothers' pensions among women activists, the movement for mothers' pensions — in contrast to woman suffrage or protective labor legislation — did not generate any prominent leaders or spokeswomen. This may be due in part to the remarkably quick passage of mothers' aid laws in most states. At any rate, it is an interesting contrast to Europe, where the protection of motherhood, in the form of widows' pensions as well as maternity insurance and motherhood endowment, was a major focus of feminist organizations like the German Bund für Mutterschutz and the British Women's Cooperative Guild. Few Americans embraced the notion of Mutterschutz; nevertheless, it is a testament to the power of the mother-protection idea that virtually the only feminist to speak out against mothers' pensions was Charlotte Perkins Gilman, fresh from her acrimonious debate with Ellen Key.

Still, only sentimental maternalists made mothers' pensions a top priority. Nearly every state affiliate of the National Congress of Mothers and Parent-Teacher Associations worked for the laws, and for several years the Congress passed a resolution supporting mothers' aid at almost every convention. Local PTAs distributed bibliographies on the subject, and members discussed the issue in mothers' study groups. Despite claiming to be uninvolved in politics, state chapters of the Mothers' Congress vigorously lobbied their legislators to enact mothers' aid laws. The work of the Oregon Congress of Mothers is illustrative. After gathering information about similar laws in other states, members drafted a bill, sent copies to every women's club, Grange, and newspaper in the state, and wrote letters and made personal calls to members of the state legislature. They secured the passage of the bill with only one dissenting vote.[13]

Although club mothers were accused of "rushing heedlessly. . . on purely sentimental grounds," their support for mothers' aid was motivated less by their "romantic, if not fanatic, idealization of home and motherhood," as one historian suggested, than by their resentment of their own social position.[14] Club mothers supported mothers' pensions because they did not want poor women to be separated from their children, because they wanted to dignify motherhood, and because they wanted to have a safety net if their husbands died or deserted them. At a time when most elite and middle-class mothers were economically dependent on men, could not vote, and did not have custody rights to their children, they felt that they shared with poor mothers a common vulnerability. As Clara Park observed, "Nothing can be more valuable to the state than the mother's contribution, but the home has no safeguards other than those which the man, with his willing or unwilling hands can give her." For poor and well-off Anglo-American women alike, motherhood was virtually the only fulfilling work open to them, but it made them vulnerable and subject to abuse because of the economic dependence that accompanied it. Resentment of economic dependence was not limited to feminists such as Charlotte Perkins Gilman; the frequency of articles on wealthy women's legal and economic dependence on their husbands in popular magazines such as the *Ladies' Home Journal* and *Harper's Bazar* demonstrates a broader concern.[15] The economic dependence of mothers was of less concern to progressive women reformers than to club mothers or feminists, perhaps because more of them eschewed marriage and motherhood for careers and social independence from men.

Activist women considered mothers' pensions part of their campaign for maternal custody rights. Indeed, William Hard launched the *Delineator's* campaign for mothers' pensions in a column concerned with the legal rights of married women. The American legal system was based on English common law, which made the father the child's sole guardian, entitled to control the child's wages and to determine his or her food, clothing, medicine, education, and punishment. Although nineteenth-century legal reforms and new "scientific" information about the child's need for mother-love increased the likelihood of mothers obtaining custody of young children, as late as 1919 the *Woman Citizen* reported that three states still gave the father the legal right to appoint another guardian for the child after his death. Even in equal guardianship states, child placement (and the determination of the mother's fitness) depended on the recommendation of a male judge. Thus mothers' pensions, which allowed "deserving" but poor mothers to retain custody of their children, seemed an important component of middle-class women's campaign for maternal rights.[16]

The maternalist justification for mothers' pensions is eloquently made in "The State's Duty to Fatherless Children," a 1911 speech by Mrs. G.

Harris Robertson, president of the Tennessee Congress of Mothers. Robertson called for mothers' aid as a way to protect homes "shattered by loss of father, the bread-winner," and to preserve mothers' dignity by recognizing the service they performed for the state. "We cannot afford to let a mother, one who has divided her body by creating other lives for the good of the state, one who has contributed to citizenship, be classed as a pauper, a dependent," she declared. "She must be given value received by her nation, and stand as one honored." Like other sentimental maternalists, Robertson assumed that all women were united by their common motherhood, dependence on men, and vulnerability to male abuse. "Mothers are bound together by a tie closer than blood. We (no matter whether we live in a palace or a hovel) have felt the same physical and mental anguish that belongs alone to motherhood."[17]

Clara Cahill Park, vice president of the Massachusetts Congress of Mothers and a member of the state's Commission on the Support of Dependent Minor Children of Widowed Mothers, also endorsed mothers' pensions as a way for impoverished mothers to obtain financial assistance from the state "without loss of self-respect." In a letter to the social work magazine *The Survey* — and reprinted by Mary Ritter Beard in *Woman's Work in Municipalities* because it expressed the attitude of "a large number" of female pension supporters — Park insisted that mothers were authorities in matters of child welfare and had a special sensitivity to the problems of poor children. "You see, mothers, in spite of the sociologists, feel themselves, for once, on their own ground in this matter; and in possession of all their faculties," she explained; "[they] will continue to think that as far as children are concerned, not they, but the learned doctors, are in the amateur class." According to Park, mothers, "and they alone," understood the importance of "care and time and money for children's needs. . . . They, and perhaps they only, can also feel the importance of preserving self-respect as an asset to be saved by the new attitude of the states [in giving mothers' pensions]." She applauded state mothers' aid as an "advance, as showing the policy of the nation, to conserve its children and its homes, and in recognizing the mother as a factor in that campaign, for the welfare of all."[18]

Despite — or because of — their assumptions about universal motherhood, maternalist justifications for mothers' pensions often reflected well-off women's matronizing attitude toward the poor. Robertson used the language of charity, not justice, to argue for extending mothers' aid to deserted wives and unmarried mothers. She lamented society's "betrayal" of "friendless" mothers, whose dreams of a home had turned to tragedy because of ignorance and economic dependence, and because they had been made the "dupe" or "toy" of men's double standard. "These mothers are so ignorant, so pitifully helplessly ignorant, that in the great industrial world there is no place for them," she proclaimed.

Although elite women appeared to identify with deserving recipients of mothers' aid, they described recipients less as sisters than as children in need of an "advisor and friend" to "supervise and [make] suggest[tions] . . . to the lonely mother." With this reasoning, they sanctioned the supervision of women's behavior that characterized the mothers' pension system.[19]

While sentimental maternalists defined woman's relationship to the state not as a citizen in her own right but as a "servant . . . bearing and rearing the future citizens," progressive maternalists and most suffragists saw no contradiction between calling for the state protection of mothers and asserting equal citizenship rights for women. Indeed, suffragists predicted that women would use the vote to secure mothers' aid, and the greatest increase in mothers' pension laws occurred in the final years of the suffrage campaign.[20] Even in the 1920s, *Equal Rights,* the journal of the National Woman's Party, supported mothers' pensions, although it advocated assistance for either parent. In any case, by the 1920s, the term "aid to dependent children" had largely replaced "mothers' pensions," making it clear that aid was designed to benefit children and was not a "special privilege" for women.[21]

There is virtually no evidence of opposition to mothers' pensions among maternalists, but in 1914 two important feminist journals did contain articles against them. These appear to be isolated examples. An article by Benita Locke in Margaret Sanger's journal, *The Woman Rebel,* referred to mothers' pensions as a "State dole," the "latest capitalist trap," which promised, "like most bourgeois reforms, to deal superficialily [sic] with a social evil." According to Locke, mothers' aid enabled children to survive merely to be exploited in capitalist factories when they were older. In addition, she observed perceptively, mothers' pensions subsidized sweatshops by prohibiting mothers from full-time work outside the home without providing them with adequate economic support. Like Locke, Charlotte Perkins Gilman objected that mothers' pensions did not address the root of women's oppression. She feared that mothers' pensions would institutionalize woman's role in the home by requiring "her own presence and labor in that family all the time." She deplored the fact that women's economic dependence required individual men to support their wives, and thought that mothers' pensions would only "saddle" "collective man" with that responsibility. Significantly, both Gilman and Locke rejected the primary feminist argument in support of mothers' pensions: that childrearing was work for which women were entitled to a salary.[22]

Salary for Mothers or Charity for Children?

The clash between reformers and social workers in favor of mothers' aid and those opposed to it appears at first to be about the merits of private charity versus public responsibility for child welfare. However, also at the heart of the struggle — one of the most bitter ever to occur within the social welfare field — was an underlying disagreement over the nature of women's work and their place in the family. While supporters of mothers' pensions maintained that mothers performed a valuable service to society and were therefore deserving of aid, opponents viewed economic assistance to poor mothers as a charity and a dole. While mothers' pension supporters insisted that the welfare of children warranted an activist state that would help fatherless families stay intact, opponents worried that state funding for single-mother households would undermine patriarchal authority in the home.[23]

Supporters of mothers' aid claimed that mothers were entitled to allowances because their labor benefited society. "Pensions are salaries earned by mothers who serve the state in giving all their time to rearing good citizens," explained The Independent, summarizing an argument for mothers' pensions. "We shall recognize that the mother of young children is doing better service to the community and one more worthy of pecuniary remuneration when she stays at home and minds her children than when she goes out charing [working] and leaves them to the chances of the street or to the care of a neighbor," wrote L. B. Hobhouse, in a statement that was widely quoted, probably because it articulated widely held ideas about woman's place in the home. William Hard, former head of the Northwestern University Settlement and the Delineator editor who publicized the pensions movement, compared the mother to any other civil servant. "He is paid for his work; she for hers. And she should be paid by those for whom she does it — all the citizens of the state, not the subscribers to the charities." The service of the mother, declared feminist Inez Milholland, was "of more value than any other in the community and therefore most deserving in the form of a pension."[24]

By using the word "pension," supporters of mothers' aid evoked the image of Civil War veterans, stressing mothers' service to the state, and challenging the priorities of a society that rewarded war but not motherhood. "It is the activities of women insisting on the value of life . . . which is bringing the question of widows' pensions forward so rapidly," Helen Todd told a New York suffrage meeting in 1915. "It is preposterous that we should be willing to pension veterans for having blown the lives out of people and not pension women for putting life into people. Inez Milholland agreed. "The State must safeguard its female soldiers on the field of life, every bit as much as it safeguards its male soldiers in the field of death," she maintained. "All women who have borne or are about to bear children are [should be] looked upon as wards of the State, to be cherished, protected and nourished. As pensions for mothers is a distinct step in this direction, pensions for mothers must become part of the policy of an enlightened State."[25]

The claim that mothers' aid was a salary for childrearing inevitably raised the possibility of paying all mothers. Influenced by the German Bund für Mutterschutz and the European campaign for motherhood endowment, a handful of feminists, such as Hard, claimed that mothers' pensions were a step toward national maternity insurance and the "gradual recognition of the principle of the endowment of motherhood." They took advantage of sentimental ideas about motherhood to campaign for sweeping social reforms. Hard, for example, publicized German feminists' demands for paid maternity leave, family allowances, and maternal health care in the *Delineator*. "The legislatures were in no position to resist an appeal on behalf of the poor widow," Katharine Anthony reflected in 1922, "and so nicely narcotized were they by their traditional tender-heartedness that they failed to perceive the socialistic basis of this new [state-funded] kind of widows' pensions."[26]

The views of Hard and Anthony notwithstanding, most active supporters of mothers' aid were not feminists or socialists, but maternalists, juvenile court justices, and social workers who had a fairly traditional understanding of family responsibilities and the division of labor in the home. Most mothers' pension supporters agreed with their opponents that men should be the family breadwinners. Yet while charity workers assumed that financial hardship (even widowhood!) was caused by individual deviance or moral failure, advocates of mothers' aid stressed its economic and environmental causes. They believed that industrialization had weakened women's position in the family by thrusting men into paid work and making women and children dependent on their income. They held society largely responsible for women's and children's poverty — whether the father did not earn enough to support his family, whether he refused to do so, or whether he had died or been disabled by a preventable disease or industrial accident.[27]

Most advocates of mothers' pensions did not challenge paternal authority in the family, but argued instead that the state could be a benevolent — and paternal — substitute for the head of the household if the father was unwilling or unable to fulfill his responsibility. "The State is a parent," a speaker told the National Congress of Mothers in 1912, "and a wise and gentle and kind and loving parent should beam down upon each child alike.... From the fountain head — *the state* — all benefits should issue." Juvenile court judge Ben B. Lindsey, a leading advocate of mothers' pensions, insisted that the state, the "over-parent" of the child, assume responsibility for children's health and morality. "It is not the purpose of the Parenthood of the State to usurp the function of the home or to permit the natural parent to shirk," he wrote, "but rather to see that the home performs its functions where it is careless, and to see that no child suffers because of poverty where the home is helpless. The State must preserve the home for the child."[28] The state would thus take over the father's dual role of maintaining discipline and providing financial support.

While advocates of mothers' pensions believed that the state should support women and children when men could not, opponents objected to public aid precisely because it seemed to undermine the male provider's role. C. C. Carstens, general agent of the Massachusetts Society for the Prevention of Cruelty to Children, objected that mothers' pensions would weaken other family members' sense of responsibility for their poor relations. Edward Devine, secretary of the New York Charity Organization Society, insisted on "personal responsibility of the individual for his own welfare and for that of those who . . . are naturally dependent upon him." In his view, mothers' aid was an "an insidious attack upon the family, inimical to the welfare of children and injurious to the character of parents." Otto Barnard, vice president of the Charity Organization Society, perceived mothers' aid as a step toward such socialistic measures as old age pensions and free food. "It is not American;" he wrote, "it is not virile."[29]

Opponents of aid for poor mothers especially objected to the idea that a mothers' pension was a salary for childrearing, potentially extended to all mothers. "Sympathy and not the payment of a financial obligation explains [the mothers' pension]," insisted Devine; "Need and not exchange is its basis." Mary Richmond, director of the Charity Organization Department of the Russell Sage Foundation and a pioneer in modern casework, complained about the "mixture and confusion of two ideas" — "service pensions" to all mothers and "relief grants" only to those who were poor. "There are many . . . who urge motherhood as such upon our attention as a service which justifies endowment by the state," she warned in 1913, "and those who take this view are writing in favor of and campaigning for the public relief measures (miscalled mothers' pension bills) that are now before fourteen legislatures. They regard them as an entering wedge to another and quite different social policy."[30]

Richmond and Devine need not have worried. Given voters' hostility to public welfare expenditures and to single mothers, few pension supporters dared suggest that aid be given to every mother in need. Instead, they insisted that the allowances should go only to those who raised their children properly. "Not supervision, but instruction, possibly compulsory — for all mothers," William Hard proposed. "A woman may be a mother, ten times over, and she may be in the most desperate distress imaginable and yet she does not therefore become eligible to an allowance. The allowance is not at all to reward her for having become a mother, nor is it primarily to cure her distress. . . . The mother gets an allowance on a condition. The condition is that she earn it by providing home care for the children."[31] At a time of Anglo-American anxiety about juvenile delinquency and race suicide —

when the claim of the experts that there was only one scientific way to raise children seemed especially compelling — no reformer could expect to achieve state aid for all mothers, including immigrants and women of color whose beliefs about childrearing and family life differed from Anglo-American norms.

Two conflicting ideas thus lay at the heart of the maternalist argument for mothers' pensions: (1) that motherhood was a service that benefited the state (not just the family) and was therefore deserving of a salary; and (2) that mothers and children should live in families headed by men and supported by the family wage. Pension supporters who described mothers as employees of the state found themselves in a contradictory position when they tried to limit eligibility to widows or "deserving" mothers. Despite Hard's claim that women were entitled to allowances in return for the service of raising children, his approval of maternal supervision and payments only to "fit" mothers ensured that the pensions would never really be considered a salary for childrearing. Ultimately, the position of pension advocates was not terribly different from that of charity workers after all.

The confusion created by the contradictory ideas behind mothers' pensions are evident in the 1914 report of the New York State Commission on Relief for Widowed Mothers. Historians have seen the 1915 passage of a mothers' pension law in New York, a stronghold of private child-saving agencies, as the crucial defeat for social workers opposed to mothers' aid.[32] Although the victory for poor mothers should not be minimized, the New York bill law represented a compromise with private charities and the triumph of the individualized casework perspective. Despite the fact that members of the Commission that designed the bill included strong pension advocates, such as Hard, it rejected the term "pension" in favor of "allowance" precisely because it implied payment for childrearing and could therefore be extended to all mothers.

> Were this the basis of the contention for widows' pensions, it would have to be extended to include all mothers of all classes of society. Those who have favored the adoption of this legislation [the proposed bill for widows only] believe it to be, rather, a payment by the State for services to be rendered in the future in the proper home education of the child. Regarded in this light, such assistance is very properly restricted to those families of which death has claimed the natural protector.

The Commission limited aid to widows because pensioning them would not "in any way increase the number of worthy families in distress" and opposed extending aid to deserted or unmarried mothers because doing so "would, undoubtedly, have the effect of a premium upon these crimes against society."[33] Yet in limiting eligibility to widows and ignoring the fact that deserted and unmarried mothers, and those with able husbands, also rendered the service of childrearing, the Commission undermined its own assertion that the allowance was a payment for the mother's services.

The Administration of Mothers' Aid

That any understanding of a welfare system must come from examining the administration of services, rather than the political campaign or ideology behind them, is nowhere as true as in the case of mothers' pensions. Despite the early rhetoric portraying mothers' aid as a salary for childrearing, the administration of public mothers' pension programs differed little from private charity in its emphasis on casework and family rehabilitation over economic support. Although the enactment of state-funded mothers' aid was achieved by a highly politicized women's movement that asserted the common ground between impoverished and privileged mothers, its implementation accentuated the differences among women and actually contributed to the depoliticization of mother-work.

Women's active role in the administration of mothers' aid was presumed in most state pension laws. The majority of states administered mothers' pensions through juvenile courts, a branch of the legal system in which women had some influence, and therefore women had more authority over pension administration than they might have had if mothers' aid had been subsumed under public relief. Moreover, a number of states specifically provided that women be appointed to the investigatory commissions or agencies that administered the pensions. For example, in Massachusetts, where widows' pensions were administered by the overseers of the poor, the law stipulated that a woman supervisor direct the five female employees who investigated and supervised recipients.[34] These administrative requirements, like the "need" for women to investigate and supervise welfare clients, created new job opportunities for educated women, who thus profited from the maternalist claim that women were more nurturant than men. However, after the passage of the laws, the majority of middle-class activists saw mothers' pensions more as a child-welfare service to be administered by experts, than as a political matter of concern to all mothers.

From their inception, mothers' pension programs were marked by local variation in administration and a chronic shortage of funds. Because counties raised most of the funds for mothers' aid, grant levels varied considerably. Large cities were more likely than rural areas to award higher grants and to provide assistance to immigrants and women of color. Eligibility requirements also varied from state to state. Widows were entitled to assistance in every state, although by 1926 only five states limited aid to them. In six states, the law applied to "any mother with dependent children." Three states included provisions for unmarried mothers. Nevertheless, widows continued to be the primary recipients of aid, even in states that specifically granted pensions to any needy mother. A 1921 study of mothers' aid in five states found that widows comprised 75 percent of recipients. Unmarried mothers accounted for only 1 percent of the seven thousand pension recipients in Michigan that year.[35]

Citizenship and residency requirements also varied widely. Almost every state had a one- to five-year residency requirement. In 1921 eight states required recipients to be U.S. citizens, and several others demanded that the widow file for citizenship. Even after a lawsuit successfully challenged San Francisco's citizenship requirement, pension administrators "observed" that immigrants who had not taken out their citizenship papers had lower standards of home life than Americans and were therefore less likely to be awarded a pension. They "urged" foreign-born recipients to file citizenship papers and learn English.[36]

Because limited funds, eligibility requirements, and their maternalist ideology required social workers to restrict assistance to "suitable" mothers, aid went disproportionately to white, English-speaking widows. Divorced and deserted women were often excluded from the rolls because officials were afraid of encouraging families to break up and because support for children with able-bodied fathers would have challenged the idea of the family wage. African American women, the poorest people in the nation, were underrepresented in the recipient group throughout the United States. For example, although blacks constituted 21 percent of the population of Houston, Texas, not one black family there received mothers' aid. In 1931, only 3 percent of mothers on welfare rolls nationally were black.[37]

Discrimination also operated within the pension system, as some counties used different budgets for different nationalities. Of forty-five agencies represented at a 1922 Children's Bureau Conference on Mothers' Pensions, only thirty used a standard budget schedule. Of those thirty, eleven deviated from the standard budget on account of nationality. For example, one agency provided lower allowances to Czech and Italian families, while another reported a "Mexican problem which affected the use of the schedule." Another agency added 10 percent to the food allowance of "high-type" families, and at least one said that it "did not reduce the widow of a clerical worker or skilled mechanic to the same standard as the widow of a laborer."[38]

Ethnic and class profiles of pensioned mothers show that, although some ethnic groups received aid in proportion to their representation in the population, others were more—or less—likely to receive aid. Of 497 San Francisco families receiving pensions in 1915, more than two-thirds were born in the United States, Ireland, and Germany. Native-born whites represented 65 percent of the San Francisco population in 1910 but comprised only 48 percent of the recipient group, no doubt because of their lesser need. In contrast, Irish and German immigrants comprised just 11 percent of the population, but accounted for 21 percent of the recipient group. Approximately 38 percent of mothers' pensions in San Francisco went to the widows of skilled workers. In Hamilton County, New York, 75 percent of the allowances were awarded to widows, and 64 percent to women born in the United States. African Americans received fewer pensions (4 percent) than their proportion of the population.[39] In the ethnically diverse city of Chicago, where native-born whites accounted for only 20 percent of the population, white "Americans" received 31 percent of the pensions. First- and second-generation European immigrants, who comprised 78 percent of the population, received 60 percent of the pensions. African Americans received 3 percent of mothers' pensions, slightly less than their proportion in the population as a whole. According to investigators, 44.7 percent of the recipients had been married to unskilled laborers and 35.9 percent had been the wives of skilled workers.[40]

Despite the rhetoric of stay-at-home motherhood that helped secure the passage of mothers' pension laws, the chronic lack of funds and fear of welfare 'chiselers' caused social workers to abandon the view that poor mothers should stay home with their children. Most state laws permitted recipients to work outside the home when it did not interfere with their family responsibilities; indeed, recipients were frequently forced to engage in outside work because there was "no other way to get an adequate income for the family." A 1923 Children's Bureau study of mothers' pensions in nine locations found that at least 52 percent of the 942 mothers receiving aid were known to be wage earners. More than half of them worked outside the home, 59 percent at housework and 16 percent in factories. Of the 188 mothers who did wagework at home, 60 percent were engaged in laundering or sewing.[41] In Cook County, Illinois, two-thirds of mothers' aid recipients between 1913 and 1915 worked for wages, 61 percent of them in the arduous job of washerwoman. In Philadelphia, fully 84 percent of mothers receiving aid in 1920 were gainfully employed, most of them in some form of domestic service. Most welfare administrators agreed with the Children's Bureau that maternal wagework could have a "wholesome influence in the family life" if limited in time and properly supervised; the majority set the maximum a mother might acceptably do outside wagework at three days a week. By not paying single mothers enough to stay at home but preventing them from (openly) working full time, the mothers' pension system perpetuated women's marginal position in the wage-labor market and reinforced their economic dependence on other family members.[42]

Investigation and supervision of recipients, modeled on the "friendly

visiting" of private charities, was the heart of mothers' pension administration. Even though pension bureaus distinguished mothers' aid from a
"charity dole" because they handled only "high type homes," supervision
was considered necessary to maintain standards of home life thought appropriate — and to catch anyone "wrongfully" receiving aid. The predominantly female caseworkers investigated clients' finances, instructed them
in scientific childrearing and efficient housekeeping methods, monitored
children's progress at school, and made sure that homes were sanitary,
adequately ventilated, and not overcrowded. Catching cheaters was a principal concern; as a Maine official tactfully remarked, not all recipients were
"thoughtful enough" to relinquish aid voluntarily. Yet because recipients
were not given enough money to live on, but might lose their pensions if
they were resourceful and got some money from another source, cheating
became part of the system. Recipients were forced to hide jobs, income, and
lovers from their caseworkers.[43]

The enormous disparity between policymakers' rhetoric about maternal
dignity and the actual charity-like administration of mothers' aid is documented in Edith Abbott's and Sophonisba Breckinridge's study of the Illinois
Aid-to-Mothers law, published by the Children's Bureau in 1921. The original
Funds to Parents Act, passed in 1911, made funds available to either parent
and placed no restrictions on nationality, family status, property ownership,
or length of residence in the state. By 1913, however, lawmakers disturbed
by the vague wording of the law and the growing expense of the program
revised the bill and restricted eligibility. The new law, renamed the Funds-
to-Mothers Act, instituted a three-year residency requirement and explicitly
prohibited property owners, convicts' wives, and deserted, divorced, and
"alien" women from receiving aid. Two hundred women, most of them
immigrants, were dropped from the rolls in the month after the new law
went into effect. In 1915 the law was again amended to make immigrant
women with American-born children eligible for a pension if they applied
for U.S. citizenship, although efforts to make deserted women and property
owners eligible for aid were defeated.[44]

As in other states, investigation and supervision of recipients was the
essence of the Cook County mothers' pension program. First, applicants for
mothers' pensions underwent the initial verification of "need" that took
from two to four months. Then, as recipients, they were "taught" efficient
techniques of cooking and cleaning, and scientific information about child
nutrition and hygiene. Their household budgets were checked, and children's progress at school was observed. Fully 85 percent of families who
received aid more than two years were visited more than once a month.
Although caseworkers sometimes provided information useful to immigrant
mothers adjusting to the unfamiliar ways of American cities, their major

function was to protect the county's funds by making sure that women did not hide lovers or income from the state.[45]

Pensioned Mothers

The case histories of two Chicago recipients, documented in Sophonisba Breckinridge's *Family Welfare Work,* show how welfare policy shaped the working lives of poor mothers. The stories of Mary Legaikas, a Lithuanian widow with five children under ten years old, and Elizabeth Meyer, a Jewish widow with three school-age boys, illuminate the conflicts between recipients' struggle to maintain their families and social workers' efforts to enforce maternalist ideas about housekeeping and child care. They illustrate the relationship between private and public assistance and the "catch 22" of the mothers' pension system: although recipients were not given enough money to live on, if they were resourceful and survived on little money, they might lose their pensions. Indeed, Meyer eventually decided that the money she received from the county was not worth the hassle of the mothers' pension program.[46]

Mary Legaikas, the widow of a factory pieceworker, waited a full year before the county granted her aid and then faced the constant threat of being removed from the rolls. The case record begins in July 1918—two weeks after Mr. Legaikas died from an unnecessary gall stone operation — when a visiting nurse from the Family Welfare Agency, a private Chicago charity, visited the Legaikas household. Although the investigator reported that the family lived in a "decent" house with a garden, eight chickens, and a "well-kept lawn," they had no food and owed $325 in unpaid physician's and hospital bills. Mrs. Legaikas, who did not speak English, was described as being "very depressed and worried over her responsibilities." Yet she was not eligible for a mothers' pension because she was not a U.S. citizen and had more than the $1,000 worth of money and property allowed under the law. She owned a Liberty Bond, a house valued at $2,000 (on which she had an $800 mortagage through the Lithuanian Building and Loan Company), was due to receive assistance from two benevolent societies, and had a brother whom the county expected to help support the family. The social worker helped Mrs. Legaikas take out citizenship papers, cash her Liberty Bond, and purchase a less expensive home.[47]

While waiting for public assistance, the Legaikas family survived through a combination of maternal wage earning, aid from private charities, and support from relatives and neighbors. During the year it took county investigators to determine that she was a fit mother and "sufficiently necessitous" for a mothers' pension, Mrs. Legaikis received a small allowance from the private Family Welfare Agency. She received $13.26 per month from the charity, assistance from relatives and Lithuanian benevolent societies, and occasional grants from the county for food, coal, and shoes. Although Mrs. Legaikas' brother could not provide financial support because he had a large family of his own, he helped around the house and, after opening a small grocery store, sold her groceries at cost.

Both because of the cultural differences between social worker and recipient and the difficulty maintaining a home amid ill health and poverty, the Legaikas household received a remarkably different evaluation each time it was visited by the Family Welfare Agency visitor. Shortly after helping Mrs. Legaikas with her budget in January 1919, the visitor reported that the widow "expressed appreciation of what the Agency had done for her." She described the house as "very nice and clean" and wrote that Legaikas seemed to be "very economical" about using coal. Yet just two weeks later, the social worker remarked that Mrs. Legaikas was "quite hopeless in her attitude. Does not know how to manage very well and is constantly worrying." She warned the Legaikas children to improve their behavior in school. Six months later, she found the "house very dirty and upset."[48]

Not surprisingly, the major confrontations between Mrs. Legaikas and her caseworker occurred over money. After the social worker discovered that the widow had $140 in the bank, she reported that Mrs. Legaikis "seemed rather nervous about [the] visitor knowing this." Upon learning that she could not receive aid if she had so much money, Mrs. Legaikas spent fifty dollars on a bed, a comforter, and embroidery but did not leave enough to buy food. The Agency informed her that she "should not have spent the money so rashly" and made her return the goods she had purchased.[49]

Despite — or because of — a theoretical commitment to family solidarity, the mothers' pension program drove a wedge between the widow and her family. Even after the Juvenile Court accepted Mrs. Legaikas's application for a mothers' pension in August 1919, thirteen months after her first application, it insisted that her brother contribute $3 a week to her support. Desperately afraid that she would again be denied aid, the widow "tearfully" told the caseworker that her brother had a large family of his own and could not afford to support hers. The agency's efforts to force her brother to provide financial assistance to her family had strained the relations between them, she said. At this point, the Lithuanian community helped Mrs. Legaikas battle the welfare system; her banker managed to convince the Juvenile Court to begin a new investigation that proved that her brother was indeed too poor to regularly give money to the widow's family.[50]

Even after Mrs. Legaikas was granted a mothers' pension in September 1919, the difference between her pension of $55.00 per month and the family budget (estimated at $89.50 by the Family Welfare Agency) made it difficult to support her family in a manner acceptable to the county investigator. To make ends meet, Mrs. Legaikas worked three days a week — at \$4.00 a day — in the factory where her husband had been employed. A neighbor cared for her children. The court approved of her employment, but kept close watch on the children through weekly home visits, school reports, and medical supervision. The visitor usually found them in "good condition" and the home "well cared for," although she sometimes reported that the house was untidy when Mrs. Legaikas was ill or at work. One child had trouble in school. At one point, the social worker noticed that the widow was cooking with cheap vegetables, convenience foods, and too much sugar since she had begun working in the factory, and she explained these "mistakes" to her.[51]

Because her children were in such good condition, the court decided that Mrs. Legaikas must have resources in addition to her county pension. She admitted receiving money from her brother-in-law in Gary, Indiana, and, occasionally, clothing from her children's school. In November the court discovered that she was also doing surreptitious work. Since the factory did not allow part-time work, Mrs. Legaikas worked a fifty-hour week, occasionally taking time off when her children needed her at home. Yet even with this extra work, she did not earn enough to meet her budget, and the court recommended a pension increase.

Although application for citizenship was an eligibility requirement for mothers' pensions, the Family Welfare Agency reported that Mrs. Legaikas took the obligation "rather lightly." Although she had learned to speak English and could read and write Lithuanian, she "refused" to learn to read or write English. In July 1922, Mrs. Legaikas's pension was stayed because her citizenship papers were overdue. In October, after she obtained the papers, her pension, now increased to \$85, was restored.[52] In March 1923, the last date included in the records, the Legaikas pension was reduced by \$15 because her oldest son turned fourteen.

Like Mary Legaikas, Elizabeth Meyer found her pension jeopardized because she was a good provider for her children. Mrs. Meyer's efforts to do what she thought was best for her children took a toll on her health and conflicted with the social workers' ideas about proper home life. Assisted by Chicago's Jewish Welfare Bureau, which took up her case six months after her husband died of diabetes in 1916, the widow was granted a county mothers' pension of \$30 per month in May 1917. Two years later her pension was increased to \$35. A proud woman who did not wish it known that she received private charity, Mrs. Meyer did not even tell her own sister that she was getting help from the Jewish Welfare Bureau, leading her family to believe that the only financial assistance she received was her county mothers' pension. Clearly, the distinction maternalists drew between mothers' pensions and charity was important to the self-esteem of women like Mrs. Meyer.[53]

Eager to do what was best for her children, Mrs. Meyer followed the Bureau's suggestions regarding diet and the children's schoolwork and worked as a seamstress to earn the difference between her budget of $95.16 and her allowance from the county. Although she worked long hours and earned very little, she was eager to be independent and self-supporting. The case-worker was sympathetic to this goal and recommended that Mrs. Meyer take a position in the Jewish Welfare Bureau's Sewing Shop. She hoped that working outside the home would regulate the widow's hours of labor, give her social contacts, and relieve her of the worry caused by the irregular income of sewing at home. She reported that Mrs. Meyer's children were happy and that she had a "certain pride and exhilaration, to think that she too is a wage-earner and not so dependent as formerly." Still, the Juvenile Court reduced her pension in January 1923.[54]

Mrs. Meyer's initiative and success at wage earning jeopardized her pension both because it added to her income and because it was thought to make her a less suitable mother. The caseworker warned her that working full-time would harm her health and family life. Because Mrs. Meyer was overworked, the worker reported, she "consequently has not enough time to attend to her household duties and cook proper meals for her children in the evening, nor has she any extra time for recreation, as most of her time is taken up with mending and sewing for herself and the boys." The social worker also explained that, even after her budget had been adjusted to allow for new expenses such as carfare, Mrs. Meyer's income was $10 more than she needed. Still she was unable to meet her expenses. Determined to give her children as much as their schoolmates had, Mrs. Meyer believed that her children should be better fed and clothed since she had a little money. According to the case records, she felt that "no matter how hard she works, how honest she was, or how good she tried to be, things never seemed any better."[55]

Eventually, Mrs. Meyer decided that the self-respect and independence of wage earning was preferable to the degradation of mothers' aid. She complained bitterly that the Juvenile Court reduced her pension after she proved she could be self-supporting and refused the offer of the Jewish Welfare Bureau to supplement her income if she worked fewer hours. She told her social worker that she had "made up her mind" to be self-supporting.[56] She apparently felt that the stigma of being dependent on charity and public welfare made the small sum to which she was entitled not worth the trouble.

Despite their problems with the mothers' pension system, Legaikas and Meyer represent its "success" stories. Many recipients had far worse experiences with their social workers; some were even threatened with the loss of their children for contesting expert ideas about child welfare. Take, for example, the experience of Anna Novak, a Czech-born widow with three young children who received an allowance from the Mothers' Assistance Fund of Pennsylvania. The friction between Mrs. Novak and her social worker may have begun at the intake interview, when the visitor observed that she "spoiled the baby a great deal by petting him" and letting him sit on her lap, even though he was almost three years old.[57] In any case, tensions erupted when all three Novak children were hospitalized for tonsillectomies. Many immigrants were terrified of hospitals, and the social worker reported that Mrs. Novak "was very much broken up" about leaving her children in one. When eight-year-old Celia contracted pneumonia in the hospital and had to extend her stay, Mrs. Novak "wept copiously and said that she wanted Celia to come home even if she died." The children had not been sick before the Mothers' Assistance Fund took them to the hospital, she protested; "she could not understand why we picked on her." The caseworker responded by informing Mrs. Novak that "if she cried this way she was not fit to look after the children" and by lecturing her about her maternal responsibilities. Probably because she feared losing her children, Mrs. Novak decided to obey her caseworker's advice; after this incident, the social worker found her "most anxious to do anything that visitor suggested."[58]

Yet even Mrs. Novak might be considered fortunate, for most poor mothers were ineligible for aid or lived in counties that provided no pensions at all. Only 38 out of 237 Philadelphia widows interviewed in 1918–19 for a study of mothers in industry even applied for pensions; only 9 women — 24 percent of those who applied and fewer than 4 percent of the total — were receiving them. The Philadelphia Mothers' Assistance Fund had a waiting list of eighteen months to two years. In Chicago, an African American woman who supported five children by cooking and taking in laundry was denied a pension even though she was considered "exceptionally skilled and competent" by investigators. She was told that the purpose of the pension was not to ease the burden of overworked mothers, but to help those who could not survive on their own (that is, to reinforce women's dependency). Conditions in rural areas were even worse: most counties in Illinois, for example, never established mothers' pension programs because of lack of funds.[59] Years after most states passed mothers' pensions laws, poor single mothers continued to lose custody of their children to asylums or foster homes.[60]

In spite of the inadequate amount and often humiliating conditions of mothers' aid, many impoverished mothers found pensions an advance over their previous options of placing children in institutions or sending them to work. Indeed, Abbott and Breckinridge found that some women received higher and more regular payments as recipients of mothers' aid than they had when their husbands were alive! Wherever mothers' aid was established, administrators were deluged with applications. A California mother explained, "My husband went a way two years ago this May and I don't know wheather he is dead or not. I have never heard a word from him. I work and try to get a long but I can't make enough to feed and clothe my four children. My Father lost his left hand So he cant help me very much."[61]

Many women who would never seek public assistance for themselves felt justified in asking for aid for their children. Some, perhaps denied help by local authorities, turned to the federal government with their requests. "I am only a poor frail little mother, left with six children," a Texas woman wrote the Secretary of the Treasury and the Children's Bureau in 1917, "I have given over my life to being a mother to my children until I would be lost without them. I do not ask for charity. . . . I care nothing for the pension only as a last resort—that is to keep me from being *seperated* from my *precious babies.*" A Pennsylvania mother, whose husband died before her last baby was born, revealed her desperation: "I am in bad means with these Children, as I have been trying to keep them together and hate so much to part them, but will hafto do some thing with them pretty soon if I dont get help from some wheres pretty soon." Counting on the fact that their childrearing work made them deserving of a pension, these mothers turned to the government when they needed aid.[62]

Many women saw mothers' pensions as a way to provide a better life for their children or to give them the education they never had. "It is my dearest wish to see my girl in school," explained a Texas mother, who was in poor health and could not find work. "I do not want to sep[a]rate from my girl as I suffered so here for all throught her life to. In fact a good mother deserves help [and] the right treatment so she can send to be trained educated her children. . . . I have been a good mother to her, because she is mine we never want to be sep[a]rated . . . if there was a mothers pens[i]on I would sure feel good."[63]

Despite the inadequate amount, unsatisfactory administration, and difficulty of obtaining pensions, many women considered publicly funded mothers' pensions—unlike private charity—to be their due. Struggling to maintain their dignity and to provide the best they could for their children, they battled with caseworkers over their lifestyles and their rights. Two letters to the Children's Bureau from a Minnesota woman who felt entitled to a county mothers' pension illustrate her frustration at being treated like a charity case. Mrs. M. S., a deserted mother of four, worked as a washerwoman to support her family. At first unaware of the mothers' pension program and later unable to obtain a pension because she could earn an income, Mrs. M. S. became eligible for aid only after washing had so destroyed her health that she was unable to work. Her allowance was cut upon her recovery.[64]

Mrs. M. S.'s letters reveal the anger and bitterness that resulted from the conflict between the claim that poor mothers were entitled to aid on the one hand, and the paltry allowance and demeaning emphasis on suitability on the other. When an investigator told her that she had too much furniture to qualify for a pension, Mrs. M. S. was angry: "I told her I could not eat my old funisher w[h]ich I have had for the last 15 years." And when the county agent told her that she would not need more money if she did not feed her children such good meals, suggesting that she take them out of school and put them to work instead, Mrs. M. S. objected that to do so "wood make slaves out of them all their lif[e]s." Despite the maternalist assertion that there was a single minimum standard for child welfare, social workers did not apply "scientific" ideas about proper nutrition and the evils of child labor to single mothers financially dependent on the state.

At the time she wrote the Children's Bureau in 1927, Mrs. M. S. had struggled for six years as a washerwoman to feed her children, take care of them when they were ill, and pay the medical bills that came so frequently. She blamed her ill health on unnecessary and unjust overwork caused by the county's refusal to grant her the aid to which she was entitled. "I seen this pi[e]ce in this paper that ever mother has a right to mothers pension," she explained, "only I was rob[b]ed of it."

> if I wood of had mothers pension and done a small amount of work I wood have better he[a]lth now. I am so sore that I had such little ed[u]cation not to [k]no[w] that my childern had a right to help and go thrue school. . . . pleas[e] help my family as for myself I can get along with one meale a day my children are all under wait. . . . I do want my children educated it is all I can give them. . . . Why cant a mother alone get it without it being used as a weapon to keep her from her Mothers pension that every single mother with minor children is entitled to.[65]

Yet, as Mrs. M. S. learned, poor mothers did not have the "right" to a pension. The county pension board responded to a Children's Bureau inquiry by saying that Mrs. M. S. was not eligible for aid in 1927 because she had received $959.72 from the county in the past four years. The Bureau then wrote Mrs. M. S. that there was nothing it could do. In spite of the rhetoric calling mothers' pensions a salary for childrearing, recipients were treated as dependents on charity. Despite maternalist claims that all children needed full-time mothers and loving homes, poverty-stricken single mothers were expected to economically support their families by doing wagework outside the home.[66]

From Mothers' Pensions to Aid to Dependent Children

Although many recipients, like Mrs. M. S., continued to regard mothers' aid as their due, by the 1920s the idea that pensions were a right in return for maternal service had virtually disappeared among the general public. As mothers' aid became part of a public welfare bureaucracy, and growing numbers of middle-class women found dignity and some economic independence in jobs outside the home, activist women generally lost interest in publicly funded mothers' pensions. The National Congress of Mothers and Parent-Teacher Associations, for example, expressed little concern about the administration of mothers' aid. "When the law was safely on the statute books the interest of the public in the humanitarian principle was overshadowed by a desire for economy," one social worker observed. In 1923, the supervisor of the Pennsylvania Mothers' Assistance Fund criticized the false distinction between mothers' pensions and other forms of relief. The maternalist campaign for mothers' dignity had metamorphosed into a charity for the poor.[67]

The waning influence of maternalism — and the depoliticization of motherhood — were reflected in the new justifications for mothers' aid. While Progressive-era activists won popular support for pensions by describing them as salaries for mothers, reformers and social workers trying to increase appropriations in the 1920s stressed that the allowances were not really intended for women, but for children. Pensions were granted "in the interest of future citizenship" to ensure the "well-being of the child under supervision," one administrator explained; she did not mention the alleviation of material distress or the protection of the mother's self-respect. Moreover, women who administered mothers' aid justified their work in terms of their professional expertise, not their maternal insight or sympathy. In 1924, the Children's Bureau announced that the term "mothers' pensions" was becoming "obsolete both in usage and in theory. . . . Aid is being administered, not as a 'pension,' but in accordance with the methods of social casework."[68]

Why were mothers' pensions less likely to be considered a women's issue in the 1920s, even though women continued to be the principal recipients and employees of ADC? The decline of maternalism, the strife between maternalists and feminists, the professionalization of social work, and the antireform climate of the decade provide some answers. So do the shortcomings of the maternalist rationale for mothers' aid. The maternalist assumption that motherhood put all women on common ground obscured the differences in real women's experience and needs. Convinced that their culturally specific ideas about home and family life were universal—and that young people needed a "suitable" home to be happy and well-adjusted— maternalists urged working-class mothers to raise their children according to certain (Anglo-American) standards. Yet impoverished women rarely lived according to middle-class norms—not the least because they had to depend on maternal wagework and child labor for economic support—and social workers frequently clashed with recipients over keeping house and raising children. Thus, although the rhetoric of mothers' pension supporters stressed the common bonds of motherhood, the welfare system increased the power some women had to take away the livelihood—and the children—of others, and it highlighted the divisions between them.

Not surprisingly, most middle-class women in the 1920s did not see government allowances as a way to ensure the dignity of motherhood or to make mothers independent of men. The intrusive investigations of recipients—and the requirement that most supplement their pensions by working in low-wage jobs—made it clear that government allowances were not a right in return for the service of childrearing, and they surely stopped many women from seeing a connection between widows' pensions and motherhood endowment.[69] Indeed, with the depoliticization of motherhood and devaluation of mother-work in the 1920s, both pensioned mothers and middle-class women who did not work outside the home were increasingly portrayed as nonworking "dependents" on the government or on individual men—and therefore potentially "dangerous" to their children. It is a bitter irony that some middle-class women escaped this fate—and obtained dignity and economic independence—by entering careers in which they supervised poor mothers receiving public aid.

The political campaign for, and apolitical administration of, mothers' pensions provides an intriguing contrast to the Sheppard-Towner Maternity and Infancy Protection Act, the other major maternalist reform of the period. The drive for Sheppard-Towner was more purely "maternalist" than the campaign for mothers' aid—both because health education did not offer the possibilities for women's autonomy that state-funded mothers' allowances did, and because Sheppard-Towner was enacted after suffrage and therefore after feminists had already begun to focus on equal rights. Nevertheless, the campaign for the "maternity bill" inspired a women's movement of enormous proportion. Its enactment was the culmination of Progressive-era efforts to politicize motherhood.

NOTES

1. Katharine Anthony, *Feminism in Germany and Scandinavia* (New York: Henry Holt, 1915), 4–5.

2. The literature on the mothers' pension movement is large and growing. The most useful published works include Mark H. Leff, "Consensus for Reform: The Mothers' Pension Movement in the Progressive Era," *Social Service Review* 47 (Sept. 1973): 397–417; Joanne Goodwin, "An Experiment in Paid Motherhood: The Implementation of Mothers' Pensions in Early Twentieth Century Chicago," *Gender and History* 4 (Autumn 1992): 323–42; Barbara J. Nelson, "The Origins of the Two-Channel Welfare State: Workmen's Compensation and Mothers' Aid," in *Women, the State, and Welfare*, ed. Linda Gordon (Madison: University of Wisconsin Press, 1990), 123–51; Theda Skocpol, *Protecting Soldiers and Mothers: The Politics of Social Provision in the United States, 1870s-1920s* (Cambridge: Harvard University Press, 1992); Mimi Abramovitz, *Regulating the Lives of Women: Social Welfare Policy From Colonial Times to the Present* (Boston: South End Press, 1988), 190–206; Roy Lubove, *The Struggle for Social Security* (Cambridge: Harvard University Press, 1968), 91–112; Susan Tiffin, *In Whose Best Interest? Child Welfare Reform in the Progressive Era* (Westport: Greenwood Press, 1982), 121–35; Ann Vandepol, "Dependent Children, Child Custody and the Mothers' Pensions: The Transformation of State-Family Relations in the Early 20th Century," *Social Problems* 29 (Feb. 1982): 221–35; Muriel W. Pumphrey and Ralph E. Pumphrey, "The Widows' Pension Movement, 1900–1930: Preventive Child-Saving or Social Control?" in *Social Welfare or Social Control? Some Historical Reflections on "Regulating the Poor,"* ed. Walter I. Trattner (Knoxville: University of Tennessee Press, 1983), 51–66.

3. Tiffin, *In Whose Best Interest,* 14–33; Hannah Kent Schoff, *The Wayward Child: A Study of the Causes of Crime* (Indianapolis: Bobbs-Merrill, 1915), esp. 80–88.

4. See Linda Gordon, *Heroes of Their Own Lives: The Politics and History of Family Violence* (New York: Penguin, 1988); Michael B. Katz, *In the Shadow of the Poorhouse: A Social History of Welfare in America* (New York: Basic, 1986), 58–84; Mary E. Richmond and Fred S. Hall, *A Study of 985 Widows Known to Certain Charity Organization Societies in 1910* (New York: Russell Sage Foundation, 1913); New York Association for Improving the Condition of the Poor, *Shall Widows Be Pensioned?* (New York: NYAICP, 1914).

5. Quoted in Leff, "Consensus for Reform," 400.

6. The National Congress of Mothers repeatedly used this quotation in its campaign for mothers' pensions. At conventions and gatherings in the 1910s, club mothers often passed resolutions which held that the mother was the best caretaker for her children and that "when necessary to prevent the breaking up of the home the State should provide a certain sum for the support of the children instead of taking them from her and placing them elsewhere at the expense of the State." "Resolutions Adopted by 2nd International Congress on Child Welfare, National Congress of Mothers," *Child-Welfare Magazine* 5 (June 1911): 193–96. Note that, contrary to the White House Conference, the Mothers' Congress called for state aid.

7. See U.S. Children's Bureau, *Laws Relating to 'Mothers' Pensions' in the United States, Canada, Denmark, and New Zealand,* Publication No. 63 (Wash-

ington, D.C.: Government Printing Office, 1919); Emma O. Lundberg, "Aid to Mothers with Dependent Children," *Annals of the American Academy of Political and Social Science* 98 (Nov. 1921): 96–105; U.S. Children's Bureau, *Proceedings of Conference on Mothers' Pensions, Providence, Rhode Island, June 28, 1922,* Publication No. 109 (Washington, D.C.: Government Printing Office, 1922).

8. U.S. Children's Bureau, *Mothers' Aid, 1931,* Publication No. 220 (Washington, D.C.: Government Printing Office, 1933), 8.

9. The following discussion is based on articles on mothers' pensions in the *Survey,* the PTA's *Child-Welfare Magazine,* popular women's magazines such as the *Delineator,* the prosuffrage *Woman's Journal,* and *Equal Rights,* the journal of the National Woman's Party. See also Edna Bullock, ed. *Selected Articles on Mothers' Pensions* (New York: H. W. Wilson, 1915).

10. Mary Ritter Beard, *Woman's Work in Municipalities* (New York: D. Appleton & Co., 1915), 251.

11. "Mothers' Pension League," typescript, Nov. 5, 1912, Grace Browning Collection, Social Welfare History Archives, University of Minnesota. Although Neil denied social workers' charges that he personally profited from the League, Judge Ben B. Lindsey resigned as its vice-president. *Survey* 29 (Feb. 1, Mar. 22, 1913): 559, 849.

12. "Mother Pensions Now Kansas Law," *Woman's Journal* 46 (Apr. 3, 1915): 103; "The Case for Widows' Aid in New York," *Survey* 33 (Feb. 20, 1915): 547; "Widows' Pension Bills in New York," *Survey* 33 (Feb. 13, 1915): 528.

13. The *Child-Welfare Magazine* contains numerous articles and resolutions on mothers' pensions. See, for example, "Sixteenth Child-Welfare Congress in St. Louis," *Child-Welfare Magazine* 6 (May 1912): 299.

14. Beard, *Woman's Work,* 251; Lubove, *Struggle for Social Security,* 100–101. See also Hace Sorel Tishler, *Self-Reliance and Social Security* (Port Washington: Kennikat Press, 1971).

15. Clara Cahill Park, letter, *Survey* 30 (Apr. 12, 1913): 74. Articles on women's economic dependence include Margaret Hamilton Welch, "The Wife's Share of the Income," *Harper's Bazar* 34 (Apr. 1901): 922–23; "The Wife and her Money," *Ladies' Home Journal* 18 (Mar. 1901): 16; "Shall Wives Earn Money?" *Woman's Home Companion* 32 (Apr. 1905): 32.

16. William Hard, "With All My Worldly Goods I Thee Endow," *Delineator* 78 (Oct. 1911): 323; idem, "When the Law Calls the Children 'His' and Not 'Hers,'" *Delineator* 79 (Feb. 1912): 99–100; "Own Your Own Child," *Woman Citizen* (Dec. 27, 1919): 633. On maternal custody rights in this period, see Michael Grossberg, "Who Gets the Child? Custody, Guardianship, and the Rise of a Judicial Patriarchy in Nineteenth-Century America," *Feminist Studies* 9 (Summer 1983): 235–56; idem, *Governing the Hearth: Law and the Family in Nineteenth-Century America* (Chapel Hill: University of North Carolina Press), chap. 7; Susan B. Anthony and Ida Husted Harper, *The History of Woman Suffrage* (Rochester, N.Y.: Susan B. Anthony, 1902), 4:603; Catherine Waugh McCulloch, "Guardianship of Children," *Chicago Legal News,* Jan. 13, 1912, clipping in Woman's Rights Collection 645, Arthur and Elizabeth Schlesinger Library on the History of Women in America, Radcliffe College, Cambridge, Mass.

17. Mrs. G. Harris Robertson, "The State's Duty to Fatherless Children," *Child-Welfare Magazine* 6 (Jan. 1912): 157–58.

18. Clara Cahill Park, letter, *Survey* 30 (Aug. 16, 1913): 669; Beard, *Woman's Work*, 252–53.

19. Robertson, "State's Duty to Fatherless Children," 158–59.

20. Schoff, *The Wayward Child*, 82; Alice Stone Blackwell, letter, *New York Times*, May 18, 1913; "Widows' Pensions and Votes," *Woman's Journal* 45 (May 24, 1913): 164. Barbara J. Nelson found that in some states, where aid to mothers was not distinguished from poor laws, mothers' pensions may have actually disenfranchised recipients. "Mothers' Aid, Pauper Laws, and Woman Suffrage: The Intersection of the Welfare State and Democratic Participation, 1913–1935" (Paper in author's possession).

21. Lavinia Dock, "Concerning Equal Rights," *Equal Rights* 12 (June 20, 1925); Emma Wold, "Mothers Pension Bills in Congress," *Equal Rights* 12 (Jan. 16, 1926). See Wendy Sarvasy, "Beyond the Difference Versus Equality Policy Debate: Post-Suffrage Feminism, Citizenship, and the Quest for a Feminist Welfare State," *Signs* 17 (Winter 1992): 329–62.

22. Benita Locke, "Mothers Pensions: The Latest Capitalist Trap," *Woman Rebel* (Mar. 1914): 4; Charlotte Perkins Gilman, "Pensions for 'Mothers' and 'Widows,' " *The Forerunner* 5 (Jan. 1914): 7–8. See Gilman's "Paid Motherhood," *Independent* 61 (Jan. 1907): 75–78, for her objection to motherhood endowment.

23. A similar interpretation of the debate over mothers' pensions can be found in Linda Gordon, "Single Mothers and Child Neglect, 1880–1920," *American Quarterly* 37 (Summer 1985): 173–92; idem, "What Does Welfare Regulate?" *Social Research* 55 (Winter 1988): 609–30.

24. "Both Sides: A Debate," *Independent* 80 (Nov. 9, 1914): 206; Hobhouse quoted in William Hard, "The Needy Mother and the Neglected Child," *Outlook* 104 (June 1917): 280–83; William Hard, "The Moral Necessity of 'State Funds to Mothers,' " in Bullock, ed., *Selected Articles on Mothers' Pensions*, 108; Inez Milholland, Speech on Mothers' Pensions, typescript, Inez Milholland Papers, Schlesinger Library. I am grateful to Nancy Cott for this reference.

25. "Helen Todd Says Support Mothers," *Woman's Journal* (Jan. 9, 1914): 14; Milholland, Speech on Mothers' Pensions. See also Ben B. Lindsey, "The Mothers' Compensation Law of Colorado," *Survey* 29 (Feb. 15, 1913): 714–16.

26. Hard, "Moral Necessity of 'State Funds to Mothers,' " idem, "Financing Motherhood," *Delineator* 82 (Apr. 1913): 263; Katharine Anthony, "The Family," in *Civilization in the United States*, ed. Harold E. Stearns (New York: Harcourt, Brace & Co., 1922), 329.

27. See, for example, Sophonisba P. Breckinridge, "Neglected Widowhood in the Juvenile Court," *American Journal of Sociology* (July 1910).

28. Quoted from Mary E. Richmond, "Motherhood and Pensions," in Bullock, ed., *Selected Articles on Mothers' Pensions*, 64; Ben B. Lindsey, "The Parenthood of the State," *Child-Welfare Magazine* 15 (Aug. 1921): 251.

29. C. C. Carstens, "Public Pensions to Widows with Children," in Bullock, ed., *Selected Articles on Mothers' Pensions*, 169; Edward Devine, "Pensions for

Mothers," in Bullock, ed., *Selected Articles on Mothers' Pensions,* 177, 179; Barnard quoted in Lubove, *Struggle for Social Security,* 103.

30. Edward Devine, "Pensions for Mothers," in Bullock, ed., *Selected Articles on Mothers' Pensions,* 177, 179; Richmond, "Motherhood and Pensions," 62; idem, "'Pensions' and the Social Worker," *Survey* 29 (Feb. 15, 1913): 665.

31. Hard, "The Moral Necessity;" idem, "Pensions for Mothers," in Bullock, ed., *Selected Articles on Mothers' Pensions,* 187.

32. For example, Lubove, *Struggle for Social Security,* 101.

33. State of New York, *Report of the New York State Commission on Relief for Widowed Mothers, Transmitted to the Legislature March 27, 1914* (Albany, 1914), 20, 126, 21.

34. Children's Bureau, *Laws Relating to 'Mothers' Pensions,'* 8; Ada Eliot Sheffield, "Administration of the Mothers' Aid Law in Massachusetts," in Bullock, ed., *Selected Articles on Mothers' Pensions,* 73.

35. Ada J. Davis, "The Evolution of the Institution of Mothers' Pensions in the United States," *American Journal of Sociology* 35 (Jan. 1930): 573–87; "Mothers' Pensions: Graft, Charity, or Justice?" *Outlook* 112 (Mar. 1, 1916): 489; Lundberg, "Aid to Mothers with Dependent Children," 99–100. On differences between urban and rural areas, see the following Children's Bureau publications: *Administration of Mothers' Aid in 10 Localities with Special Reference to Health, Housing, and Recreation* (1928); *Public Child-Caring Work in Certain Counties of Minnesota, North Carolina and New York* (1927), and *Standards of Public Aid to Children in Their Own Homes* (1923).

36. San Francisco Widows' Pension Bureau, *Annual Report* (1914); Lundberg, "Aid to Mothers with Dependent Children," 99.

37. Winifred Bell, *Aid to Dependent Children* (New York: Columbia University Press, 1965), 9–10; Children's Bureau, *Mothers' Aid, 1931,* 13. For an excellent discussion of the exclusion of African Americans from mothers' pension rolls in Chicago, see Joanne Goodwin, "The Differential Treatment of Motherhood: Mothers' Pensions, Chicago 1900–1930" (Paper Presented at the Mini-Conference on Gender and Social Policy Held in Conjunction with the Social Science History Association, Minneapolis, Minn., Oct. 1990).

38. Children's Bureau, *Proceedings of Conference on Mothers' Pensions,* 4–7.

39. San Francisco Widows' Pension Bureau, *Annual Report* (1915), 11; U.S. Bureau of the Census, *Thirteenth Census of the United States Taken in the Year 1910* (Washington, D.C.: Government Printing Office, 1913), 2:186; T. J. Edmonds and Maurice Hexter, "State Pensions to Mothers in Hamilton County," *Survey* 33 (Dec. 12, 1914): 289.

40. U.S. Children's Bureau, *The Administration of the Aid-to-Mothers' Law in Illinois,* Publication No. 82 (Washington, D.C.: Government Printing Office, 1921), 84; *Thirteenth Census,* 2:512. Comparison is difficult because the Children's Bureau study of mothers' pensions did not clearly differentiate between first-generation immigrants and members of ethnic groups born in Chicago. Joanne Goodwin notes that the underrepresentation of African Americans in the pension program is particularly striking when their higher rate of female-headed families is taken into account. "Differential Treatment," 27.

41. U.S. Children's Bureau, *Standards of Public Aid to Children in Their Own Homes,* Publication No. 118 (Washington, D.C.: Government Printing Office, 1923), 18–20. The study covered Boston; Denver; St. Louis; Haverhill, Mass.; Hennepin County, Minn.; Westchester and Montgomery Counties, N.Y.; Northampton County, Pa.; and Yellow Medicine County, Minn.

42. Goodwin, "Differential Treatment," 16; Pennsylvania State Board of Education, *1920 Report of the Mothers' Assistance Fund to the General Assembly of Pennsylvania* (Harrisburg, 1922), 4; Children's Bureau, *Standards of Public Aid,* 19.

43. San Francisco Widow's Pension Bureau, *Report of the Widows' Pension Bureau of San Francisco* (1916), 4; "Third Year of Mothers' Aid in Maine," *Survey* 43 (Feb. 28, 1920).

44. Children's Bureau, *Administration of the Aid-to-Mothers' Law in Illinois,* 12–16, 81.

45. Ibid., 26–27.

46. Sophonisba P. Breckinridge, *Family Welfare Work in a Metropolitan Community. Selected Case Records* (Chicago: University of Chicago Press, 1924). These cases are no doubt representative of the more "successful" mothers' pension cases as they are included in a text of a leading (though not uncritical) proponent of modern social work. Although they must be read critically, they nonetheless offer a better understanding of the impact of the mothers' pension program on individual women than most other published sources. See also "Source Materials: Two Mothers' Pension Investigations," *Social Service Review* 2 (Mar. 1928): 82–115, and "Source Materials: A Foreign-Born Applicant for Mothers' Aid, Mrs. Anna Novak," *Social Service Review* 3 (Dec. 1929): 632–68.

47. The Legaikas case covers pages 462–96. Quotations on p. 462.

48. Ibid., 475, 476, 483. The records do not state whether these reports are from the same social worker, but it is probable that they are.

49. Ibid., 477–78.

50. Ibid., 486.

51. Ibid., 490–91.

52. During the interval the Family Welfare Agency assumed responsibility for her care. Ibid., 490, 496. According to Breckinridge, the practice of staying pensions in situations similar to that of Mrs. Legaikas was soon abandoned in the absence of "gross negligence or of other evidence of unfitness."

53. The Meyer case covers pp. 505–17.

54. Ibid., 508.

55. Ibid., 511, 509.

56. Ibid., 517.

57. Ibid., 633.

58. "Source Materials: A Foreign-Born Applicant for Mothers' Aid, Mrs. Anna Novak," 633, 652–53, 655–56.

59. Helen Tyson, "Foreword," to Gwendolyn Hughes, *Mothers in Industry* (New York: New Republic, 1925); I. M. Rubinow, "Should Mothers' Assistance

Be Supplemented?" *Survey* 52 (May 15, 1924): 234; Children's Bureau, *Administration of the Aid-to-Mothers Law in Illinois,* 109–10, 133.

60. In a well-publicized case in Ohio, a deserted mother named Mary Strazisar killed herself and her seven children because she could not support her children and was afraid that they would be sent to the County Home. See the correspondence between Julia Lathrop and the Children's Welfare Department of the Ohio Board of State Charities on the subject, especially C. V. Williams to Julia Lathrop, August 26, 1919, File 13–11, Children's Bureau Records, Central Files, 1914–40, Record Group 102, National Archives, Washington, D.C. (hereafter cited as CB).

61. Children's Bureau, *Administration of the Aid-to-Mothers Law in Illinois,* 67; Mrs. A. P, California, May 8, 1927, to Department of Public Welfare, File 10–12–2–5 (6), CB.

62. Mrs. L. M., Texas, October 18, 1917 to Secretary of the Treasury; and Mrs. L. M., Pennsylvania, to Children's Bureau, November 2, 1917, File 9–4–4–1, CB. The letter from the Pennsylvania woman is reprinted in Molly Ladd-Taylor, *Raising a Baby the Government Way: Mothers' Letters to the Children's Bureau, 1915–1932* (New Brunswick, N.J.: Rutgers University Press, 1986), 159.

63. Mrs. V. A., Texas, to Child Welfare Bureau, April 12, 1928, File 10–12–2–5 (47), CB.

64. Mrs. M. S., Minnesota, to Children's Bureau, May 16, 1927, and August 20, 1927, File 10–12–2–5 (25), CB.

65. Mrs. M. S., Minnesota, May 16, 1927 to Children's Bureau, File 10–12–2–5 (25), CB.

66. Grace Guilford to Mrs. M. S., August 15, 1927, and Agnes Hanna to Mrs. M. S., August 24, 1927, File 10–12–2–5 (25), CB.

67. Emma O. Lundberg, "Progress of Mothers' Aid Administration," *Social Service Review* 2 (Sept. 1928): 438, as quoted in Skocpol, *Protecting Soldiers and Mothers,* chap. 9; Mary Bogue, "Ten Years of Mothers' Pensions," *Survey* 49 (Feb. 15, 1923): 634–36.

68. U.S. Children's Bureau, *Administration of Mothers' Aid in Ten Localities with Special Reference to Health, Housing, Education and Recreation,* Publication No. 184 (Washington, D.C.: Government Printing Office, 1928), 5; idem, *Laws Relating to Mothers' Pensions in the United States* (Washington, D.C.: Government Printing Office, 1924), III.

69. There were some exceptions, of course. See Sarvasy, "Beyond the Equality Versus Difference Debate."

6

"We Mothers Are So Glad the Day Has Come": Mothers' Work and the Sheppard-Towner Act

"Of all the activities in which I have shared during more than forty years of striving," reflected Florence Kelley in 1926, "none is, I am convinced, of such fundamental importance as the Sheppard-Towner Act."[1] The Maternity and Infancy Protection Act was the first federally funded social welfare measure and the first "women's" legislation to pass after the suffrage amendment. Its enactment in 1921 marked the climax of the maternalist campaign to create and control a welfare system that protected the health of mothers and children. Its repeal less than eight years later brought women's efforts to secure federal responsibility for child welfare to a discouraging end.

Designed by Children's Bureau chief Julia Lathrop, the Sheppard-Towner Act exemplifed the political philosophy and program of maternalism. Maternalists' high regard for mothers' work and service to the state was evident in their call for the government protection of motherhood; their belief that women had a special sensitivity to child welfare was manifest in their insistence that Sheppard-Towner health programs be run by women. The maternalist commitment to all children's welfare motivated Sheppard-Towner workers to extend the principles of scientific childrearing into every community and racial ethnic group, while the maternalist adherence to the family wage system was reflected in the bill's concern for women only in their maternal role. Sheppard-Towner was intended to protect the health of women and children within the family; it did not challenge married women's economic dependence on men or try to empower mothers in other social roles.

Still, the Maternity and Infancy Act was unique among maternalist reforms. For one thing, unlike mothers' pensions and protective labor legislation, Sheppard-Towner educational programs were conceived as a protection for all mothers, and not just the poor. For another, Sheppard-Towner grew out of an unusually broad alliance that included working-class and farm mothers who wanted information and material assistance with child-rearing, as well as middle-class maternalists and reformers. As we saw in chapter three, Children's Bureau chief Julia Lathrop learned from her correspondence and personal contacts with poor women how "very urgent the great question of protecting motherhood" was, and she designed the Maternity and Infancy Act with their needs and requests in mind.[2] Grassroots mothers thus played an important if indirect role in the creation of the Sheppard-Towner Act.

The maternity bill also differed from other maternalist reforms in that some of the women who campaigned for it became "clients" of Sheppard-Towner programs.[3] Although the bill was intended primarily for those who did not have access to private physicians, Sheppard-Towner "clients" included middle-class women who read *Infant Care* and attended lectures on child health, as well as impoverished women who attended free clinics or were visited by public health nurses at home. Women in both groups campaigned for the bill. Poor and middle-class mothers alike wrote letters to the government, and many also joined committees to secure the bill's passage. (Feminists, who by 1921 had already turned their attention toward equal rights, were virtually absent in the campaign for Sheppard-Towner, although most gave it lukewarm support.) Furthermore, in striking contrast to mothers' pensions, thousands of women activists worked with the federal Children's Bureau to administer the bill. The implementation of the Sheppard-Towner Act depended as much on the voluntary activities of individual and organized women as on the work of professionals.[4]

More than any other maternalist reform, the campaign for maternal and child health care reveals the intersection of women's private and public mother-work. The Maternity and Infancy Act grew out of women's personal concerns about their children's health and fears that they or their children would die. The campaign to secure the bill's passage brought these "private" concerns about infant and prenatal care into the world of politics. In turn, as we shall see, Sheppard-Towner programs altered many women's personal experience of mothering by improving and medicalizing health services, accelerating the decline of traditional beliefs about infant death and maternal suffering, and raising women's expectations for care.[5]

Although its passage was a major victory, the Sheppard-Towner Act was a compromise measure that was far from achieving all of the maternalists' goals. The final version of the bill, sponsored by Texas Senator Morris Sheppard and Iowa Congressman Horace Towner, provided federal matching grants to the states for information and instruction on nutrition and hygiene, prenatal and child health clinics, and visiting nurses for pregnant women and new mothers. It furnished no financial aid or medical care, and limited appropriations to a period of five years. Yet despite its narrow provisions, Sheppard-Towner was vigorously opposed by a coalition of medical associations and right-wing organizations who claimed it was a Communist-inspired step toward state medicine that threatened the home and violated the principle of states' rights. By 1926, when Sheppard-Towner funding was to be renewed, the bill's opponents had gained so much strength that they succeeded in forcing the bill's supporters to accept a compromise that extended funding for two more years, but repealed the law itself in 1929, thereby ensuring that all federal appropriations for maternal and infant care would cease.[6]

Given the modesty of the Maternity and Infancy Act, the intensity of emotions it raised (both pro and con) requires some explanation. How could the bill's supporters win an easy victory in 1921, but go down to a humiliating defeat just a few years later? Scholars have provided two main explanations for the bill's enactment and defeat. The first focuses on the political, noting that Sheppard-Towner was enacted when the maternalist lobby was at its strongest — paradoxically, because of women's exclusion from voting — and that it was defeated after it became clear that women did not vote as a bloc. The second ties the bill's defeat to the triumph of the male medical establishment over the public health vision of female professionals and reformers.[7] Although both explanations contain valuable insights, they can be enriched — not supplanted — by looking at Sheppard-Towner from another angle: the backlash to the Sheppard-Towner Act was also a reaction to politicized motherhood.

The 1920s was a decade of fiscal conservatism and a backlash to feminism and progressive reform. Partly because activist women played such a large role in creating the U.S. welfare system, right-wing opposition to social welfare programs was tied to antifeminist hostility to changing gender roles and to women's visibility in public life. We have examined the right-wing attacks on reformers at the Children's Bureau and within the PTA, and we have noted the denigration of motherhood in the popular culture of the decade. In this environment, the adamantly political objective of the Sheppard-Towner Act — to educate women with an eye toward mobilizing them to demand more extensive welfare services — could hardly be more controversial. Indeed, the highly politicized character of the Sheppard-Towner Act, evident in its unusual reliance on volunteer labor and its (for the government) relatively democratic administration, may be one reason that the maternity bill — in contrast to the mothers' aid bureaucracy — did not survive the decade.

The Campaign for the Maternity Bill

Most women's organizations made the passage of the Sheppard-Towner Act a top priority. The newly created Women's Joint Congressional Committee, a coalition formed to coordinate the national lobbying activities of women's organizations, voted unanimously to make the maternity bill its top priority and appointed the indomitable Florence Kelley to head up its campaign. The National Congress of Mothers and Parent-Teacher Associations, the League of Women Voters, the General Federation of Women's Clubs, the Women's Trade Union League, the National Consumers' League, the National Council of Jewish Women, the National Association of Colored Women, the Woman's Christian Temperance Union, the Daughters of the American Revolution, and the Business and Professional Women's Clubs were among the groups supporting the bill. Indeed, so many women sent their congressmen petitions and letters urging passage of the Sheppard-Towner bill that one senator's assistant remarked, "I think every woman in my state has written to the Senator." According to Grace Abbott, who replaced Lathrop as Children's Bureau chief in 1921, the Sheppard-Towner Act "was demanded by literally millions of mothers in the country."[8]

Support for the Sheppard-Towner bill, as for mothers' pensions, was not limited to women's organizations. Magazines such as *Good Housekeeping, The Ladies' Home Journal, Woman's Home Companion,* and *McCall's* urged women to write their congressmen and provided petitions for them to circulate and sign. The American Federation of Labor testified in favor of the bill in congressional hearings, and the Democratic, Socialist, and Farmer-Labor parties included it in their platforms. Republican presidential candidate Warren G. Harding endorsed the bill. Also, in spite of the opposition of the American Medical Association (AMA), the American Child Health Association (formerly the American Association for the Prevention of Infant Mortality), the Medical Women's National Association, the National Organization of Public Health Nurses, and the AMA section on pediatrics joined the drive for Sheppard-Towner.[9]

While flowery and sentimental language characterized the most eloquent statements in favor of mothers' pensions, Sheppard-Towner supporters defended the maternity bill in the progressive reform vocabulary of efficiency, scientific progress, and justice. Julia Lathrop insisted that modern science had established health care as a "minimum standard" for child welfare, to be "provided as the public schools are provided, to be used by all with dignity and self-respect." Florence Kelley contended that the large number of preventable deaths betrayed the low value society placed on women's and children's lives. In eloquent testimony in congressional hearings, she declared that women deeply resented the fact that Congressmen legislated salary and pension increases for postal employees and veterans, but claimed that the government could not afford to provide health care for women and children. "No woman in the United States would begrudge those increases of salaries," she said angrily, "but when we are told that this country is so poor and this Congress so harassed by things of greater importance than the deaths of a quarter of a million of children a year . . . we say to ourselves, 'Surely we are not to take this seriously? . . . Why does Congress wish women and children to die?' "[10]

Like the earlier debate over mothers' pensions, the battle over Sheppard-Towner turned on sharp differences over the state's obligation for child welfare and the politicization of motherhood. However, because the Sheppard-Towner debate took place in the midst of the anticommunist hysteria of the 1920s, disagreements over state responsibility for child welfare were muddied by accusations of bolshevism and feminism. Moreover, while the influence of private charities was evident in the discussion of mothers' aid, the tone of the Sheppard-Towner debate was set by the powerful American Medical Association, which combined an attack on "state medicine" with hostility to the "lay" women in the Children's Bureau. The fight over the maternity bill occurred after progressive maternalists had achieved considerable success at establishing a women-controlled welfare system, and thus Sheppard-Towner opponents made a direct and powerful challenge to women's authority over child welfare.

Right-wing associations and medical societies objected to the proposed Maternity Act on three counts: it made a political issue of women's and children's health; it expanded the social welfare function of the state; and it increased professional women's authority over public health and welfare programs. Like opponents of mothers' pensions, the foes of the Sheppard-Towner Act portrayed it as an invasion of privacy that would replace the authority of the father with that of the state. "It is an invasion of the castle of the American citizen," warned a former antisuffragist. "This idea is to take care of all alike, or, in other words, to substitute the State for the father," deplored the editor of the right-wing *Woman Patriot*. If maternal mortality was to be stopped, declared Elizabeth Lowell Putnam, a conservative clubwoman who pioneered the development of private-sector prenatal services but was a vigorous opponent of the Sheppard-Towner Act, "the husbands and fathers of the country must see that this is done, and it is their duty to their wives to take hold of the situation and to demand proper care for them." Women should not demand care for themselves.[11]

Like the charity workers who lobbied against state mothers' pensions, foes of the Sheppard-Towner Act feared that government aid would undermine individual men's responsibility for their families. The maternity bill might save a few lives, they conceded, but it would do more harm than good by "discouraging private initiative, responsibility, and thrift." State responsibility for social welfare "tends to pauperize the people," insisted a right-wing opponent of the bill; "it tends to make the mothers believe that Uncle Sam instead of their own husbands, ought to take care of them." A conservative Congressman warned, "When the Government itself goes beyond instructing and enters into the business of taking care of the individuals constituting American citizenship, it has made a leap into the arena of paternalism from which it can never escape."[12]

Right-wingers considered communism and politicized motherhood two sides of the same coin, and they objected to both in the Sheppard-Towner Act. The family was "the very foundation of our national life," declared the president of the Massachusetts Anti-Suffrage Association; "those who would overturn present Governments consider it the first point of attack. Abolish the family and the whole structure must fall." Insisting that Sheppard-Towner was a step to motherhood endowment and birth control, superpatriots quoted statements advocating motherhood endowment by feminists Helen Todd and Harriot Stanton Blatch to discredit the bill. A reference in a Children's Bureau publication on maternity benefits to a study by Soviet feminist Alexandra Kollontai was widely cited as an example of the Bureau's ties to Bolshevik leaders.[13] "No one in this House can deny that those who have propagated this maternity bill really advocate the maintenance of indigent, pregnant women, both before, during, and after labor; child control by the State; mothers' pensions; the doctrine of eugenics; birth control; and other notions of the sort born out of purely socialistic brains," one Congressman warned.[14]

Right-wing patriots attacked the main proponents of the Maternity Act as feminists, communists, and unwomanly spinsters incapable of caring for children. One opponent of the bill objected that Julia Lathrop was "one of the Hull House crowd," while another accused her of endorsing the "feminist ideals of the unspeakable Madam Kollontai."[15] The caustic remarks of Missouri Senator James Reed, a leading critic of the bill, illustrate right-wingers' hostility to women in public life: "It is now proposed to turn the control of the mothers of the land over to a few single ladies holding Government jobs at Washington. I question whether one out of ten of these delightful reformers could make a bowl of buttermilk gruel that would not give a baby the colic in five minutes. [Laughter.] We would better reverse the proposition and provide for a committee of mothers to take charge of the old maids and teach them how to acquire a husband and have babies of their own. [Laughter.]"[16]

Significantly, the earliest statements of medical opposition to Sheppard-Towner played as much on popular fears of feminism and communism as on the issue of medical expertise. Dominated by male specialists engaged in private practice, the AMA objected to public health programs — especially when provided by women — as a threat to male doctors' incomes and control over the health care system. The AMA campaign against Sheppard-Towner began in February 1921 with an editorial in the *Journal of the American Medical Association,* and it grew stronger and more effective over the course of the decade.[17]

Doctors also questioned the ability of the "lay" women on the Children's Bureau staff to administer maternity and infancy programs. Overlooking the fact that a female physician headed the Maternity and Infancy Division of the Children's Bureau, medical leaders argued that, if passed, the maternity bill should be administered by the (male) doctors in the Public Health Service, rather than by the (female) social workers at the Bureau. Conservative health reformer Elizabeth Lowell Putnam, a close ally of the medical establishment and an energetic foe of the Children's Bureau staff, explained this position: "Everyone of knowledge and wisdom when confronted with a case of childbirth in their own family would call in a skilled obstetrician and not a social worker for the management of the case."[18] Interestingly, the question of Sheppard-Towner administration also divided the Children's Bureau from sentimental maternalists, who had more traditional ideas about gender roles and accorded male experts greater authority over the science of child study. Yet although National Congress of Mothers president Hannah Schoff believed that Sheppard-Towner should be administered by the Public Health Service, she agreed to actively support the bill wherever its administration was placed.[19]

The Children's Bureau focus on the social and economic dimensions of infant mortality incensed doctors and right-wingers alike. Elizabeth Lowell Putnam, who headed up an innovative experiment in prenatal care under the auspices of the Boston Women's Municipal League between 1909 and 1914, insisted that infant mortality was "a medical question, pure and simple;" the best way to reduce maternal and infant death was to require better medical school training in obstetrics. In keeping with the denigration of maternal skills by childrearing experts of the 1920s, Sheppard-Towner opponents asserted that mothers were capable of being educated only to the extent of finding good medical care and "of cooperating with it by carrying out the doctor's orders." The only purpose of health education was to convince women of the "enormous benefit of proper medical care," Putnam remarked, for the mother "cannot possibly be educated to take care of herself to any further extent than this."[20]

Putnam's conception of women's intelligence presents a striking contrast to that of the bill's supporters, who insisted that women had a right to know what to expect during pregnancy and childbirth. Women activists who were pro Sheppard-Towner believed that educating women about infant and prenatal care would remove the mystique surrounding reproduction and give them more control of their health during pregnancy and childbirth. "One of the opinions I have always fought is that a woman is too delicate or too sensitive to know about her chief function — child bearing — and her chief contribution to civilization — the bearing and rearing of children," Bureau physician Dorothy Reed Mendenhall remarked. Maternalists and grassroots mothers, living at a time when many women were not taught vital information about reproduction, supported Sheppard-Towner for the same reason some doctors resisted it: it promised them more knowledge about reproduction and their bodies.[21]

In spite of its vigorous campaign against the bill, the anti–Sheppard-Towner coalition made little headway in 1921. Congress passed the Maternity and Infancy Act by a wide margin — 63-7 in the Senate and 279-39 in the House of Representatives — and President Warren G. Harding signed it into law on November 23, 1921. Congressmen may have been afraid of provoking the wrath of newly enfranchised women voters or the powerful maternalist lobby, or they may have heeded women's requests for the "protection of maternity and infancy" out of chivalry and sentimentalism. In any case, most observers agreed that congressional support for the bill was soft. "On a secret ballot I don't think it would have got 50 votes," observed Alice Robertson, the only woman in Congress and a staunch opponent of the bill. "Nineteen men who voted for it — so one of them told me — were cursing it and themselves at once in the cloak room."[22]

Although unable to prevent passage of the bill, Sheppard-Towner opponents did manage to effect compromise. Even though the bill originally designed by Lathrop provided medical and nursing care in addition to instructional programs, the final bill was purely educational. Moreover, the Children's Bureau chief took pains to disassociate herself from socialism and to reaffirm her commitment to the family wage when she testified in congressional hearings on the bill. Admitting that cash maternity benefits might be necessary for poor families in Europe, Lathrop said that the preferred solution in the U.S. was to increase men's wages so that they could support their wives and children. "If the country has that it will not have to endow motherhood," she explained.[23]

Children's Bureau officials went to great lengths to quell the medical opposition to the bill. In an attempt to placate doctors worried that Sheppard-Towner would lead to state medicine, they carefully distinguished between publicly funded health education and private medical care. Sheppard-Towner clinics would only advise parents on the care of healthy children, they contended; doctors still cured the sick. "We are not giving medicines"; Josephine Baker testified during Congressional hearings, "we are not treating sick people; we do nothing of that kind. We simply teach people how to keep well and readjust as far as we are able the bad effects of wrong environment. . . . Infant mortality is very largely a social problem and an economic problem." The Bureau maintained (correctly, as it turned out) that prenatal and child health clinics would increase doctors' patients, not compete for them. "Your private practice should immediately reflect its [Sheppard-Towner's] work, which is to discover remediable conditions and stir up parents to visit their doctors for the necessary treatment and supervision," read a letter distributed to physicians by Sheppard-Towner administrators in Pennsylvania.[24]

As a result of the need for compromise, the final version of the Sheppard-Towner Act was considerably weaker than the initial bill introduced in 1918 by Representative Jeannette Rankin and Senator Joseph Robinson. The Rankin-Robinson bill provided "medical and nursing care at home or at a hospital when necessary," as well as instruction in hygiene, and it specifically targeted rural areas, where mortality was thought highest. By contrast, Sheppard-Towner furnished no hospital or medical care, reduced the Children's Bureau's authority over administration, and sharply cut appropriations. Although the original Sheppard-Towner bill requested an appropriation of 4 million dollars, the version that passed allocated only 1.48 million for fiscal year 1921–22 and 1.24 million for the next five years. No more than fifty thousand dollars was given to the U.S. Children's Bureau for administrative expenses. Five thousand dollars went to each state outright and an additional five thousand to states that provided matching funds. Furthermore, funds were only appropriated for five years, requiring the bill to be approved again in 1927.[25]

The administrative structure of the Sheppard-Towner Act was another compromise. Unlike the Rankin-Robinson bill, which invested administrative authority in the Children's Bureau, Sheppard-Towner kept responsibility for the bill's daily administration with the Children's Bureau, but transferred ultimate authority to a newly created Federal Board of Maternity and Infant Hygiene, composed of the Surgeon General of the Public Health Service, the U.S. Commissioner of Education, and the Children's Bureau chief. It gave states wide discretion in the development of maternity and infancy programs and required each state to pass special enabling legislation and provide a plan for implementing the program before it could receive funds. The bill also prohibited government agents from entering any home or taking charge of any child over the objection of either parent. Finally, in reaction to feminist advocates of motherhood endowment, it explicitly prohibited using Sheppard-Towner funds "for the payment of any maternity or infancy pension, stipend, or gratuity."[26]

As a purely educational program, Sheppard-Towner was both less subversive and less coercive than mothers' pensions. Although a bill that did not provide medical treatment or financial aid could not entirely protect infant health or increase mothers' autonomy, Children's Bureau officials knew from experience that a mandate limited to education could be turned to advantage. For one thing, public education — in contrast to material assistance or medical care — had already been established as a right available without loss of dignity or self-respect to people of all classes. For another, although government-sponsored instruction could be intrusive, Sheppard-Towner educational programs were not compulsory, at least not for mothers. While recipients of mothers' pensions risked losing income if they did not follow the childrearing or housekeeping suggestions of their social workers, Sheppard-Towner clients were generally free to accept or ignore the experts' advice. Furthermore, Sheppard-Towner agents in the field frequently did perform preventive health examinations, assist women during childbirth, and work with the Red Cross and local women's groups to provide much-needed clothing and furniture to impoverished families. In the actual implementation of the bill, the line between health education, nursing care, and even material assistance was often blurred.

Most maternalists were thrilled with the passage of even a moderate Sheppard-Towner Act. However, some feminists thought the compromise had been too great. Writing in the National Woman's Party journal *Equal Rights*, Madeleine Doty judged the bill's passage to be "in reality a defeat." In her view, women had been duped but were "too dazed and weary to protest" a compromise bill that reduced appropriations and gave mothers only instruction, and no real help, with child care. "If a woman hadn't money, she must die without aid, clutching the *knowledge* of what ought to have been done and hadn't, to save her and the child," she wrote. Another writer argued that the initial bill would do little in the way of dignifying motherhood: "Requests for grants of money to teach rules which the mother had no money to carry out are futile. Much more than that will have to be gained before the mother takes her place beside her self-supporting sister, a complete and self-respecting personality."[27] Unlike mothers' pensions, which some feminists saw as a step toward women's independence, the educational programs of the Sheppard-Towner Act did not challenge women's dependent position in the family.

Still, most mothers appear to have welcomed the bill. Those who lacked vital information about reproduction and their bodies, who had suffered a difficult pregnancy or birth, or who had lost a child, were desperate for any information that could give them more control over their health. Some women wrote the Children's Bureau to express their appreciation of its work and to find out how the bill might benefit them. "I do hope it will help us Poor Country people who need help," a Texas mother wrote. "I am

27 yrs. old and have Five little one's to Care for besides my husban[d] and his Father."[28]

The Administration of Sheppard-Towner

Most states responded quickly and enthusiastically to the Sheppard-Towner Act. Forty-one passed enabling legislation in 1922, and eventually only three states (Massachusetts, Connecticut, and Illinois) refused to do so. Almost every state used Sheppard-Towner funds to hold health conferences, make home visits, promote birth registration, and distribute literature, especially the Children's Bureau pamphlets *Infant Care* and *Prenatal Care*. A number of states also ran mobile health clinics (called "child-welfare specials"), organized training programs for midwives, immunized children against diptheria and smallpox, and encouraged the use of silver nitrate to prevent blindness in infants. Some used Sheppard-Towner funds to do research into maternal and infant mortality or to investigate local hospitals, maternity homes, and day nurseries. By 1929, the bill's last year of operation, the Children's Bureau estimated that Sheppard-Towner workers held 183,252 prenatal and child health conferences and helped establish 2,978 permanent health clinics. Public health nurses visited 3,131,996 homes between 1923 and 1929 and distributed 22,030,489 pieces of literature in the last five years of the act. According to the Bureau, Sheppard-Towner reached more than 4,000,000 babies and 700,000 expectant mothers in its last four years alone.[29]

Most female supporters of the Sheppard-Towner Act assumed that women would staff the new maternity and infancy programs, both because of their special maternal sensibility, and because of their expertise and leadership role in child welfare reform. Indeed, Sheppard-Towner did significantly increase employment opportunities for female physicians and nurses. The staff of the federal Bureau stayed small; only nine women — three physicians, three nurses, and three clerks — worked in its Maternity and Infancy Division in 1926. However, most of the state agencies charged with the administration of the act were headed and staffed by women. According to historian Robyn Muncy, women comprised almost half of the Sheppard-Towner doctors working full-time in the states (at a time when only 5 percent of all doctors were women) and at least 75 percent of the state directors of maternity and infancy programs. Most of the new employment opportunities fell to public health nurses, however. In 1929, 900 nurses, probably all women, were paid out of Sheppard-Towner funds. Nurses also headed child health agencies in ten states.[30]

In contrast to mothers' pensions, which provided job opportunities for female professionals but had no place for volunteers, the implementation as well as passage of the Maternity and Infancy Act depended on the unpaid services of women activists. Even after the enactment of the federal bill, supporters had to lobby state legislatures to pass enabling legislation, appropriate funds, and (in some states) make sure the bill did not get diluted or repealed. The Children's Bureau also depended on volunteers to conduct prenatal and child health conferences, publicize Sheppard-Towner programs, and research local health conditions. In 1929 the Bureau reported at least 7,339 volunteer workers in the twenty states and Territory of Hawaii that kept records. Of these, 700 were nurses, 1,614 were physicians, and 4,683 were "lay persons." The PTA gave assistance to Sheppard-Towner administrators in 42 states, the Federation of Women's Clubs in 30 states, and the American Red Cross and League of Women Voters helped with maternity and infancy work in 18 states each. (By contrast, state medical associations cooperated with Sheppard-Towner in just 14 states.) Clearly, the fate of the Maternity and Infancy Act was tied to that of the women's movement.[31]

Like mothers' aid, the Sheppard-Towner Act was marked by local variation in funding and support. The bill's decentralized administration had the advantage of allowing communities to devise programs that suited their needs, but it also made maternity work vulnerable to political opposition and incompetent administration. This meant that Sheppard-Towner work varied with state and local politics, the personnel in the state bureaus of child health, the attitudes of local physicians and civic leaders, and climate and geography (such as snow, mountains, floods, and poor roads). Consequently, while the Maternity and Infancy Act had a tremendous impact in states where child health was politicized and the Children's Bureau worked effectively with activist women and physicians, it had little impact in others.

Where the Sheppard-Towner Act was most successful, states used federal funds both to teach individual mothers about nutrition and hygiene and to build a political campaign for maternal and child welfare. Take the example of literature distribution. Women often shared Children's Bureau publications on childrearing and prenatal care with friends and relatives, passing on much-needed information and creating a wider demand for health care. After the Oklahoma Bureau of Maternity and Infancy placed an advertisement for its monthly "prenatal letters" in a farm journal, it received so many requests that the director estimated that the agency would soon be sending letters to one-fifth of the pregnant women in the state. By 1929, the last year of Sheppard-Towner operation, the Children's Bureau estimated that almost one-half of all babies born in that year had been affected by its child care advice.[32]

Prenatal and child health conferences also functioned both as a useful service and as an effective tool for building political support for the maternal and infant health campaign. In rural areas, child health conferences were social as well as educational events: some communities closed schools, businesses, and stores so that everyone could attend the festivities. Families came for the movies, refreshments, prizes, and carnival atmosphere of the clinics, as well as for physical examinations and childrearing advice. At an Alabama county fair, nurses ran a baby "check room" that enabled mothers to tour the exhibits without babies in tow and to receive free pamphlets, advice, and physical examinations when they collected their children. Although attendance could be small at a poorly organized clinic, conferences actively supported by local club women, civic leaders, and physicians were generally well attended. For example, over two hundred women attended a meeting in a remote county in Mississippi in 1924. Mothers frequently rode horseback or walked several miles carrying small children to attend the conferences in one-room schoolhouses or local churches; one enthusiastic father brought two children in a wheelbarrow to a clinic in Georgia.[33]

Although literature distribution and health conferences were effective means of providing services and building the baby-saving campaign in most states, they had little impact in very isolated areas where few people could read. When difficult terrain, inclement weather, lack of roads, or a busy harvest season made it difficult to get a crowd to clinics, nurses spent most of their time on home visits. They went to women's homes to treat sick children, to show mothers how to prepare modified milk and get the house ready for childbirth, and to help during delivery. In New Mexico, a fourteen-month old baby weighing less than nine pounds gained weight after the nurse taught his mother how to keep milk cool, clean, and free from flies. The same nurse also dispensed medicine that cured an eye infection and saved the sight of the woman's other child, a three-month-old baby who weighed only five pounds.[34]

Building public support for the federal baby-saving campaign was a vital part of Sheppard-Towner work. Public health nurses met with doctors, civic leaders, and club women to lay the groundwork for health conferences, and they lectured on child hygiene before a wide range of groups, including missionary societies and the Girl Scouts. In 1927, nurses in Mississippi were forced to temporarily abandon their maternity work and midwife classes because a flood had destroyed the homes of most of the midwives. Instead, they helped with flood relief, vaccinated refugees, and cooked breakfast for rescue workers. In the process, they built local support for their campaign.[35]

Many grassroots mothers welcomed Sheppard-Towner programs, but some resented government intervention into their "private" affairs. In Florida, six white women left a meeting of twenty because the nurse's discussion of prenatal care violated their beliefs about feminine modesty and maternal suffering. "The Lord gives and the Lord takes and we have no business talking of such things," they reportedly said. Yet evidence from the Children's

Bureau records suggests that many expectant mothers wanted to be examined. "We find there is a great demand for examination on the part of women who are suffering from lack of care at previous childbirths," reported a North Dakota official. However, some women worried that their wishes were unjustified because their families considered prenatal care to be an unnecessary indulgence. A few, who were embarassed to seek help for themselves, borrowed neighbors' children so they could justify going to the clinics. Others fought with their families for their right to prenatal care, slowly changing social attitudes.[36]

Like other maternalists, Children's Bureau officials felt a sense of responsibility for the welfare of all children and thus made a serious effort to reduce infant and maternal mortality in all racial and ethnic groups. Although most Sheppard-Towner workers were white, the Children's Bureau encouraged states with large minority populations to employ nurses and midwives from communities of color. Thus a small number of Spanish-speaking nurses conducted health conferences and made home visits among Mexican Americans in the southwest, a few Native American nurses worked on the reservations, and some African American nurses carried out Sheppard-Towner programs in black communities. The federal Bureau employed black physician Ionia Whipper to work in the rural south and train "granny" midwives.[37] Still, Sheppard-Towner promoted ideas about science and medicine that were rooted in the cultural beliefs of the Anglo-American middle class. Bureau officials tried to save lives by providing up-to-date medical care to women of color and suppressing what they considered the superstitious and dangerous healing practices of immigrants and African Americans. They assumed that educating women about new scientific thinking on child care would convince them that infant deaths were preventable and lead them to demand better medical and nursing care.

Maternalists' secular faith in science and medicine sometimes put a wedge between Sheppard-Towner nurses and their patients. Poor mothers were often grateful for medical care, but most rejected the efforts of Sheppard-Towner agents to replace traditional healing with modern medicine. For example, the family of a New Mexico woman who had been in labor for six days refused to relinquish the midwife's services, even though the doctor refused to help if the midwife were there. Similarly, a Sheppard-Towner nurse in Montana reported with annoyance that a Native American family refused to allow whites to intervene in a difficult case they considered the domain of the traditional healer.[38]

The cultural presumptions of Sheppard-Towner agents frequently hampered baby-saving efforts in states with large populations of color. This was particularly evident in maternity and infancy work among Native Americans. Although infant mortality was extremely high on the reservations, and most state children's bureaus reported great interest in child welfare there, Sheppard-Towner activity among American Indians varied tremendously. In Minnesota, two Chippewa (Ojibwe) nurses and a white woman who had missionary experience worked full-time on the reservations, and hundreds of Native mothers attended infant health clinics and mothers' classes there. In contrast, the director of the Nebraska Division of Child Hygiene discontinued work among Native Americans, whom she described as "entirely indifferent" to the suggestions of the (Native) nurse. Instead, she recommended directing the limited Sheppard-Towner funds to white women who had already "proven" their interest in the program, perhaps because they shared her cultural values.[39]

Although most of the Anglo-American nurses working with Native Americans tried to be sensitive to their culture, they were often shocked by customs that deviated from middle-class ideas about scientific childrearing. The migratory nature of some American Indian cultures challenged agents' views of proper home life and frustrated their efforts to make follow-up visits. Nurses objected to customs — such as keeping babies tightly clothed in papoose — which they considered unhealthy. Although they approved of the fact that Native Americans breastfed their babies, Sheppard-Towner nurses condemned older children's diet of beans, potatoes, and condensed milk. "The mothers do not understand how to feed them," reported the director of the New Mexico program, attributing children's inadequate diet to parental ignorance rather than to poverty.[40]

Recognizing that poor health among Native Americans derived in large part from U.S. government policy, some Sheppard-Towner workers urged the authorities to treat them better. "The Indian has had such a rough deal that I would like him to feel the hand of Government from a new angle — possibly a shade gentler!" wrote New Mexico physician Gertrude Light. Sympathetic field-workers described Native American interest in their children's welfare as "genuine and delightful," and stressed the need for government workers to appreciate Native American customs and taboos. One nurse remarked on the cultural gulf between whites who had permanent homes to keep clean and Native Americans who, she said, simply moved their teepees when they were dirty. Yet their language betrayed the nurses' feeling of superiority. A Montana nurse, shocked but delighted when a man came to a baby conference with his face painted crimson in honor of child welfare, reminded her superiors that American Indian customs were "entitled to consideration if not approval." A Minnesota agent tried to defend Native Americans by saying that they were "just as human as the rest of us" and had "almost a childlike simplicity."[41]

Racial ethnic mothers should not be seen simply as victims of maternalists' missionary zeal, however. Although Sheppard-Towner workers did try to impose Anglo-American ideas about scientific childrearing on their clients, mothers were free to accept or refuse government assistance, and many were enthusiastic about Sheppard-Towner services. For midwives, however, Sheppard-Towner programs were compulsory. Although Children's Bureau officials maintained that the care given by trained midwives was just as good as medical care, they condemned what they considered the superstitious and unhygienic practices of African American and immigrant midwives. Ignoring their own findings about the correlation between poverty and infant deaths, progressive maternalists blamed traditional lay midwives for the high infant and maternal mortality rates in black and Mexican American communities. They concluded that lives could be saved by educating midwives and stopping the oldest and most "dangerous" of them from practicing.[42]

In the thirty-one states that established midwife training programs, efforts to license and regulate midwives—most of whom were women of color—depended on the legal authority of Sheppard-Towner agents. Public health nurses who were unfamiliar with local customs had the power to grant or withhold licenses, and thus to threaten the livelihood of local midwives. Most did not hesitate to take advantage of what they considered midwives' "very wholesome fear" of license-granting agencies. Sheppard-Towner classes were the first direct experience many midwives had with the state, and they may have felt that the government had more power than it actually did. Even in states where public health workers could legally deny permits to midwives, the limited resources of Sheppard-Towner administrators meant that prosecution for practicing without a permit was unlikely to occur, even if the nurse thought it desirable. Nevertheless, as a result of Sheppard-Towner training programs, the number of midwives dropped from over 6,000 to 4,339 in Virginia and from 4,209 to 3,040 in Mississippi. Some birth attendants were probably driven underground, continuing to practice but living in fear of prosecution, but others undoubtedly left the work out of fear or because of the reduced demand for their services.[43]

Although some midwives resisted Sheppard-Towner instructional programs, evidence suggests that others enjoyed the classes. Perhaps they saw midwife meetings as a recognition of their work or a way to facilitate the difficult task of collecting fees. They may have believed that, despite their cultural differences, nurses shared midwives' commitment to the health and well-being of infants and mothers. Or perhaps they simply found midwife meetings—which were festive affairs that included songs, prayers, refreshments, prizes, and films—a welcome break in routine. In any case, many women willingly traveled long distances to attend the meetings. One midwife, a mother of seventeen, rode thirty miles on horseback; a seventy-year-old woman walked five miles in the freezing rain. After arriving 1½ hours late to a midwife meeting because her car had been stuck in the mud, a Mississippi nurse marveled at the sixty-year-old midwife who had to walk 8½ miles but always arrived on time.[44]

The most important lesson of midwife classes was cleanliness. While birthing women traditionally lay on old quilts and wore their husband's clothes, Sheppard-Towner instructors stressed aseptic procedures and required midwives to scrub, shave, and bathe their patients. Concern about a sterile, germ-free environment was a legitimate public health concern, for puerperal septicemia was the major cause of maternal deaths.[45] However, the obsessive attention to midwives' personal appearance suggests that concern with cleanliness went beyond the desire for a healthy environment. Anglo-American nurses described African American midwives as "dirty" and "untidy," and tried to change their appearance. Claiming that women who were not "spotlessly clean" were "unworthy" to care for new babies, they promoted their own cultural values of order, purity, and discipline. Sheppard-Towner administrative reports chronicle numerous "successes," such as the transformation of a "disorderly" group of tobacco-chewing midwives wearing fancy hats and wool dresses into an eager, well-behaved class wearing starched dresses. Clean, sterile, and dressed in white, African American midwives were symbolically cleansed of their race, their sexuality, and their motherhood.[46]

In addition to teaching midwives to use sterile procedures and remember their place in the medical hierarchy, Sheppard-Towner training programs aimed to raise midwives' expectations for their patients' health. And they apparently succeeded, at least in part. Anxious to save lives and improve health, many midwives abandoned some traditional remedies and combined other practices with medical procedures they considered useful. A growing proportion provided prenatal care, followed sanitary procedures such as substituting newspaper pads for old quilts during childbirth, and called on doctors during difficult deliveries. But they continued to use herbal treatments, favor traditional birth positions, and follow established rituals, such as placing a knife under the bed to "cut the pain" and burying the placenta. The Sheppard-Towner Act accelerated the medicalization of birth and permanently changed women's experience of pregnancy and delivery. Yet midwives and mothers also contributed to the direction of childbirth by choosing to follow some modern procedures while ignoring others, and by refusing to abandon traditional ways.[47]

Maternalists' bias against traditional healing unquestionably impeded efforts to reduce infant and maternal mortality in communities of color, but the administrative structure of the Sheppard-Towner Act was even more to blame. Despite efforts by the Children's Bureau to extend health services to all sectors of the population, the decentralized administration of the

Sheppard-Towner Act perpetuated discriminatory practices by allowing states to provide inferior services to people of color. For example, although Native American infants in Montana were more than 2 1/2 times as likely to die as whites, the state did not have a full-time nurse on the reservations.[48] Similarly, despite extremely high infant mortality among African Americans, the Georgia State Board of Health tried to save money by providing inferior services to the black community. At least one African American nurse could not do her work because she was not provided with transportation at the same time as her white co-workers. In addition, the Board of Health hired an inexperienced nurse to work with black midwives because it considered the salary demanded by an experienced nurse "too much for any negro." The Children's Bureau staff, perhaps unwilling to jeopardize support for the Sheppard-Towner Act among white voters and politicians, did not comment.[49]

The Defeat of Sheppard-Towner

Curiously, the medical and right-wing opposition to the Sheppard-Towner Act both fostered and frustrated democracy within the Children's Bureau's baby-saving campaign. On the one hand, the political attacks against the Maternity Act increased the Bureau's dependence on grassroots women's support, and the bill's underfunding required administrators to rely heavily on volunteer labor. On the other, the persistent opposition to Sheppard-Towner pressured Children's Bureau officials to depoliticize child health services in order to make them a permanent part of a public health bureaucracy. Hostility to the bill—and to the women running it—may have encouraged Bureau officials to justify their administration of the Maternity Act only in terms of their professional expertise, not their womanly sensitivity, thereby strengthening the hierarchy of women welfare professionals over untrained volunteers. Eventually, the contradictions between the bill's two goals of politicizing and professionalizing maternal and child welfare could be contained no longer; professionalization won out.

The attacks on Sheppard-Towner and the Children's Bureau staff continued through the 1920s. There were two constitutional challenges to the bill's legality, both dismissed by the U.S. Supreme Court in 1923, and the medical establishment conducted an energetic campaign against the bill. Medical opposition was probably the major reason Illinois and Massachusetts refused to accept Sheppard-Towner funds in the first place. Moreover, although thousands of small-town doctors cooperated with the Children's Bureau, the state directors of maternity and infancy programs found that AMA opposition to Sheppard-Towner had a growing impact on local doctors. The director of the Minnesota Division of Child Hygiene complained that the head of the state medical association was discrediting Sheppard-Towner work. It was "disgusting" that one man could create such a disturbance, she wrote.[50]

The anti–Sheppard-Towner coalition forced the Children's Bureau staff to make a number of compromises in the process of lobbying for and administering the Sheppard-Towner Act. These concessions weakened the bill's impact, especially in communities of color, and contributed to its ultimate defeat. For example, although most progressive maternalists believed that universally-available medical and nursing care was a "minimum standard" for child welfare, Children's Bureau supporters approved a bill that provided no medical care and gave the Children's Bureau little real control over Sheppard-Towner administration in the hopes of making it acceptable to medical and right-wing organizations. However, the passage of a moderate bill changed the Bureau's position from leader of a campaign to get the government to assume responsibility for child welfare into the administrator and defender of an existing — and inadequate — social service. Marginal and on the defensive within the federal bureaucracy, the Bureau staff were caught between their roles as reform-minded "outsiders" who had little power in government and as pragmatic "insiders" who administered a social service bureaucracy and had to defend their own positions in government to protect the welfare programs for which they had fought so hard.[51]

Fighting the persistent and increasingly influential opposition to the bill drained the time and energy of federal and state administrators. The energy of the federal Children's Bureau staff was diverted away from administering the bill to defending it in court and lobbying Congress for renewal. In addition, since the law required each state to pass enabling legislation and renew funding in order to receive federal grants, there were constant political battles in the states. At first, the Bureau staff naively assumed that a well-organized women's movement would crush the opposition. "With the women of your state well organized, one does not have to take their [doctors'] action too seriously," Bureau physician Anna Rude told Michigan director Blanche Haines in 1922. Yet two years after thirty thousand Michigan women signed petitions and succeeded in getting their state to accept Sheppard-Towner funds, Haines (who went on to head the Maternity and Infancy Division of the Children's Bureau) faced another round over appropriations. "If anything has made me want to get out of my job it is facing the situation," she complained. Similarly, just two years after the Sheppard-Towner administrator in Oklahoma complained that she had "wasted" three months fighting proposed legislation to get rid of her agency, she had to fight a new Health Commissioner's efforts to stop distributing prenatal literature — the most successful part of the state's Sheppard-Towner program.[52]

That support from local women and physicians was necessary for the successful delivery of health services and, ultimately, for popular support of the Sheppard-Towner Act, is evident in Nevada, one of two or three states that Grace Abbott felt was "not making some real headway." The poor administrative skills of the Nevada director were compounded by physicians' objections that the agency that administered Sheppard-Towner funds was not directed by a medical professional. As a result, Sheppard-Towner programs in Nevada languished. A nurse in one of the richest counties in the state had no supplies except for scales. The child health conferences she ran were poorly organized; in one community, only two mothers attended a four-hour clinic. A nurse in another county had only three cases one year. Discouraged by the ineffective services, some women activists lost the enthusiasm needed to sustain them during the difficult battles for renewal. "I am so thoroughly disgusted with the situation that I feel that I cannot waste any more time in trying to do something . . . so long as the present people are in charge," complained the president of the Nevada League of Women Voters.[53]

The Nevada experience notwithstanding, Sheppard-Towner workers in most states considered the program a success. Although the accomplishments were often intangible and difficult to quantify, nurses' monthly reports to the Children's Bureau document their perception that local women were becoming interested in their work and that it was changing prenatal and childbirth practices. "Last summer, I distributed literature to as many expectant mothers as I could find, hardly daring to hope that it would be read," a Mississippi nurse reported in 1926. "On my rounds the other day, I find that the literature has been read and passed on to others and that they are all going directly by the instructions, even to having paper pads and other equipment ready when the midwives arrive." "Sometimes while on my daily rounds I feel that I am not accomplishing much," confided a New York nurse, "but when I look at this record I cannot help feeling encouraged. . . . The number of new cases on roll shows more people are interested. Lately many mothers are calling on me to visit them or their friends, and many are coming to the consultations without being visited." A Colorado physician noted women's increasing knowledge about infant and prenatal care: "It has become a very rare thing to have a call on a confinement case at the onset of labor without having seen the patient before."[54]

Women's enthusiasm for Sheppard-Towner services is documented in the letters they wrote to the federal and state children's bureaus. "I trust you'll find by many letters that your work is doing much and will continue it," wrote a West Virginia mother of twins. "There are many who do not Pay attention But It Is a great Benefit to those that do." A Georgia woman agreed, "I don't see how we poor mothers could do without them [prenatal clinics].

It has meant so much to me and so many more mothers to[o]. . . . I am the mother of 14 children, and I never was cared for till I begin going to the good will center clinic. . . . We mothers do learn a lot from the kind nurses. We are so glad the day has come when we have someone to care for our babies when they get sick."[55]

A further indication of the program's success was the significant decrease in infant mortality during the Sheppard-Towner years. According to the Children's Bureau, infant deaths in the birth registration area dropped from 76 to 69 per 1,000 live births between 1921 and 1928, and declined by 11 percent in states that had been in the birth registration area before Sheppard-Towner began. Deaths due to gastrointestinal disease, most easily prevented by educational programs, dropped 47 percent. The Bureau attributed a slight rise in maternal deaths (from 68 per 10,000 live births in 1921 to 69 in 1929) to the inclusion of predominantly African American counties with high death rates into the birth registration area for the first time. Maternal mortality declined from 67 to 64 per 10,000 live births in states that had been in the birth registration area the entire time.[56]

Yet deaths remained high among babies of color. When Sheppard-Towner began in 1921, 108 babies of color died for every 1,000 live births; by 1928, the infant death rate had fallen only slightly, to 106 (compared to 64 for whites). The 1921 statistics were probably artificially low since several states with high African American death rates had not yet joined the birth registration area. Moreover, most rural people of color were so poor, and conditions in their communities so dire, that the meager resources of the Sheppard-Towner Act were unable to make much more than a dent in improving their health. The decentralized administration of the Sheppard-Towner Act and maternalists' bias against traditional healing probably also reduced the effectiveness of maternity and infancy work among racial ethnic groups.[57]

White farm wives appear to have been the chief beneficiaries of the Sheppard-Towner Act — unlike mothers' pensions programs, which principally benefited white widows in cities. This is partly because health agencies were already established in cities, but it is also no doubt because Julia Lathrop and her staff had been profoundly influenced by their correspondence and personal contacts with rural women, who were the main audience for *Infant Care* and *Prenatal Care*. Indeed, the original maternity bill specifically targeted rural areas, even though Children's Bureau statistics actually showed a slightly higher infant mortality rate in cities than in the country (possibly because birth registration lagged behind there). Targeting the country was astute not only because white farm women already shared the Bureau's cultural values regarding family life and science but also because there was less danger of conflict with the medical profession, since the specialists who dominated the AMA had less influence in rural areas.[58]

The popularity and moderate success of the Sheppard-Towner Act notwithstanding, activist women were unable to win its renewal. The 1924 elections brought into power President Calvin Coolidge, an ally of big business and critic of a strong federal government, and a Congress more concerned with cutting taxes than with providing for social welfare. Furthermore, politicians who supported the maternity bill in 1921 because of the sentimental appeal to motherhood and their fear of the unknown female vote knew by the end of the 1920s that women did not vote as a bloc and that they had nothing to fear. Consequently, when the Children's Bureau tried to extend Sheppard-Towner appropriations (which were to expire in June 1927), the American Medical Association and the right-wing Sentinels of the Republic and Woman Patriots moved to defeat the bill itself. Using basically the same arguments as they had in 1921, opponents described Sheppard-Towner as an "entering wedge" to socialism and an attack on the sanctity of the family. They denounced Lathrop, Abbott, and Kelley as Bolsheviks. These allegations, which carried little weight in 1921, apparently seemed more convincing after the defeat of the child labor amendment in mid-decade. The Catholic church, which was initially indifferent to the Sheppard-Towner bill, began speaking out against government intervention into family affairs, and the Daughters of the American Revolution, a warm supporter of the Maternity Act in 1921, became a vigorous opponent in 1926.[59]

Although the bill to renew Sheppard-Towner passed the House easily by a vote of 218 to 44, right-wing senators blocked it in the Senate for eight months, forcing the Children's Bureau to agree to a compromise measure that extended appropriations for two years until 1929, and then automatically repealed the law itself. Between 1928 and 1932, fourteen bills that would reverse the repeal of the Sheppard-Towner Act were introduced in Congress. All of them failed. The Children's Bureau itself opposed many of the renewal bills because they transferred responsibility for overseeing maternity and infancy work to the Public Health Service.[60]

The tensions between maternalists and their adversaries in the medical profession exploded at the 1930 White House Conference on Child Health and Protection. Called by President Herbert Hoover, the conference was clearly intended to establish medical authority over child health and to rescue public health services from "lay" women's control. Secretary of the Interior Ray Lyman Wilbur, a past president of the AMA and outspoken opponent of the Sheppard-Towner Act, was the conference chair. Children's Bureau chief Grace Abbott, who had been secretary of the 1919 White House conference, was given only a minor role. In contrast to 1919, when maternalists set the conference agenda, the 1930 White House conference was shaped by male physicians who rejected the Bureau's belief in children's right to federally funded health care and who wanted to return responsibility for child welfare to the private sector. In the midst of the Depression, they virtually ignored the economic causes of ill health.

Maternalists were furious when conference officials tried to sneak through a resolution recommending the transfer of maternity and infancy programs from the Children's Bureau (and women's control) to the medically run Public Health Service. Hundreds of women attending the conference pro-tested the proposal and forced its withdrawal. They made it plain that they preferred no maternity bill at all to one that asserted men's authority over women's and children's welfare, that was administered by doctors who had a narrowly medical conception of children's health needs, and that intended ultimately to depoliticize maternal and child health programs and return them to the private sector. Yet although maternalists managed to stop the transfer of Sheppard-Towner programs to the Public Health Service, they no longer had the political clout necessary to pass their own maternity bill. The White House Conference signaled the triumph of the medical profession over maternalists and the defeat of politicized motherhood.[61]

Ironically, the success of the Maternity and Infancy Act contributed to its eventual defeat. By raising individual women's expectations for their health and making them more knowledgeable about prenatal and well-baby care, Sheppard-Towner convinced physicians to incorporate preventive health education into their private practices and to improve obstetrical training in medical schools. The improvements in — and easier access to — both private- and public-sector prenatal and well-baby health services were important factors in the drop of the white infant mortality rate. Sadly, when the health of white women and children improved, publicly funded health care ap-peared less urgent to middle-class voters and stopped being an important political concern of women activists.

Contrary to the intentions of its female supporters, the Sheppard-Towner Act also hastened women's loss of control over health policy and care. Because of maternalists' faith in modern science and desire to maintain good relations with the medical profession — and because of their failure to secure a bill that provided publicly funded medical or nursing care — Shep-pard-Towner clinics encouraged women to seek private medical care and thus accelerated the medicalization of childbirth and infant care. In the process, they inadvertently undermined both the Bureau's wholistic ap-proach to child welfare and "lay" women's claim to expertise in the field. Although individual women continued to play a prominent role in the development and administration of child health services, by the mid 1930s male physicians and public health bureaucrats dominated both public- and private-sector health services. Once maternity and infancy programs were professionalized and rendered part of the government bureaucracy, they were no longer considered a special women's concern. All but three of the forty-eight state directors of child welfare programs had been women when Sheppard-Towner began in 1922, but by 1939 three-quarters of them were men.[62]

The repeal of the Sheppard-Towner Act in 1929 reasserted the principle that Progressive-era maternalists and feminists had spent their lives trying to change: that children's welfare was primarily the responsibility of individual mothers, not of society. Although twenty-one states tried to continue maternity and infancy work after Sheppard-Towner was repealed, the removal of federal funds reduced public support for the program. "In other words," observed the Children's Bureau, "the participation of the Federal Government contributed something else as important as money." The financial constraints of the Depression forced some states to drop maternity and infancy work entirely, making health care once again unavailable to women who could not afford private physicians or who lived in remote areas — the women who benefited most from the Maternity and Infancy Act. Federal monies for maternal and infant care were restored under the 1935 Social Security Act, but maternal and child health services were no longer considered an entitlement for women of all classes. Instead, they were needs-based and limited to the poor.[63]

Maternalists lost their battle to dignify motherhood and make children's welfare a societal concern, but their campaign for the state protection of mothers and children left a permanent mark on women's work of reproduction and caregiving and on the future welfare state. The Sheppard-Towner Act eased the burden of countless mothers by improving the health of their children, and it served as a bridge between Progressive-era maternalism and public welfare expansion during the New Deal. Yet, like maternalism itself, it left an ambiguous legacy. Sheppard-Towner expanded employment opportunities for professional women while leaving women's responsibility for child care unquestioned. It extended some health services to women and children of color, but demanded that they follow Anglo-American prescriptions about childrearing and medicine. It created a women-controlled public health system and mobilized thousands of women activists to help run it, but set up a public health bureaucracy that eventually supplanted them. Ironically, the Children's Bureau's success at one goal — professionalizing maternal and child welfare services — contributed to the failure of another — sustaining a broad-based women's movement to demand further welfare reform. Maternalism's greatest achievement thus inadvertently paved the way for its final defeat.

NOTES

Portions of this chapter previously appeared in my article, "'Grannies' and 'Spinsters': Midwife Education under the Sheppard-Towner Act," *Journal of Social History* 22 (Winter 1988): 255–75.

1. Florence Kelley, *The Autobiography of Florence Kelley: Notes of Sixty Years,* ed. Kathryn Kish Sklar (Chicago: Charles H. Kerr Publishing, 1986), 31.

2. Julia Lathrop to Mrs. A. P., reprinted in Molly Ladd-Taylor, *Raising a Baby the Government Way: Mothers' Letters to the Children's Bureau, 1915–1932* (New Brunswick, N.J.: Rutgers University Press, 1986), 50.

3. Linda Gordon points out that clients also played a role in the formation of mothers' pensions. Linda Gordon, "Single Mothers and Child Neglect, 1880–1920," *American Quarterly* 37 (Summer 1985): 173–92; idem, *Heroes of Their Own Lives: The Politics and History of Family Violence* (New York: Penguin, 1988).

4. In 1929, for example, Sheppard-Towner had 1,054 paid employees and at least 7,339 volunteer workers. U.S. Children's Bureau, *The Promotion of the Welfare and Hygiene of Maternity and Infancy for the Fiscal Year Ending June 30, 1929,* Publication No. 203 (Washington, D.C.: Government Printing Office, 1931), 6.

5. See Nancy Schrom Dye and Daniel Blake Smith, "Mother Love and Infant Death, 1750–1920," *Journal of American History* 73 (Sept. 1986): 329–53.

6. "Appendix A: Text of the Act for the Promotion of the Welfare and Hygiene of Maternity and Infancy," in Children's Bureau, *Promotion of the Welfare . . . 1929,* 127–29. See J. Stanley Lemons, *The Woman Citizen: Social Feminism in the 1920s* (Urbana: University of Illinois Press, 1975), 153–80.

7. Political explanations are emphasized in Lemons, *Woman Citizen,* and Theda Skocpol, *Protecting Soldiers and Mothers: The Politics of Social Provision in the United States 1870s-1920s* (Cambridge: Harvard University Press, 1992). The role of the medical profession is emphasized in Sheila Rothman, *Woman's Proper Place: A History of Changing deals and Practices, 1870 to the Present* (New York: Basic, 1978); Robyn L. Muncy, *Creating a Female Dominion in American Reform, 1890–1935* (New York: Oxford University Press, 1990); and Richard A. Meckel, *Save the Babies: American Public Health Reform and the Prevention of Infant Mortality, 1850–1929* (Baltimore: Johns Hopkins University Press, 1990).

8. Secretary quoted in Lemons, *Woman Citizen,* 155; Abbott to Mrs. L. G., in Ladd-Taylor, *Raising a Baby,* 195.

9. See Lemons, *Woman Citizen,* and Skocpol, *Protecting Soldiers and Mothers,* for more detailed examinations of the political campaign for the bill.

10. Julia Lathrop, "Child Welfare Standards a Test of Democracy," Presidential Address to the National Conference of Social Work, June 1919, Box 60, Folder 10, Grace and Edith Abbott Papers, Regenstein Library, University of Chicago; House Committee on Interstate and Foreign Commerce, *Public Protection of Maternity and Infancy, Hearings on H.R. 10925* 66th Congress, 3d Session, Dec. 21, 1920, 28.

11. House Committee on Interstate and Foreign Commerce, *Hearings on H.R. 10925,* Dec. 23, 1920, 116; Senate Committee on Education and Labor, *Hearings*

on *S. 1039, Protection of Maternity,* 67th Congress, 1st Session, Apr. 25, 1921, 62; Mrs. William Lowell Putnam, "Why the Appropriations for the Extension of the Sheppard-Towner Act Should Not be Granted," n.d., Box 4, Folder 53, Elizabeth Lowell Putnam Papers, Arthur and Elizabeth Schlesinger Library on the History of Women, Radcliffe College, Cambridge, Mass.

12. Senate Committee on Education and Labor, *Hearings on S. 1039,* Apr. 25, 1921, 121; House Committee on Interstate and Foreign Commerce, *Hearings on H.R. 2366, for Public Protection of Maternity and Infancy,* 67th Congress, 1st Session, July 21, 1921, 177; *Congressional Record,* 66th Congress, 3d Session, vol. 60, Dec. 17, 1920, 457.

13. Senate Committee on Education and Labor, *Hearings on S. 1039,* Apr. 25, 1921, 52; House Committee on Interstate and Foreign Commerce, *Hearings on H.R. 2366,* 173–74. The reference to Kollontai is in U.S. Children's Bureau, *Maternity Benefit Systems in Foreign Countries,* Publication No. 57 (Washington, D.C.: Government Printing Office, 1919), 9.

14. *Congressional Record,* 67th Congress, 1st Session, vol. 61, Nov. 1, 1921, 7145.

15. Elizabeth Lowell Putnam to Peggy [Rice], May 14, 1921, Folder 301, Putnam Papers; Eden Burnstead, "Soviet Committees for all America," Mass. Civic Alliance, July 23, 1921, in National League of Women Voters Records, Series 2, Box 38, Library of Congress.

16. *Congressional Record,* 67th Congress, 1st Session, vol. 61, July 21, 1921, 8764.

17. Lemons, *Woman Citizen,* 164. On the medical opposition to Sheppard-Towner, see Muncy, *Creating a Female Dominion;* and Ronald L. Numbers, *Almost Persuaded: American Physicians and Compulsory Health Insurance* (Baltimore: Johns Hopkins University Press, 1978), 107.

18. Elizabeth Lowell Putnam to Miss Bacon, Apr. 26, 1921, Folder 301, Putnam Papers.

19. W. F. Bigelow to Harriet Anderson, Mar. 25, 1920, File 10,406, Children's Bureau Records, Central Files 1914–50, Records Group 102, National Archives, Washington, D.C. (hereafter cited as CB.)

20. Putnam, "Why the Appropriations for the Extension of the Sheppard-Towner Act Should Not be Granted"; Elizabeth Lowell Putnam to Mr. Kellogg, May 17, 1921, Folder 300, Putnam Papers. See Sonya Michel and Robyn Rosen, "The Paradox of Maternalism: Elizabeth Lowell Putnam and the American Welfare State," *Gender and History* 4 (Autumn 1992): 364–86.

21. Dorothy Reed Mendenhall, Autobiography, Typescript, J. p. 23–24, Sophia Smith Collection, Smith College. For evidence of women's desire for information on reproduction, see the letters in Ladd-Taylor, *Raising a Baby,* and Margaret Sanger, *Motherhhood in Bondage* (New York: Brentano's, 1928).

22. Alice Robertson to Elizabeth Lowell Putnam, Nov. 21, 1921, Folder 300, Putnam Papers.

23. House Committee on Interstate and Foreign Commerce, *Hearings on H.R. 2366,* July 23, 1921, 241.

24. House Committee on Interstate and Foreign Commerce, *Hearings on H.R. 2366*, July 12, 1921, 21; Charles H. Miner, M.D. to My dear Dr. —, in "Report of Work Done Under the Maternity and Infancy Act in the State of Pennsylvania," July 1, 1925 to June 30, 1926, File 11–40–8, Children's Bureau Records, Correspondence and Reports Relating to Surveys and Programs, 1917–54, Record Group 102, National Archives, Washington, D.C. (hereafter cited as C&R, CB).

25. See Joan E. Mulligan, "Pregnant Americans, 1918–1947: Some Public Policy Notes on Rural and Military Wives," *Women & Health* 5 (Winter 1980): 23–38; Louis J. Covotsos, "Child Welfare and Social Progress: A History of the United States Children's Bureau, 1912–1935" (Ph.D. diss., University of Chicago, 1976).

26. "Text of the Act," 129.

27. Madeleine Z. Doty, "The Maternity Bill," *Equal Rights* 8 (Jan.-Feb. 1921): 353–54; Eleanor Taylor, "Wages for Mothers," *Suffragist* 8 (Nov. 1920): 273.

28. Mrs. L. W., Alabama, Mar. 13, 1922, reprinted in Molly Ladd-Taylor, *Raising a Baby*, 193. See also pp. 54–56, 195 in that volume.

29. Children's Bureau, *Promotion of the Welfare . . . 1929*, 27.

30. Skocpol, *Protecting Soldiers and Mothers*; Muncy, *Creating a Female Dominion*, 108, 140; Children's Bureau, *Promotion of the Welfare . . . 1929*, 5.

31. Children's Bureau, *Promotion of the Welfare . . . 1929*, 5–6, 24–25.

32. Lucile Spire Blachly to Florence Kraker, Apr. 6, 1925, and Lucile Blachly to Blanche Haines, Feb. 4, 1926, File 11–38–1, CB; Children's Bureau, *Promotion of the Welfare . . . 1929*, 21.

33. "Semi-Annual Report of Maternity and Infancy Work [Alabama]," July 1, 1923 to Dec. 31, 1923, File 11–2–8, C&R, CB; [Mississippi], "Narrative and Statistical Report," Mar. 1924, File 11–26–1, CB; "Semi-Annual Report of Maternity and Infancy Work [Georgia]," Jan. 6, 1923. File 11–12–8, C&R, CB.

34. Dorothy Anderson to G. S. Luckett, Oct. 6, 1926, File 11–33–8, CB.

35. Mississippi Department of Health, Bureau of Child Welfare, "Narrative and Statistical Report," Mar. 1924, File 11–26–1, CB; "[Mississippi] Narrative and Statistical Report," Apr.-Aug. 1927," File 11–26–8, CB. See also the 1926 reports of Dorothy Anderson, R.N., Sheppard-Towner Special Agent in New Mexico, File 11–33–8, CB.

36. Division of Maternity and Infancy Hygiene, Bureau of Child Welfare, Florida State Board of Health, "Biennial Report," July 1, 1922 to Dec. 31, 1922, File 11–11–8, C&R, CB; "Semi-Annual Report of Maternity and Infancy Work [North Dakota]," Jan. 1 to June 30, 1923, File 11–36–8, C&R, CB; "Conference of Directors of State Divisions Administering the Federal Maternity and Infancy Act held under the Auspices of the Children's Bureau," Sept. 19–21, 1923, page 39, File 11–0, C&R, CB.

37. U.S. Children's Bureau, *The Promotion of the Welfare and Hygiene of Maternity and Infancy for the Fiscal Year Ending June 30, 1928*, Publication No. 194 (Washington, D.C.: Government Printing Office, 1929), 26–27. Most studies on women of color and the public health system focus on African American women in a slightly later period. See Edward Beardsley, *A History of Neglect: Health Care for Blacks and Mill Workers in the Twentieth-Century South* (Knox-

ville: University of Tennessee Press, 1987); Darlene Clark Hine, *Black Women in White: Racial Conflict and Cooperation in the Nursing Profession, 1890–1950* (Bloomington: Indiana University Press, 1989), and Susan L. Smith, "Black Activism in Health Care, 1890–1950" (Paper Delivered at the Conference on Black Health: Historical Perspectives and Current Issues, University of Wisconsin-Madison, Apr. 1990).

38. Dorothy Anderson to G. S. Luckett, Oct. 6, 1926, File 11–33–8, CB; Child Welfare Division, Montana State Board of Health, "Narrative Report of Activities," July 1 to Dec. 31, 1924, File 11–28–8, C&R, CB. Sandra Schackel argues that Anglo health workers in New Mexico adjusted their ideas about modern health practices to fit Hispanic and Native American customs. *Social Housekeepers: Women Shaping Public Policy in New Mexico, 1920–1940* (Albuquerque: University of New Mexico Press, 1992).

39. Adelia Eggestine, "A Defense of our Minnesota Indians," June 1928, enclosed in "Report of Work Done Under the Federal Maternity and Infancy Act in the State of Minnesota," July 1, 1927 to June 30, 1928, File 11–25–8, C&R, CB; "Semiannual Report of Maternity and Infancy Work [Minnesota]," July 1, 1923 to Dec. 31, 1923, File 11–25–8, C&R, CB; "Semi-Annual Report of Maternity and Infancy Work [Nebraska]," Jan. 1, 1925 to June 30, 1925, File 11–29–8, C&R, CB.

40. Eggestine, "A Defense of our Minnesota Indians;" Child Welfare Division, Montana State Board of Health, "Narrative Report of Activities," July 1 to Dec. 31, 1924, File 11–28–8, C&R, CB; Janet Reid to Grace Abbott, Sept. 28, 1923, File 11–33–1, CB.

41. Gertrude Light to Ethel Watters, Jan. 5, 1924, File 11–33–1, CB; Kansas Division of Child Hygiene, "Annual Report," July 1, 1928 to June 30, 1929, File 11–18–8, C&R, CB; Child Welfare Division, Montana State Board of Health, "Narrative Report of Activities," July 1 to Dec. 31, 1924, and Jan. 1, 1925 to June 30, 1925, File 11–28–8, C&R, CB; Eggestine, "A Defense of our Minnesota Indians," File 11–25–8, C&R, CB.

42. Ladd-Taylor, "'Grannies' and 'Spinsters,' 255–75.

43. "Report of Work Done Under the Maternity and Infancy Act in the State of New Mexico," July 1, 1925 to June 30, 1926, File 11–33–8, C&R, CB; "Report of Work Done Under the Federal Maternity and Infancy Act in the State of Virginia," July 1, 1928 to June 30, 1929, File 11–50–8, C&R, CB; "Report of Work Done Under the Federal Maternity and Infancy Act in the State of Mississippi," July 1, 1928 to June 30, 1929," File 11–26–8, C&R, CB.

44. "Semi-Annual Report of Maternity and Infancy Work [Virginia]," Jan. 1, 1923 to July 1, 1923, File 11–50–8, C&R, CB; "Report of Midwife Classes Held in Halifax County, Virginia," [1924] File 11–50–8, C&R, CB; Mississippi State Board of Health, Bureau of Child Hygiene, Division of Maternity and Infancy, "Report," June 1925, File 11–26–1, CB.

45. U.S. Children's Bureau, *Maternal Mortality,* Publication No. 158 (Washington, D.C.: Government Printing Office, 1926), 22. See also idem, *Maternal Deaths: A Brief Report of a Study Made in 15 States,* Publication No. 221 (Washington, Government Printing Office, 1933), 37.

46. "Midwife Activities in Mississippi," 1928, File 11-26-8, C&R, CB. Georgia State Board of Health, "Lessons for Midwives [1922]," reprinted in *The American Midwife Debate: A Sourcebook on Its Modern Origins*, ed. Judy Barrett Litoff (Westport, Conn.: Greenwood Press, 1986), 200-207, is an example of instructions given to midwives.

47. See Ladd-Taylor, "'Grannies' and 'Spinsters.'"

48. In Montana the infant mortality rate among Native Americans was 185.4, compared to only 69.1 for whites. "Report of Work Done Under Federal Maternity and Infancy Act in the State of Montana," July 1, 1926 to June 30, 1927, File 11-28-8, C&R, CB.

49. [Georgia] Division of Child Hygiene, "Annual Report," 1925, File 11-12-8, C&R, CB; Clark Goreman, Georgia Committee on Interracial Cooperation, to Blanche Haines, July 8, 1926, File 11-12-2, CB. It is likely that black nurses also faced discrimination in salaries. In 1926, a black nurse in Georgia earned $1,000 while two white nurses earned $1,200 and $1,800 respectively. Joe P. Bowdoin to Grace Abbott, Apr. 20, 1926, File 11-12-1, CB.

50. Lela B. Costin, *Two Sisters for Social Justice: A Biography of Grace and Edith Abbott* (Urbana: University of Illinois Press, 139-40; Lemons, *Woman Citizen*, 171-72; Annie S. Veech to Grace Abbott, Dec. 12, 1924, File 11-0-11, CB; Ruth Boynton to Grace Abbott, May 5, 1926, File 11-25-1, CB.

51. See Judith Sealander, *As Minority Becomes Majority: Federal Reaction to the Phenomenon of Women in the Work Force, 1920-1963* (Westport, Conn.: 1983), 3-11, for discussion of a similar phenomenon in the Women's Bureau.

52. Anna Rude to Blanche Haines, Oct. 31, 1922, File 11-24-2, CB; Blanche Haines to Anna Rude, Feb. 26 and Apr. 19, 1923, File 11-24-2, CB; Blanche Haines to Grace Abbott, Jan. 8, 1925, File 11-24-1, CB; "Narrative Report of the Bureau of Maternity and Infancy, State Department of Public Health, State of Oklahoma," January 1, 1925 to July 1, 1925, File 11-38-8, CB; Lucile Blachly to Blanche Haines, July 1, 1927, File 11-38-1, CB.

53. Grace Abbott to Lillie M. Barbour, July 13, 1925, File 11-30-1, CB; Marie Phelan to Florence Kraker, Oct. 30, 1924, File 11-30-1, CB; Marie Phelan to Blanche Haines, June 15-20, 1925, File 11-30-1, CB; Lillie Barbour to Grace Abbott, July 2, 1925, File 11-30-1, CB; Mrs. J.B. Clinedinst to Grace Abbott, Jan. 2, 1928, File 11-30-8, CB.

54. Mississippi State Board of Health Bureau of Child Hygiene, "Report," May 1926, File 11-26-8, CB; New York State Division of Maternity, Infancy, and Child Hygiene, "Report," Dec. 1927, File 11-34-8, CB; Dr. E. H. Munro to Estelle Mathews, Mar. 18, 1926, File 11-7-1, CB.

55. West Virginia Division of Child Hygiene and Public Health Nursing, "Extracts from Statements of Mothers Who Took Motherhood Correspondence Course," enclosed in Katharine Lenroot to Julia Lathrop, Sept. 23, 1926, File 11-0, CB; "Letters from Georgia Women Attending Prenatal Clinic," enclosed in Joe Bowdoin to Dorothy Kirchwey Brown, Apr. 30, 1929, Box 2, Folder 39, Dorothy Kirchwey Brown Papers, Schlesinger Library.

56. Children's Bureau, *Promotion of the Welfare . . . 1929*, 24, 28-34, 37. Eigh-

teen states and the Territory of Hawaii joined the birth registration area during the Sheppard-Towner years.

57. The white infant mortality rate was 72 in 1921. Children's Bureau, *Promotion of the Welfare . . . 1929,* 27–37, 132.

58. In 1921, 78 urban infants died for every 1,000 live births, while 74 died in rural areas. By 1928, the infant mortality rate had declined to 69 in the cities and 68 in rural areas. Children's Bureau, *Promotion of the Welfare . . . 1929,* 31.

59. See House Committee on Interstate and Foreign Commerce, *Hearing on Extension of Public Protection of Maternity and Infancy Act,* 69th Congress, 1st Session, 1926. For a good discussion of Sheppard-Towner's defeat, see Muncy, *Creating a Female Dominion,* 124–50.

60. Joseph Chepaitis, "The First Federal Social Welfare Measure: The Sheppard-Towner Maternity and Infancy Act, 1918–1932" (Ph.D. diss., Georgetown University, 1968), 278.

61. White House Conference on Child Health and Protection, *Official Proceedings, November 19–22, 1930* (New York: American Child Health Association, 1931); Costin, *Two Sisters for Social Justice,* 167–69.

62. S. Josephine Baker, *Fighting for Life* (New York: Macmillan, 1939), 201.

63. Children's Bureau, *Promotion of the Welfare . . . 1929,* 39; Costin, *Two Sisters,* 134, 221–26.

Conclusion

With the defeat of the Sheppard-Towner Act, maternal and child welfare stopped being a central issue of the women's movement. Although individual women continued to work for welfare reform, they did so not as part of a broad-based women's movement, but as professionals — social workers and public health officials — or as clients affected by the system. Paradoxically, federally funded maternal and child welfare programs expanded in the 1930s and 1940s, even as grassroots interest declined. This is largely because the Roosevelt administration gave individual maternalists unprecedented influence in government. Indeed, the three most powerful women in the administration, First Lady Eleanor Roosevelt, Secretary of Labor Frances Perkins, and Molly Dewson, head of the Women's Division of the Democratic National Committee, came of age in progressive maternalist circles. Roosevelt and Perkins worked in settlement houses; all three were members of the National Consumers' League and energetic advocates of protective labor legislation. Consequently, when political support for social welfare reform returned during the Depression, government leaders turned to progressive maternalists who had years of experience in maternal and child welfare administration.[1]

Since maternalists had long sought to establish government responsibility for social welfare, it is not surprising that the Department of Labor, which housed the Children's and Women's Bureaus, produced the most enduring welfare accomplishments of the New Deal: the 1935 Social Security Act and the 1938 Fair Labor Standards Act. Mothers' pensions, maternal and child health care, protective labor legislation, and the abolition of child labor — all made nationwide by these laws — had long been part of the maternalist agenda. Indeed, Children's Bureau officials authored the children's provisions of the Social Security Act. At the request of Secretary of

Labor Frances Perkins and of Edwin Witte, head of Roosevelt's Committee on Economic Security, retired Bureau chief Grace Abbott, her successor Katharine Lenroot, and Martha May Eliot, who was later appointed the fourth director of the agency, drafted a proposal based on their knowledge about the mothers' pensions system and experience with the Sheppard-Towner Act.[2]

The three Children's Bureau women recommended increasing federal support for child welfare through four programs: an expansion of mothers' pensions, by then known as aid to dependent children; grants-in-aid for maternal and child health programs modeled on the Sheppard-Towner Act (but only for those unable to afford private medical care); welfare services for homeless, neglected and delinquent children; and an entirely new Crippled Children's Services to provide medical care to disabled youth. Although they expected that the Children's Bureau would administer all four programs, to their great disappointment, Congress decided at the last minute to place the administration of Aid to Dependent Children (ADC) in the hands of the newly created Social Security Administration.

Given the bitter fight over the Sheppard-Towner Act, the relative absence of opposition to the children's provisions of the Social Security Act is striking. Right-wing organizations and the medical establishment were so alarmed about "socialist" proposals for health insurance, unemployment compensation, and old-age pensions, that they did not seriously protest the children's sections of the Social Security Act — even though they had objected to similar programs under Sheppard-Towner. The maternalist agenda seemed moderate when compared to the more militant demands of workers, leftists, the unemployed, and the elderly. Moreover, women reformers in government were no longer tied to a grassroots movement; they were simply social workers with administrative expertise in child welfare. As a result, the children's portions of the Social Security Act were less political (in the sense of involving women at the grassroots) than previous maternalist reforms. Although the National Congress of Parents and Teachers and General Federation of Women's Clubs testified in congressional hearings and organized what one Roosevelt appointee called a "very helpful" lobbying campaign, women's organizations played little role in the design of the Social Security bill and virtually none in its administration. Federally funded health and welfare services had become the domain of social workers and public health professionals in government.[3]

Signed by Roosevelt on August 14, 1935, the Social Security Act was the first permanent acknowledgment of federal responsibility for maternal and child welfare, and its passage was a great victory for maternalists and for poor women and children. Title V revived and expanded Sheppard-Towner maternal and child health programs; Title IV nationalized Aid to Dependent

Children. By establishing uniform state residency requirements and requiring states to operate ADC in every county, the Social Security Act significantly increased the numbers of children getting assistance. Only three hundred thousand children received aid under existing state mothers' allowance programs when ADC began in 1936; within three years, the number had more than doubled to seven hundred thousand.[4]

Yet the Social Security Act also wrote the inadequacies of maternalist welfare policies into the law. Maternal and child health programs remained primarily educational and focused on rural areas. Title V, like Sheppard-Towner, required each state to pass enabling legislation, submit a plan for implementation, and show that it had a special child health agency to administer the bill before it could receive funds. In a step back from Sheppard-Towner, the Social Security Act slighted the social and economic aspects of infant and maternal health and treated it exclusively as a medical issue; the bill even gave state and local medical societies the authority to reject programs. Moreover, the new bill served only the economically disadvantaged and not women and children of all classes.[5]

Similar weaknesses beset Aid to Dependent Children. Although Abbott had hoped ADC would provide "a reasonable subsistence compatible with decency and health," the final version of the Social Security bill established a maximum — and inadequate — ceiling on grant levels. Congress allocated less money and established lower matching grants for ADC than for other welfare programs. Because the law permitted broad freedom to the states in determining ADC benefit levels and eligibility, discrimination pervaded the system. Moreover, although the "suitable home" clause was not written into the federal law, states were permitted to include it among eligibility requirements; in 1935, only two states did not have such a provision. Since eligibility was determined not by need, but by social workers' notions of suitability, most states discriminated against the children of unmarried mothers and women of color.[6]

In contrast to mothers' pensions, which were initially described as a salary for childrearing, Aid to Dependent Children barely acknowledged the mother's existence. Astonishingly, it did not even give an allowance to the mother until 1950! Congress established the maximum ADC grant as eighteen dollars per month for the first child, the same amount payable to children of servicemen who lost their lives in the first World War. However, while widows of veterans received an additional thirty dollars for themselves, the "caretaker" grant was omitted in ADC. Thus, an ADC mother and one child were expected to live on only eighteen dollars per month. (Old-age pensioners — who had a stronger lobby in Congress — got thirty dollars per month.) According to Edwin Witte, director of the Committee on Economic Security, the House Ways and Means Committee noticed the omission of the caretaker grant but did not correct it because there was "so little interest." If, as historian James Patterson argues, the failure of Congress to grant a separate allowance for the mother was due to "simple negligence by the framers," that negligence reflects the absence of a strong maternalist movement and the invisibility of mothers' work.[7]

Many of the shortcomings of the Social Security Act were the result of necessary compromises with states' rights conservatives and opponents of social welfare spending, and women reformers were not responsible for them. However, the Social Security Act also reflected the weaknesses of maternalism — particularly its family-wage ideology and presumption that (Anglo-American middle-class) experts knew what was best for impoverished children. Despite insisting that mothers' aid was not poor relief, Abbott, Lenroot, and Eliot constructed Aid to Dependent Children according to a social work/charity model, making the "education" and supervision of mothers' work and morality by professionally trained caseworkers a central part of the program.

The Children's Bureau women designed a bill that did not encourage women's economic independence, but provided assistance only when male wage earners failed to support them. Although recipients were expected to do some wagework, they were discouraged from seeking economic self-sufficiency through employment. The restrictive eligibility requirements and inadequate grant levels of ADC forced mothers to take low-paying jobs, while the omission of most women's jobs (such as domestic and agricultural work) from the unemployment and old-age sections of the bill further reinforced their economic dependence on men. By incorporating maternalist ideas about dependent motherhood into the Social Security Act, Abbott, Lenroot, and Eliot built New Deal social welfare policy on the values of a bygone era. They ignored the fact that growing numbers of mothers were gainfully employed outside the home, slighted feminist proposals for motherhood endowment and equal rights in the labor market, and disregarded the concept of universal entitlement exemplified in proposals for old-age pensions and workers' compensation put forth by men.[8]

Unfortunately, maternalism and its compromises continue to shape U.S. family policy. Current family and welfare legislation is still based on the notion that fathers are the primary breadwinners — despite the fact that two-thirds of all women and more than one-half of mothers of young children are currently in the paid labor force. One consequence of this family wage assumption is that the federal government provides no direct assistance, in the form of family allowances or child care to "intact" families. Another is that public assistance programs (such as AFDC and Medicaid health services) for "dependent" women and children are distinguished from entitlements like Social Security or unemployment insurance, which are tied to wage labor and therefore mainly benefit men. They are thus stig-matized as charity and cut off from mainstream political support. A third consequence of the maternalist assumptions behind U.S. welfare and family policy is the differential treatment of mothers. Women without husbands who stay home with their children are criticized as nonworking dependents; those with husbands are not. AFDC recipients are required to "work," although tax policies encourage mothers with husbands to stay out of the labor force. Finally, most employed mothers are denied federal funding for child care, even as the 1988 Family Support Act mandates child care for welfare recipients so that they can "work" off their grants.[9]

Despite the family wage assumptions of its authors, Aid to Dependent Children contained a potential challenge to dependent womanhood, for it provided an invaluable economic cushion for some single mothers. When the Social Security Act was enacted, no one imagined that ADC (later renamed Aid to Families with Dependent Children) would expand so dra-matically. The fact that most AFDC payments today are made not to widows but to divorced and unmarried mothers suggests that, in a sense, opponents of mothers' pensions had been correct in their assessment of welfare's effect on the family. By making it a little easier for women to leave untenable family situations and raise their children themselves, AFDC altered women's experience of mothering. It subverted the "family" (meaning women's and children's dependence within the family) and gave some women some economic independence from men.[10]

The persuasive appeal of maternalism as a political movement of Anglo-American women in the Progressive era is precisely what now seem its weaknesses: the presumption of gender difference and the repression of diversity. Despite the differences among them, all maternalists believed that women were more nurturing and sensitive to children than men and that the welfare of children — and therefore the future of the nation — depended on the preservation of the home. At a time of increasing heterogeneity in family styles and childrearing practices, both sentimental and progressive maternalists clung to a singular conception of family life. Elite white women, who despite their privilege were denied political, economic, and legal rights equal to men of their class, saw in the defense of "home" and "motherhood" a promising source of dignity and power.

Paradoxically, maternalism grew out of the weak economic and legal position of Anglo-American upper- and middle-class women, but depended on (and eventually increased) their political clout. Progressive-era maternalists assumed that they shared with poor women a vulnerability to male abuse and commitment to child welfare. However, as we have seen, they tended to view mother-work hierarchically, to "mother" those deemed less fortunate than themselves and to judge mothers of other social groups as fit or unfit

according to their own cultural norms. As lobbyists who influenced policymakers (and sometimes as policymakers themselves), well-off maternalists
were often deaf to the wants of working-class mothers unless — as in the
case of child health — they converged with their own. Thus they supported
protective labor laws for women workers and the abolition of child labor,
but opposed maternity benefits (because they might increase the number
of wage-earning mothers), and were relatively unconcerned with helping
working-class mothers obtain economic self-sufficiency or equal opportunity
in employment. Furthermore, maternalism lost its force as a social movement when Anglo-Americans won improvements in health care and professional opportunities in the expanding welfare system. It is ironic that some
maternalists escaped the vulnerability of stay-at-home motherhood and obtained a degree of economic independence by staffing health and welfare
programs that defined poor women as mothers and kept them "dependent"
on the state.[11]

In spite of the success of maternalist efforts to politicize motherhood and
establish public responsibility for all children's welfare, the absorption of
welfare programs into the government bureaucracy had the unexpected
result of making maternalism less political and less capable of mobilizing
grassroots support. The philosopher Nancy Fraser has pointed out that administrative and social work discourses tend to depoliticize social movements: in the language of welfare administrators, recipients become individual "cases" rather than members of a social group. "In addition," writes
Fraser, "they are rendered passive, positioned as potential recipients of pre-
defined services rather than as agents involved in interpreting their needs
and shaping their life conditions."[12] This is exactly what happened to mothers' pensions and, after the defeat of the Sheppard-Towner Act, to publicly
funded maternal and child health care. Mothers' highly political need for
material assistance, health care, and dignity was redefined as a personal need
for services to be administered on a case-by-case basis.

The hostile political climate of the 1920s surely contributed to the depoliticization of maternalist welfare services. While club mothers reacted
to the anticommunist attacks of the early 1920s by turning the PTA away
from reform, progressive maternalists responded by claiming authority over
child welfare on the basis of their professional expertise rather than their
maternal sensitivity, by strengthening the Children's Bureau's position in
the government bureaucracy and not its political base, and by insisting on
the duty of mothers to stay home with their children. Progressive reformers'
hostility to the Equal Rights Amendment may have further hardened their
commitment to the family wage. In any case, despite evidence of their
increasing approval of married women's employment and even birth control
in the 1920s, Children's Bureau officials designed the children's sections of

the 1935 Social Security Act on outdated maternalist ideas of dependent womanhood.[13]

The welfare system we have today is in many ways a legacy of the parochialism of the maternalist network. Activist women whose politics might have been more empowering to grassroots mothers had little influence on maternalists — or on welfare policy. African American club women, for example, had a politics of motherhood that was very different from maternalism. Black women activists were far more likely than whites to value women's economic independence and accept their right to combine wage-work and family. Moreover, because black women were historically denied the right to protect and care for their children, their appeals to motherhood challenged both gender relations and white supremacy in a way that those of Anglo-American maternalists did not. The welfare services they established were generally conceived as self-help for the community, instead of individualized assistance for the "dependent" poor. However, black women were largely excluded from maternalist organizations, and their potential contribution to social welfare policy was overlooked.[14]

Socialist feminists provided another alternative to the maternalist politics of motherhood. Crystal Eastman and a handful of others retained progressive maternalists' recognition of mothers' work and concern about women's poverty, but rejected their ideas about women's dependence and need for protection. They worked simultaneously for legal equality and the remuneration of mothers. Unlike maternalists, who described motherhood as a "service" deserving of a salary only if the breadwinner was absent, they described caregiving as an occupation that entitled the worker to a wage. Yet such feminist politics of motherhood were short-lived, and by the end of the 1920s most self-defined feminists focused their political energy almost exclusively on winning equal rights. The welfare system we have today reflects both the failure of maternalists to challenge traditional ideas about women's responsibility for childrearing and the failure of most feminists to create an alternative vision of the welfare state.

Although it is easy to criticize maternalism (and the welfare programs it helped create) from the perspective of the 1990s, we must remember that the policies that passed were all compromise measures and thus only a partial illustration of the maternalist welfare vision. At its best, as articulated by the women in the Children's Bureau network, maternalism stood for the allocation of society's resources away from war and toward children and families; the social recognition of mothering and other forms of household labor; an awareness of the interdependence of people and therefore of the responsibilities of privilege; and democratic mobilization for welfare reform. As we approach the twenty-second century with a widening gap between rich and poor and nearly one-fourth of the nation's children living in poverty, we would not do badly to remember Lathrop's insistence that "the power to maintain a decent family living standard is the primary essential of child welfare." Or to heed her words: "If we really want to help Democracy prevail we must set ourselves to the task, the long insistent stern task of abolishing poverty. Comfortable women cannot evade responsibility."[15]

The political, economic, and demographic changes that have reshaped women's lives in the late twentieth century call for a rethinking of the politics of motherhood. Laws establishing women's right to vote and sit on juries, to birth control and abortion, and to equality in employment, education, and pay, establish women's relationship to the state as citizens and not as mothers. At the same time, the falling birth rate, the decline in infant and maternal deaths, and women's increasing labor force participation make childrearing less central to women's lives than it was earlier in the century. The majority of women still become mothers, but they have fewer children and are increasingly likely to combine childrearing with work outside the home. As a result, many, perhaps most, women no longer identify exclusively as mothers but consider mothering only one of many social roles. Still, motherhood remains a central experience of most women in the United States, and poor women today (like almost all women in the presuffrage era) relate to the state primarily as mothers and clients of welfare programs, and not as citizen-voters.[16]

The opposition between maternalism and feminism that was set in the 1920s still echoes in the contemporary feminist debate over "equality" versus "difference." Fortunately, many scholars and theorists appear to be moving away from such dichotomous thinking, for the majority of mothers are served neither by a focus on "equality" that ignores the fact that women do most of the nation's caregiving work, nor by a focus on "difference" that might lock them into that job.[17] Certainly, as the history of motherwork shows, few mothers profit from a public policy based on sentimental ideas about motherhood and women's capacity for nurture, for those ideas are founded on a middle-class Anglo-American understanding of family life, and the social policies based on them are invariably confining.

Instead, a feminist politics empowering to mothers should be founded on a commitment to economic and racial justice, on an acknowledgment of cultural diversity in childrearing practices and the experience of mothering, on the inclusion of women from every social group in the political process, and on the social recognition of women's (and men's) work of caregiving and reproduction. A feminist politics of motherhood calls for a redefinition of work itself: to challenge the artificial boundaries between "mothering" and "working," between domestic and market employment, and between welfare and labor policy. Constructing feminist family and welfare policies along these lines cannot be easy. But as Crystal Eastman noted prophetically in 1920, for feminists, achieving equal rights — an objective still not fully realized — "is the easiest part of our program."[18]

NOTES

1. See Susan Ware, *Beyond Suffrage: Women in the New Deal* (Cambridge: Harvard University Press, 1982), and Robyn L. Muncy, *Creating a Female Dominion in American Reform, 1890–1935* (New York: Oxford University Press, 1990), 150–57.

2. Lela B. Costin, *Two Sisters for Social Justice: A Biography of Grace and Edith Abbott* (Urbana: University of Illinois Press, 1983), 221–26.

3. Remarking on the success of the lobbying efforts of women's organizations and the Fraternal Order of Eagles in getting the bill out of committee, Edwin Witte wrote: "The total amount of work of this character was not very great at this stage or any other, but I believe that it was very helpful." Edwin Witte, *The Development of the Social Security Act* (Madison: University of Wisconsin Press, 1962), 97n. See House Committee on Ways and Means, *Economic Security Act, Hearings on H.R. 4120,* 74th Congress, 1st Session, Jan.-Feb. 1935.

4. James T. Patterson, *America's Struggle Against Poverty, 1900–1985* (Cambridge: Harvard University Press, 1986), 67–71. Mimi Abramovitz notes that, despite the federal legislation, "most states delayed putting the ADC program into place. . . . By early 1939, ten states still lacked the program for dependent children." Mimi Abramovitz, *Regulating the Lives of Women: Social Welfare Policy from Colonial Times to the Present* (Boston: South End Press, 1988), 316. See also Winifred Bell, *Aid to Dependent Children* (New York: Columbia University Press, 1965).

5. Richard A. Meckel, *Save the Babies: American Public Health Reform and the Prevention of Infant Mortality* (Baltimore: Johns Hopkins University Press, 1990), 222–24.

6. Grace Abbott, *The Child and the State* (Chicago: University of Chicago Press, 1938), 238; Bell, *Aid to Dependent Children,* 6.

7. Witte, *The Development of the Social Security Act,* 164; Patterson, *America's Struggle Against Poverty,* 70.

8. For an illuminating discussion of the contrast between men's support for social insurance and women social workers' reliance on casework, see Linda Gordon, "Social Insurance and Public Assistance: The Influence of Gender in Welfare Thought in the United States, 1890-1935," *American Historical Review* 97 (Feb. 1992): 19–54.

9. See Mimi Abramovitz, "Why Welfare Reform is a Sham," *The Nation* (Sept. 26, 1988): 221, 238–41.

10. See Linda Gordon, "What Does Welfare Regulate?" *Social Research* 55 (Winter 1988): 625–27.

11. On Grace Abbott's objection to maternity benefits, see Grace Abbott to

Mollie Ray Carroll, July 27, 1925, Box 36, Folder 4, Grace and Edith Abbott Papers, Regenstein Library, University of Chicago.

12. Nancy Fraser, "Struggle Over Needs: Outline of a Socialist-Feminist Critical Theory of Late-Capitalist Political Culture," in *Women, the State and Welfare,* ed. Linda Gordon (Madison: University of Wisconsin Press, 1990), 212.

13. On the maternalist (or "social feminist") rethinking of married women's employment, see Sybil Lipschultz, "Social Feminism and Legal Discourse: 1908–1923," *Yale Journal of Law and Feminism* 2 (Fall 1989): 131–60, and Sophonisba Breckinridge, "The Home Responsibilities of Women Workers and the 'Equal Wage,'" *Journal of Political Economy* 31 (1928): 521–43. On their ideas about birth control, see Martha May Eliot Interview, 420–22, Family Planning Oral History Project, 1973–76, Arthur and Elizabeth M. Schlesinger Library on the History of Women in America, Radcliffe College, Cambridge, Mass.

14. Linda Gordon, "Black and White Visions of Welfare: Women's Welfare Activism, 1890–1945," *Journal of American History* 78 (Sept. 1991): 559–90.

15. Julia Lathrop, "Child Welfare Standards a Test of Democracy: Presidential Address Before the National Conference of Social Workers, June 1919, Box 60, Folder 10; Julia Lathrop, "Speech at the Federation of Women's Clubs," Apr. 1918, Box 60, Folder 9, Abbott Papers.

16. Barbara J. Nelson, "Women's Poverty and Women's Citizenship: Some Political Consequences of Economic Marginality," *Signs* 10 (1984): 209–31.

17. For example, Martha Minow, *Making All the Difference: Inclusion, Exclusion, and American Law* (Ithaca: Cornell University Press, 1990).

18. Crystal Eastman, "Now We Can Begin," in *Crystal Eastman: On Women and Revolution,* ed. Blanche Wiesen Cook (New York: Oxford University Press, 1978), 54. See Deanne Bonnar, "Toward the Feminization of Policy: Exit From an Ancient Trap by the Redefinition of Work," in *For Crying Out Loud: Women and Poverty in the United States,* ed. Rochelle Lefkowitz and Ann Withorn (New York: Pilgrim Press, 1986), 285–99.

Index

Molly Ladd-Taylor teaches U.S. history at York University in Toronto, Canada. She is the editor of *Raising a Baby the Government Way: Mothers' Letters to the Children's Bureau, 1915–1932.*

Books in the Series
Women in American History

7824